EMPOWERING STUDENTS, CHALLENGING BIAS:

A Middle School Curriculum

Anti-Defamation League
605 Third Avenue
New York, NY 10158-3560
(212) 885-7700/885-7800
(212) 867-0779/490-0187 (Fax)
www.adl.org

CONTENTS

Unit V. Challenging Bias and Injustice 199

Appendix. Correlation of Lessons to the Common Core Learning Standards

INTRODUCTION

Empowering Students, Challenging Bias: A Middle School Curriculum is a teaching guide designed for middle school educators who want to promote anti-bias concepts in order to create safe, inclusive and respectful classroom and school environments. The materials have been designed to assist educators and students in exploring ways to ensure that the principles of respect for diversity, freedom and equality become realities. The curriculum provides teachers with lessons that encourage students to reflect on their identity, understand and appreciate differences, explore societal issues arising from bias and discrimination, understand how historically people have combatted prejudice and injustice and take leadership roles in promoting justice and equity in their schools, communities and society at large. By teaching this curriculum, you will be making an important contribution by helping children explore valuable principles that they will bring into their social and peer interactions throughout their lives.

About ADL

ADL is a leading anti-hate organization. Founded in 1913 in response to an escalating climate of anti-Semitism and bigotry, its timeless mission is to stop the defamation of the Jewish people and to secure justice and fair treatment to all. Today, ADL continues to fight all forms of hate with the same vigor and passion. ADL is the first call when acts of anti-Semitism occur. A global leader in exposing extremism, delivering anti-bias education and fighting hate online, ADL's ultimate goal is a world in which no group or individual suffers from bias, discrimination or hate.

About A World of Difference® Institute

ADL's A World of Difference® Institute is a market leader in the development and delivery of anti-bias and diversity training and resources. Human relations and education professionals design training modules and produce curricula that provide the necessary skills, knowledge and awareness to promote and sustain inclusive and respectful learning environments.

The origins of the A World of Difference Institute date back to 1985, when ADL and WCVB-TV in Boston initiated the A World of Difference campaign, a year-long series of education and media-driven programs designed to combat prejudice and create effective tools to address these issues in the classroom and community. The campaign's immense success led to ongoing programs in Boston and 28 U.S. cities as well as several national awards, including a Peabody, Gàbriel and Scripps-Howard. In 1992, in an effort to meet the increasing demand for its services and to formalize and coordinate its anti-bias research, programming and training efforts, ADL created and officially launched A World of Difference Institute.

A World of Difference Institute training programs and curricular materials are developed and evaluated by a research department that interacts on an ongoing basis with professionals in the field. The Institute collaborates with universities, colleges and national funding sources to study and enhance the efficacy of its programs. These collaborations have included formal studies with prominent institutions, including Yale University, Columbia University Teachers College, Claremont Graduate School and the University of Pennsylvania.

Through the development and delivery of its programs and resources, the Institute seeks to help participants recognize bias and the harm it inflicts on individuals and society; explore the value of diversity; improve intergroup relations; and combat racism, anti-Semitism and all forms of prejudice and bigotry.

Goals of A World of Difference® Institute

The following are the overall goals of A World of Difference for all audiences:

- To promote respectful, inclusive and safe learning environments and communities,
- To build understanding of the value and benefits of diversity,
- To improve intergroup relations,
- To eradicate anti-Semitism, racism and all forms of bigotry, and
- To encourage personal responsibility in the promotion of justice and equity.

The Rationale for Anti-Bias Education

Schools in the United States have long played a vital role in supporting the nation's democratic ideals. Providing all students with a quality education—one in which academic and social development are inseparable goals— is essential to creating equal access to opportunity and fostering responsible citizenship. The challenges of fulfilling this obligation are heightened in an educational climate whose primary focus is accountability for student achievement as measured by standardized test scores. Recognizing the need to prepare students to live and work successfully in a pluralistic national and a global community, educators can engage in a collaborative process to achieve the ideals of justice and equality upon which the nation was founded.

The inequities and social tensions that exist in U.S. society are also present in the hallways of our nation's schools. Because schools are both educating and socializing institutions, the potential exists for them to establish frameworks that challenge intolerance and promote safety, fairness and respect. Students' successful pursuit of academic excellence depends on their ability to learn in a safe and inclusive environment.

The rapidly increasing diversity of our nation presents both a windfall of benefits and new challenges. When diversity—differences in race, religion, sexual orientation, language, culture, learning style, socioeconomic class, body type and ability—is not understood, valued or respected, the resulting fear and misunderstanding can fuel intergroup tension. The potential for conflict, bullying, discrimination and scapegoating is high when bias and stereotypes go unchallenged or are ignored. Left unexamined, biased attitudes can lead to biased behaviors, which have the potential to escalate into violent acts of hate. Youth violence, hate crimes, bullying and harassment occur today at alarming rates, have a powerful impact on the entire educational community and underline the imperative for schools to address prejudice and discrimination directly.

Biased behavior can be subtle or overt. In schools, name calling and acts of social exclusion are the common examples of discriminatory behavior and prejudicial thinking. Although children are not born prejudiced, from as early as six months of age, infants can distinguish differences in physical appearances and by ages 3–5, children may also begin to develop negative attitudes toward differences. In an attempt to minimize the development of prejudice, well-meaning adults often teach children to ignore differences and focus only on similarities—also known as being "color blind"—and do not teach children about bias and discrimination. Just as common experiences are part of the "glue" that holds communities together, understanding and respecting differences are essential for successful multicultural societies.

References

Henze, Rosemary, A. Katz, E. Norte, S.E. Sather and E. Walker. 2002. *Leading for diversity: How school leaders promote positive interethnic relations.* Thousand Oaks: Corwin Press.

Stern-LaRosa Caryl, and E.H. Bettmann. 2000. *Hate Hurts: How children learn and unlearn prejudice.* New York: Scholastic.

What Is Anti-Bias Education?

Anti-bias education is a comprehensive approach to learning designed to actively challenge stereotyping, prejudice and all forms of discrimination. Anti-bias education incorporates curricular content that reflects diverse experiences and perspectives; it includes instructional methods that advance the learning of all students and tools to establish and sustain a safe, inclusive and respectful learning environment and school community. Ultimately, anti-bias education engages students in the exploration of social problems and empowers them to take active steps to create a more just and peaceful world, where all groups share equal access to opportunity and every person can flourish.

With comprehensive anti-bias education, the mastery skills that participants acquire include the following (specific activities and curricula are tailored for each age group):

- Young people understand the various dimensions of identity and apply this understanding to their thinking and behavior.

- Young people develop an understanding of basic terms and concepts relating to prejudice and discrimination and apply this understanding to their interactions with others.

- Young people increase their understanding of the impact of culture on communication and apply this understanding to their interactions with others.

- Young people develop the capacity to recognize and acknowledge bullying, prejudice and discrimination in themselves, in others and within institutions.

- Young people develop and put into practice skills to challenge bullying, bias and discrimination in themselves and others.

ABOUT THIS CURRICULUM

Empowering Students, Challenging Bias: A Middle School Curriculum is divided into five instructional sections and each section includes lessons for grades 6–8. Educators may find it useful to use a specific lesson or lessons from a particular unit to support ongoing curricular content; however, we encourage the consideration of using the units sequentially. By progressing through the units in this manner, students build a strong foundation for analyzing and confronting bias.

The social and emotional development of students is a core part of their school experience. We suggest making *Empowering Students, Challenging Bias: A Middle School Curriculum* a regular part of your weekly lesson plans. With thirty lessons in total, it is ideal to do one lesson per week. Each lesson has a core activity as well as extension ideas and many include writing activities and fit within English Language Arts (ELA) curriculum. The curriculum can also be used in Advisory, Social Studies and Health classes as well as integrated into other subject areas. Advisors for after-school diversity and affinity clubs can use the lessons to help students understand issues and build upon that knowledge to create change in their school and community. An integrated approach to anti-bias education is significantly more powerful than tying it to one subject area.

Overview of Units

Below is an overview of the curriculum, including the goals for each section as well as the specific lessons for each grade level.

Unit I: Setting a Respectful Classroom Tone provides lessons to build a solid foundation for students' social and emotional skill development. The lessons help students feel safe in their classroom; expand their feelings vocabulary and empathize with others; communicate effectively; manage conflict; and learn to work as a team member.

Unit II: Identity and Differences provides lessons to build a sense of self and explore the concepts of identity and differences. The lessons help students consider various aspects of identity and the identity groups to which they belong; examine the positive and negative aspects of diversity; and explore groups, cliques and friendship.

Unit III: Analyzing Where We Get Information provides lessons to build students' critical thinking skills in analyzing the information they receive and absorb. The lessons help students differentiate fact from opinion; explore the concept of perspective; consider various information sources; assess and analyze online information; reflect on misinformation, rumors and gossip; and learn about advertising and propaganda.

Unit IV: Understanding Bullying, Bias and Injustice provides lessons to build an understanding of the bias and injustice young people see in their world. The lessons help students understand what stereotyping and bias are; explore the different forms bias takes; reflect on bullying, identity-based bullying and cyberbullying; explore how media perpetuate bias; and gain insight into the escalation of hate.

Unit V: Challenging Bias and Injustice provides lessons to empower students to do something about the bias, discrimination and bullying they encounter. The lessons help students understand how to be an ally; challenge bias in words, actions and online; explore the differences between equality and equity; and engage in other projects that improve their school, community and world.

Overview of Lesson Structure

Each section consists of 5–7 lessons. All of the lessons build upon the previous lessons/units and are highly interactive, modeling a participatory process that encourages students to actively engage with issues that affect their classroom, school and community. As students work together, share diverse perspectives and backgrounds, solve problems, brainstorm and discuss the material, they learn to communicate respectfully, cooperate and improve their critical thinking skills. Research indicates that all of these abilities are associated with decreased discriminatory behavior.

Lesson Structure

Rationale: A statement that identifies the purpose of the lesson and the topic(s) to be explored.

Objectives: The anticipated student outcomes that will occur as a result of the lesson.

Handouts/Support Documents: Additional materials that are needed to implement lessons can be found at the end of the lesson they accompany.

Other Materials: Additional items needed to implement the lesson that can likely be found in most middle school classrooms (e.g., paper, art supplies) or a website that will need to be used.

Procedures: Step-by-step teacher instructions to implement the lesson. Also included throughout this section are special considerations and cautions to the teacher, highlighted as NOTE (👆) as well as alternative methods for a procedure, highlighted as 👆. Notes are numbered based on the lesson instruction they refer to.

Extension Activities: A list of additional activities to continue and extend students' learning of the lesson's concepts.

Time: The suggested block of time that teachers will need to schedule for the lesson. Most lessons are 45 minutes.

Academic Standards: A list of Common Core Learning Standards that are met by teaching the lesson (See the Appendix for a comprehensive list of the standards).

Strategies and Skills: A list of instructional techniques (e.g., role play) and skills (e.g., writing skills) practiced or reinforced in the lesson.

Key Words and Phrases: A list of vocabulary, organized alphabetically, which students will need to know in order to effectively participate in the lesson (see the Appendix for a comprehensive list of all key words).

Flipped Classroom Idea: Suggestions for "flipping" your classroom which include videos you can make and have students watch prior to the lesson. These ideas are designated by the symbol 📷◀.

Instructional Methods and Strategies

A variety of instructional methods are used to implement the lessons in this curriculum. The strategies provide opportunities for students to talk with each other in order to connect and learn. They also provide opportunities for students to tie historical and contemporary information to their own understanding of bias and discrimination. Other methods invite students to examine information critically and personally clarify their own opinions on a variety of topics. The following five methods are used most often through the curriculum although other techniques are also used.

1. **Directed Discussions:** The lessons include discussion questions that are intended to help facilitate student discussions in pairs, small groups and as a whole class. Some of the questions assess student comprehension of the concepts presented and others ask students to formulate feelings and opinions, draw conclusions or connect material to parallel situations.

    The material in Unit I, "Setting a Respectful Classroom Tone," provides a helpful framework for having these discussions. The material in this section should be reviewed and reinforced regularly and especially when sensitive topics are under discussion.

2. **Small Group Work:** Numerous opportunities for students to work collaboratively are provided throughout. Teachers may want to enlist a variety of grouping methods, including randomly assigned groups, self-selected groups and teacher-selected groups. Providing opportunities for students to interact with as many of their classmates as possible will increase the likelihood that students will be exposed to a greater number of perspectives and communication styles. The instructional techniques also give students the opportunity to learn the behaviors that foster and support effective group process. To maximize student participation in small group work, teachers should make sure that all students clearly understand what is being asked of them and circulate around the room during small group work.

3. **Brainstorming:** Brainstorming sessions are often used as a springboard for discussing new concepts. Because the process of coming up with ideas is distinct from the process of judgment, brainstorming provides an opportunity to generate ideas that have no right or wrong answers. The process can often lead to creative ideas because students build on each other's thoughts. It is important to remind students throughout brainstorming sessions not to criticize any of the ideas that are shared, to work quickly, not to censor their own ideas and, whenever possible, to expand on the ideas of others.

4. **Role Playing:** One of the most effective ways to get students involved in the learning process is through role play. By experimenting with various roles and considering the implications of each, students begin to understand the complexity of social issues and to develop empathy. Stress to students that the purposes of role playing are to practice new responses, to consider alternative points of view and to experience some of the feelings that occur in real-life situations. Whenever students are asked to develop or act out role plays, it is important that they not use real names of other students or teachers or details about a situation that would reveal something that should be private. It is also important that they act as realistically as possible and avoid the use of stereotypical behaviors during role plays.

5. **Defining Terms:** It is critical that students gain an understanding of the language of diversity, bias and social justice as well as the distinction between words. Often in the lessons, there is a discussion about terminology that is related to the concepts being taught, including words and phrases for which many students may be unfamiliar. In most cases, we suggest providing an opportunity for students to reflect on and share what they may have heard or already know about the term and then provide the definition for the students as well as an example to help them better understand the word. All key words and phrases used throughout the curriculum are defined in the "Glossary."

Additional Resources

In addition to the resources used to conduct the activities in the lessons, you may also find many of the ADL's online education resources useful at www.adl.org/educator-resources including:

Anti-Bias Education, www.adl.org/what-we-do/promote-respect/anti-bias
Provides information on anti-bias trainings, programs, webinars and other resources offered for schools and campuses.

Curriculum Resources, www.adl.org/educator-resources
A collection of free original lesson plans and resources that help K-12 educators integrate culturally responsive, anti-bias and social justice themes into their curricula.

BACKGROUND INFORMATION FOR EDUCATORS

Creating an Anti-Bias Learning Environment

Educational environments that reflect the rich diversity of the community, nation and world assist in opening students' minds and actively engaging them in their own learning. Research has shown that prejudice is countered when schools and classrooms foster critical thinking, empathy development and positive self-esteem in students.

It is important for teachers to consider how they can most effectively raise complex issues of identity, hate, bias, bullying and exclusion with their students. Educators should keep in mind that conversations about understanding and respect should not be limited to commemorative events or special programs, celebrations and holidays but should be a part of everyday classroom life. Creating inclusive, respectful classrooms where students feel comfortable talking about difficult but important issues is an ongoing effort and working for social justice is a life-long endeavor.

To prepare for successful learning of anti-bias concepts in the classroom, teachers should consider making the following practices an integral part of their everyday practice.

1. **Self-exploration:** Examine your own cultural biases and assumptions. Explore your perceptions and understanding of situations by developing an awareness of your cultural "filters."

2. **Comprehensive Integration:** Integrate culturally diverse information and perspectives in all aspects of your teaching. Relegating equity issues to special "multicultural" times sends a message to students that such lessons are unimportant relative to other aspects of the curriculum.

3. **Time and Maturation:** Allow time for the process to develop. Introduce less complex topics first and create time to establish trust. Develop ground rules for discussion which allow for honest conversation within a respectful context.

4. **Accepting Environment:** Establish an environment that allows for mistakes. Since most of us have been unconsciously acculturated into prejudicial and stereotypical thinking, we may not be aware that certain attitudes are harmful to ourselves and others. Model how to respond in a non-defensive manner when told something you said or did was offensive. Assume good will and make that assumption a common practice in the classroom.

5. **Intervention:** Be prepared to respond to purposefully directed acts of bias. Students will carefully observe how you intervene when someone is the target of discriminatory or bias-motivated behavior. Silence in the face of injustice conveys the impression that the behavior is condoned or not worthy of attention. Make it clear to students and their families that you will not allow name-calling in the classroom.

6. **Lifelong Learning:** Keep abreast of current issues and discuss them with students. Clip articles from newspapers and magazines and post them in the classroom. Use our lesson plans (www.adl.org/lesson-plans) to discuss those topics with your students. Let students know that you consider yourself a learner in these issues as well and see yourself as part of the learning process.

7. **Discovery Learning:** Avoid "preaching" to students about how they should speak or behave. Research indicates that exhortation is the least effective methodology for changing prejudiced attitudes; in fact, it often produces a result opposite from the desired effect. Provide opportunities for students to resolve conflicts, solve problems, work in diverse teams and think critically about the information they learn.

8. **Life Experiences:** Provide opportunities for students to share life experiences and choose literature that will help students develop empathy. Make your classroom a place where students' experiences are embraced and appreciated, as opposed to marginalized or invalidated. Prejudice and discrimination have a unique impact on each individual, and it is not fruitful to engage in a debate over who has suffered the most.

9. **Resources Review:** Review materials so that classroom displays and bulletin boards are inclusive of all people. Insure that supplemental books and videos do not reinforce existing stereotypes. When you see such examples in literature, textbooks and the media, point them out to students and encourage them to think critically about and challenge them.

10. **Home-School-Community Connections:** Involve parents, caregivers, family members and the community in the learning process. Find opportunities to invite family and community members into the classroom as teachers and learners. We cannot view the school and the home or school and the community as isolated from one another; we must examine how they interconnect and provide opportunities to share these connections with students.

11. **Examine the Classroom Environment:** What is present and absent in the classroom sends a message to children about whom and what is important. Make every effort to create a setting that is rich in possibilities for exploring cultural diversity. Such an environment assists children in developing their ideas about themselves and others, creates the conditions to initiate conversations about differences and provides teachers with a setting for introducing activities about diversity.

Social and Emotional Development

Social and emotional learning (SEL) is the process through which children, teens and adults acquire and effectively apply the knowledge, attitudes and skills necessary to understand and manage emotions, set and achieve positive goals, feel and show empathy for others, establish and maintain positive relationships, and make responsible decisions. Before students can understand and address bullying, bias, discrimination and injustice, they first need skills in communicating effectively, empathizing with others, understanding and managing their feelings and the feelings of others and working collaboratively. As such, we have provided social and emotional skill development as part of the first section's lessons and we encourage the review of these and other lessons when topics arise in the classroom.

For more information about the connection between anti-bias education and SEL, read "Anti-Bias Education: The Power of Social-Emotional Learning" at www.adl.org/news/op-ed/anti-bias-education-the-power-of-social-emotional-learning.

Responding to Name-Calling and Bullying in the Classroom

Being the target of bullying can be painful and damaging. When students are targeted based on their identity (frequently called "identity-based bullying" or "bias-based bullying"), it can be particularly harmful and hurtful. Identity-based bullying is any form of bullying related to characteristics considered part of a person's identity or perceived identity group, such as race, religion, disability, immigration status, sexual orientation, gender identity, physical appearance, etc. It can cause young people to internalize negative messages about that part of their identity and harm their self-esteem in lasting ways. A 2015 study from the Gay, Lesbian, and Straight Education Network of U.S. students ages 13 to 18 reveals that identity-based name-calling and bullying are widespread and often based on personal characteristics. Just over half (50.9%) of U.S. middle and high school students reported being verbally harassed at school based on appearance or body size, and the numbers for bullying based on other identity markers are also cause for concern: race/ethnicity (30.3%), gender expression (21.9%), sexual orientation (19.4%), gender (18.1%), religion (18%) and disability (12.7%).

Below are strategies for preventing name-calling, harassment and bullying in the classroom and for addressing it when it does arise. In addition, there are several lessons in the *Empowering Students, Challenging Bias: A Middle School Curriculum* that address name-calling and bullying directly.

- Provide students with opportunities to develop cooperative learning and conflict resolution skills, both as independent opportunities and as part of routine instructional methods.

- Provide students who engage in bullying behaviors with opportunities to discuss these behaviors with counseling staff and to develop more effective strategies for managing peer relationships.

- Avoid focusing efforts to eliminate bullying on a few students who are the aggressors. Understand and communicate the expectation that all members of the school community are needed to create positive change. Those people not directly involved in bullying are often bystanders who can become active allies by supporting those targeted by bullying.

- Implement strategies to increase student reporting of bullying. Have "share boxes" available where students can leave anonymous notes for administrative staff about incidents or problems that occur in the school.

- Offer "ally-building" activities for students to strengthen their skills, teach techniques to prevent or respond to future incidents and build self-esteem.

- Engage students in a campaign to develop a school motto that communicates a commitment to address bullying, e.g., "All students should feel safe in all areas of the school at all times."

- Organize a group or club for students to take action against name-calling and bullying and to develop skills to be allies to targeted students, e.g., "friendship groups."

- Help students develop informal ways to build peer support.

For more information about bullying and bullying prevention, visit www.adl.org/education/resources/tools-and-strategies/bullying-and-cyberbullying-prevention-strategies.

Enhancing the Social and Psychological Development of Young Adolescents[1]

Addressing the social and psychological development of young adolescents is critical. Five areas that affect students' social and psychological development are self-esteem, achievement motivation, social skills, coping skills and aspirations.

Self-Esteem
Although school achievement affects self-esteem and vice versa, the focus on improving student self-esteem should not be connected solely to improving academic achievement. A formal program is not necessary to nurture

students' self-esteem; daily interactions with teachers and the environment they create in classrooms have a significant effect on self-esteem.

Although positive feedback from others is important, how students interpret and process the feedback ultimately determines its effect on their self-esteem. Teachers can help nurture students' self-esteem in several ways. For example:

- Use learning activities for which students receive feedback that helps build confidence.
- Work with students' "significant others" (parents/guardians, grandparents, family members and other students) to reinforce their positive accomplishments in school.
- Share success stories of adults whose childhood backgrounds and accomplishments were similar to those of your students.
- Help students identify their strengths and resources, and consider how to use them to achieve educational and personal goals.
- Emphasize the relationship between success in and outside of school.
- Reduce competition between students; cooperative learning takes place in groups under the teacher's guidance.
- Monitor interaction in the classroom to eliminate teasing, bullying and negative feedback.

Achievement Motivation

Achievement motivation is the student's drive, desire and persistence to master a goal or task. Students with high achievement motivation have "stick to it" behaviors (sometimes referred to as grit) that often lead them to accomplish what they set out to do.

It is important for students to believe they can be successful in school and that their goals are worthwhile. Further, students need positive feedback for what teachers may view as a small accomplishment to prompt the student to put forth continued effort to accomplish the next tasks. It is also important for students to have input about what happens in their classrooms. Strategies to enhance achievement motivation include:

- Structure activities so that every student's achievement is recognized.
- Create challenges that build on students' existing strengths.
- Create ways for students to assess and discuss their progress.
- Offer "personal best" awards and other incentives for attendance, grades, and/or achievement.
- Structure classroom experiences so that students feel responsible for their actions.
- Have students evaluate their own work performance as they work to produce a quality product.
- Structure lessons to prompt active participation from all students.

Social Skills

Social skills pertain to students being able to work and interact productively with others in meaningful ways. Students who have good social skills know how to develop positive interpersonal interactions, avoid using negative and violent behaviors and have tolerance for those whom they may view as "different." Productive interpersonal relations often contribute to a positive self-esteem.

Strategies for enhancing students' social skills include:

- Assign informal small-group learning activities in a space for groups to congregate and to cooperate in developing peer-help programs.
- Use activities that emphasize social interaction with a heterogeneous mix of students.
- Eliminate social subgroups that ostracize others.
- Help students accept and appreciate individual differences.
- Emphasize the need to be sensitive to the feelings of other people.
- Reduce competition when it can lead to negative relationships.
- Teach diversity in the context of showing how differences among people are strengths, especially for problem solving.
- Demonstrate positive social skills in the way you interact with students and others.

Coping Skills

Students who consistently experience failure at tasks can fall into a state of "learned helplessness." They may feel they have so little control over outcomes that are important to them that they develop the attitude of "why even try?"

Coping skills can help students overcome adversity. Strategies for enhancing coping skills include:

- Incorporate activities that encourage students to talk about their emotions, listen to their classmates express their feelings and reflect on what motivates people. Provide stress-free learning environments.
- Encourage nonjudgmental and non disruptive venting of emotions rather than negative verbal and physical aggression.
- Stress to students that they can have control over what happens to them.
- Teach students various methods of relaxation, such as deep muscle relaxation and deep breathing, for times when they need strategies to reduce anxiety.
- Foster a sense of belonging for the students in the classroom so they feel a connection to school.

Aspirations

The current emphasis on college and career readiness focuses not only on academic skills needed for students to maximize their potential, but also on the aspirations students need to develop the knowledge, drive and motivation to pursue future endeavors.

It is important to help students set aspirations for their future and to help them understand what it takes to reach their life goals. Strategies to help students enhance aspirations include:

- Demonstrate the relationship between schoolwork and careers by using vocational, career and other job-related examples in classroom activities. Talk to students about their interests and relate those interests to possible vocations, careers and college programs.
- Point out the relationship between success in school and success in the real world.
- Assure students that everyone has positive attributes and that those, coupled with training and aspirations, can lead to a successful and rewarding career.

- Expose students to a variety of careers and vocations so they can become "career wise" across curriculum areas.
- Explain to students what "career and college readiness" means by using activities designed to pique their aspirations.
- Use advisory time to teach life and employment skills.

Self-esteem, achievement motivation, social skills, coping skills and aspirations are critical to the development of middle school students. Teachers make important contributions to students' present and future lives through these five areas. Reviewing and reflecting on the practices presented here will be beneficial to teachers and, in turn, students.

Endnote

[1] Reprinted with permission from David E. Bartz, "Enhancing the Social and Psychological Development of Young Adolescents," *AMLE Magazine* 4(2016): 12–13, www.amle.org.

Teacher and Classroom Self-Assessment

The following self-assessment checklist assists educators in reflecting on and gaining insight into their personal, professional and institutional beliefs and attitudes about diversity and anti-bias education. These questions can be used as part of a larger conversation about anti-bias education or by individual teachers to assess their own practice.

Part I. Assessing Yourself

How effective are you in promoting a bias-free educational environment?	I haven't thought about this.	I need to do this better.	I do this well.
1. Have you recently read any books or articles, or watched any documentaries to increase your understanding of the particular hopes, needs and concerns of students and families from the different cultures that make up your school community and beyond?	[ ]	[ ]	[ ]
2. Have you participated in professional development opportunities to enhance your understanding of the complex characteristics of racial, ethnic and cultural groups in the U.S.?	[ ]	[ ]	[ ]
3. Do you try to listen with an open mind to all students and colleagues, even when you don't understand their perspectives or agree with what they're saying?	[ ]	[ ]	[ ]
4. Have you taken specific actions to dispel misconceptions, stereotypes or prejudices that members of one group have about members of another group at your school?	[ ]	[ ]	[ ]
5. Do you strive to avoid actions that might be offensive to members of other groups?	[ ]	[ ]	[ ]
6. Do you discourage patterns of informal discrimination, segregation or exclusion of members of particular groups from school clubs, committees and other school activities?	[ ]	[ ]	[ ]
7. Do the curricular content and wall displays in your classroom reflect the experiences and perspectives of the cultural groups that make up the school and its surrounding community?	[ ]	[ ]	[ ]
8. Have you evaluated classroom materials and textbooks to ensure they do not reinforce stereotypes and that they provide fair and appropriate treatment of all groups?	[ ]	[ ]	[ ]
9. Do you use classroom methods, such as cooperative learning, role-playing and small group discussions to meet the needs of students' different learning styles?	[ ]	[ ]	[ ]
10. Do students have opportunities to engage in problem-solving groups that address real issues with immediate relevance to their lives?	[ ]	[ ]	[ ]
11. Do you use a range of strategies, in addition to traditional testing methods, to assess student learning?	[ ]	[ ]	[ ]

Part II. Assessing Your School

How effective is your school in promoting a bias-free educational environment?	We haven't thought about this.	We need to do this better.	We do this well.
1. Does the school's mission statement communicate values of respect, equity and inclusion?	[ ]	[ ]	[ ]
2. Do students typically interact with one another in positive, respectful ways?	[ ]	[ ]	[ ]
3. Do the school's symbols, signs, mascots and insignias reflect respect for diversity?	[ ]	[ ]	[ ]
4. Do celebrations, festivals and special events reflect a variety of cultural groups and holidays?	[ ]	[ ]	[ ]
5. Is the school staff (administrative, instructional, counseling and supportive) representative of the racial, ethnic and cultural groups that comprise the surrounding community?	[ ]	[ ]	[ ]
6. Are staff or volunteers available who are fluent in the languages of families in the school community?	[ ]	[ ]	[ ]
7. Do students, families and staff share in the decision-making process for the school?	[ ]	[ ]	[ ]
8. Has the school community collaboratively developed written policies and procedures to address harassment and bullying?	[ ]	[ ]	[ ]
9. Are consequences associated with harassment and bullying policy violations enforced equitably and consistently?	[ ]	[ ]	[ ]
10. Do the instructional materials used in the classroom and available in the school library, including text books, supplementary books and multimedia resources, reflect the experiences and perspectives of people of diverse backgrounds?	[ ]	[ ]	[ ]
11. Are equitable opportunities for participation in extra- and co-curricular activities made available to students of all gender, ability and socioeconomic groups?	[ ]	[ ]	[ ]
12. Do faculty and staff have opportunities for systematic, comprehensive and continuing professional development designed to increase cultural understanding and promote student safety?	[ ]	[ ]	[ ]
13. Does the school conduct ongoing evaluations of the goals, methods and instructional materials used in teaching to ensure they reflect the histories, contributions and perspectives of diverse groups?	[ ]	[ ]	[ ]

UNIT I. SETTING A RESPECTFUL CLASSROOM TONE

For most young people, middle school is the first time they will switch classes for different subject areas. As a result, they will interact with several different teachers and a large group of students each day. Most middle school teachers will only see their students for 45 minutes each day and do not have the luxury of getting to know those students well or spending a great deal of time creating a safe and inclusive classroom environment. Therefore, establishing a positive and inclusive tone in the classroom and teaching social and emotional skills from the onset is critical. Further, in the context of teaching anti-bias skills, it is particularly important that students have opportunities to develop social and emotional skills and that their classroom environments are safe, respectful and inclusive.

In Unit I of this curriculum, students will have the opportunity to develop ground rules for working together so that all students feel safe, ready and able to participate. To help them express their feelings effectively as well as building empathy skills, they will expand their feelings vocabulary, reflect on their own feelings and learn how to empathize with the feelings of others. Middle schoolers will explore the magnitude of communication in our daily lives, reflect on the ways in which communication can be most effective and develop skills and strategies to improve their communication. Handling conflict is not only a critical life skill; it is essential in effectively responding to issues of bias and bullying because often conflicts arise when grappling with these topics. Students will learn more about conflict and reflect on their own conflict styles in order to expand the strategies they use when encountering conflict. Finally, learning to work as a team is an essential part of being a member of the school community as well as an important life skill.

1. WHAT I NEED TO FEEL SAFE

Rationale

The purpose of this lesson is to begin to create a classroom environment where students feel safe, included and engaged. Developing ground rules that everyone agrees to will help students feel safe in the classroom, especially when they are discussing challenging and/or sensitive topics. This lesson provides an opportunity for students to reflect on what they need to feel safe, share with others and develop buy-in to the classroom ground rules.

Objectives

- Students will consider what ground rules are and the purpose they serve.
- Students will reflect on what they need in the classroom to feel safe and will share those thoughts and feelings with others.
- Students will establish classroom ground rules so that everyone feels safe.

What's Needed

Post-it Notes® (at least five per student), construction paper (10 sheets), chart paper or smart board, markers

Advance Preparation: Write the following on chart paper or smart board:

Question 1: What do you need to feel safe?
Question 2: What do you need to feel included?
Question 3: What do you need to feel engaged (i.e., interested in what's going on)?
Question 4: What do you need to feel open to learning?
Question 5: What do you need to be yourself?

TIME
45 minutes

COMMON CORE STANDARDS
Writing, Speaking & Listening

STRATEGIES AND SKILLS
large and small group discussion, consensus building, concentric circles

KEY WORDS AND PHRASES
concentric, consensus, engaged, ground rules

Procedures

1. Begin the lesson by explaining to students that as a class, they are going to develop some ground rules so that everyone feels safe, respected and able to participate. Explain that the ground rules will be part of the class going forward, especially as they are engaged in the learning about bias, bullying and social justice. Ask: *What are ground rules? Why are ground rules important especially when we are discussing challenging or sensitive topics?*

NOTE 2

If concentric circles are not possible due to logistics or spacing limitations in your classroom, instead play some music and have students mill around the classroom. When you stop the music, they should talk with the person to whom they are standing closest.

2. If space is available in the classroom, create concentric circles by assigning half the class the number "1" and the other half the number "2." Explain that concentric circles provide an opportunity to have short conversations with several different people. Have the "1" students come to the center of the room and form a tight circle. They should be facing inside. When they are situated in the circle, have them all turn around so they are facing outward. Next, have all the "2" students come and face one of the "1" students so that two concentric circles have formed with each student facing another student.

3. Explain to students that you are going to ask a series of questions and each pair will respond to each question by taking turns talking. They should decide who talks first before responding. When time is up, you will give instructions as to who moves and how. Tell students they won't take notes during the activity but that they should make a "mental note" of what they shared.

4. Read the following five questions one at a time and give 60 seconds for the pair (30 seconds for each student) to respond to the question. Let students know when 30 seconds is up and it is time to switch who is speaking. After each question is completed (i.e., both students have talked), have either the inner circle ("1" students) or outer circle ("2" students) move one or more places to the left or right so that they are facing a new student. Do not make this part overly complicated because the focus should remain on the questions, not the partners.

   Question 1: What do you need to feel safe?

   Question 2: What do you need to feel included?

   Question 3: What do you need to feel engaged? (i.e., interested in what's going on)

   Question 4: What do you need to feel open to learning?

   Question 5: What do you need to be yourself?

5. Have students return to their seats and distribute five *Post-it Notes®* to each student. Remind them of the five questions by posting them on the smart board or chart paper (after the concentric circle activity). Have students reflect on their concentric circle conversations and record any needs, ground rules or guidelines that come to mind after discussing

what they need to feel safe, included, engaged, open to learning and to be themselves. When they are finished, have students (a few at a time) post their notes on the board or on a wall in the classroom.

6. As students are placing their needs and ground rules on the board, organize them so that similar ideas and rules are grouped together. You may want to enlist the help of two or three students to do this task.

7. If space is available, have students come up and look at the board and if not, read aloud the responses and how you grouped similar ideas or rules together. Engage students in a group discussion by asking the following questions:

   a. Are there any patterns that you notice?

   b. Are there some ground rules that are listed more than once? A lot? Which?

   c. Are there some ground rules that are listed just once or a few times? Which?

   d. Are there any conflicting ground rules?

   e. What is your sense of what people need to feel safe, included, engaged, open to learning and to be themselves?

8. As a class, come up with 6–8 ground rules and get consensus that everyone can agree to the ground rules. Define **consensus** as "general agreement" and explain that everyone should feel like they can agree to or "live with" the decision made by consensus.

9. Once the rules are created, divide the students into 6–8 small groups and give each group one of the ground rules. Distribute one sheet of construction paper to each small group and have the groups create signs that have the rule written clearly, a drawing to illustrate the rule and one sentence about why the rule is important (e.g., "no interrupting" can have a picture of two people talking over each other with a line through it and a phrase like "It is rude."). Give students ten minutes to complete this task.

10. When students are done, have each group present their ground rule poster. After all groups have presented, post all of the posters somewhere in the classroom for easy viewing. Ask again for consensus to abide by all the ground rules.

Extension Activities

◼ Have students interview their parent or another adult family member or friend to find out what kind of rules and guidelines they have at work and the purpose and goal of the rules or ground rules. After having that conversation, they will record what the rule is, why they have the rule, how it is enforced and what happens if someone doesn't follow the rule.

◼ Have students construct a short persuasive essay on a rule (either in their school, community or country) they disagree with and why they disagree with that rule. They should explain what the rule is, why they think the rule was created (i.e., what purpose it serves) and why they disagree. It can be written in the form of a letter or an op-ed.

2. FEELINGS AND EMPATHY

TIME
45–60 minutes

COMMON CORE STANDARDS
Reading, Writing, Speaking &
Listening, Language

STRATEGIES AND SKILLS
small group discussion, writing, role
play, small group work

KEY WORDS AND PHRASES
constructive, destructive, emojis,
empathy

Rationale

The purpose of this lesson is to help students understand their feelings and learn how to be empathic to the feelings of others. As students discuss sensitive and sometimes difficult topics, feelings arise and it is helpful to be aware of these feelings and act accordingly. This lesson provides an opportunity for students to expand their feelings vocabulary, reflect on how they are feeling and why, be mindful of how they respond to strong feelings and promote empathy for others' feelings.

Objectives

- Students will be able to identify how they are feeling and why.
- Students will analyze how different feeling words represent the intensity of the feeling.
- Students will reflect on constructive and destructive responses to anger and other feelings.
- Students will consider the ways in which they can learn how others are feeling.

What's Needed

Handouts and Resources: Feelings Scale Strips Template (for facilitator only), *Emojis and Feelings* (one for each student)

Other Material: Sheets of paper with 1, 25, 50, 75 and 100 written on them, chart paper and markers

Advance Preparation:

- Place signs on the walls around the room in order as follows: (1) 1, (2) 25, (3) 50, (4) 75 and (5) 100.
- Read through the lesson and determine which of the following two methods you will use for the *Feelings Scale Strips Template* (see Procedure #2).

    a. Cut all of the *Feelings Scale Strips* to distribute one to each student. Be sure to mix them up before passing out.

b. Cut the *Feelings Scale Strips* and group them as categorized on the template to distribute a categorized group of words to each small group.

■ Make a copy of the *Feelings Scale Strips Template* for your reference.

Procedures

1. Begin the lesson by asking students: *How are you feeling today?* Allow a few students to answer briefly. Then ask: *On a scale of 1 to 100, 1 being the lowest (worst feeling) and 100 being the highest (best feeling), how are you feeling today?* Tell students to place themselves around the room according to how they're feeling on a scale of 1–100. Explain that they can either stand right near the sign with the number (e.g., if they are feeling 50) or in between (e.g., if they are feeling 10). Give students a few minutes to situate themselves. Then ask some students to share why they are standing where they are. Record any feeling words on chart paper or on the board/smart board. Define any words that may be unfamiliar.

2. Explain to students that many feelings' words have degrees (mild to strong) that illustrate the intensity of that feeling. For example, on a given day you may be feeling fine or you may be feeling fabulous. Explain to students that they are going to work in small groups and will look at a variety of words that convey similar feelings to different degrees. Based on the option you selected in preparation of this lesson, distribute the *Feelings Scale Strips* according to one of the following processes:

    a. Distribute one *Feelings Scale Strip* to each student and have the students get into groups by finding each other according to the feelings word they have (i.e., all anger words together, all sad words together, etc.). This is the preferred process but will take longer.

    b. Divide the students into small groups of 4–5 students each and give each group a collection of words for a specific category (i.e., all anger words, all sad words, etc.). It's okay if more than one group has the same collection of words.

3. Explain that working in small groups, they will discuss all of the words they have, define each of them and try to come to agreement on the order the words go in based on the intensity of the feeling. Let them know they should try to agree but agreement may not be reached. If students are unfamiliar with any words, they should try to figure out the meaning or look up in dictionary if necessary. Give students 5–7 minutes to work in their small groups to complete this task.

4. When the time is up, everyone should come back to the large group and each small group will present their word category and their order of intensity. They will also share whether they came to agreement or not and if not, explain their areas of disagreement.

5. Engage students in a class discussion by asking the following questions:

    — Which of these words were unfamiliar?

    — Was it difficult or easy to come to agreement on the order of the words?

    — What is useful about using different words to convey different levels of intensity about how we are feeling?

    — Why it is useful to expand our "feelings vocabulary?"

6. Ask students, "What are emojis (or emoticons)?" When and how do we use them? Elicit from students that we usually use emojis to convey a feeling or emotion and they are especially used in texting, email and social media where we cannot convey a feeling as we normally do in person. Ask, "How do we convey the feeling in person?" Elicit from students that we use tone of voice, facial expression and body language to convey feelings that go along with the words we are speaking.

7. Distribute one copy of the *Emojis and Feelings* handout to each student and explain that students will take a few minutes to look at each emoji on the sheet and write a word underneath it on the blank line that best describes

FLIPPED CLASSROOM IDEA

Make a short video of you sharing about a recent time you were very angry about something. Use different feelings words to describe your anger and explain what happened, why you got angry, what you did and what the result was in the end.

the feeling conveyed in the emoji. Give students five minutes to complete this task. Have students then turn and talk to a person sitting next to them and share what they recorded on their handout. Have them notice if they came up with different or similar words to describe the emojis.

8. Explain to students that we are going to discuss the emotion of anger in greater detail.  Have students think about a time that they were very angry. Ask, "What happened? Why did you get angry? What did you do? What was the outcome and how did you feel?" Have students think about the incident or situation silently and then focus on the last question ("What did you do?") for discussion. Record some of their responses on the board, which may look something like this:

— Screamed at the person I was angry at

— Listened to music

— Got revenge on social media

— Hit a wall

— Walked away

— Asked for mediation

— Talked to or texted my best friend

— Went into my room and did nothing

— Cried to myself

— Confronted the person and told them how I felt

— Played sports

— Blew up at my brother or sister

9. Elicit from students that when we have strong feelings about something, there can be many different ways to respond. Sometimes what we do makes us feel better and makes the situation better. Other times, our expression of feelings makes us feel better but makes the situation worse. And sometimes, we feel worse and the situation is worse. Go through the items on the board and ask: Was this a constructive ("helping to improve") response to the angry feeling or a destructive ("causing destruction or damage") response? As students share their thoughts, write a "C" (constructive) or "D" (destructive) and note where there is disagreement. Have students elaborate on the reason for their response.

10. Engage students in a discussion by asking: How can we make sure that the way we respond to strong feelings is constructive rather than destructive?

11. Have students write a short story (either during class or for homework) about a time they had strong feelings about something. In the essay, they should share (1) what happened, (2) how they felt, (3) what they did and (4) what happened after they acted on their feelings. If they were dissatisfied with the way the situation ended, have them share in the essay what they might have done differently if they could re-do the situation and how they think the outcome would be different. Have some of the students share their stories aloud.

12. In order to facilitate a discussion about how to understand and "read" other people's feelings, act out one of the scenarios below. You will need a student volunteer to act out the role of the person listening to you. After role playing the scenario, ask students the following questions:

   — What was the person feeling? What words would you use to describe the feelings?

   — How do you know how the person is feeling?

   — What do you see, hear and notice?

   — What can you do to find out what the person is feeling that is not possible to see and hear from this scenario?

13. If time permits, use the other scenarios below or ones you create to generate a discussion about how other people feel. You may ask for volunteers of two students to play the parts and engage students in a discussion by asking others to notice how they're feeling.

   Scenario 1: You just found out that your best friend is dating someone you like. Your best friend knows how much you like this person and has been keeping the fact that they're dating from you for several weeks. You are talking to a mutual friend about it.

   Scenario 2: You are talking to your mom about a party you want to go to this weekend. She reminds you that your grandparents are coming to visit and you can't go because there are a lot of plans she has made. This is an important party. You are talking to your mom about it.

   Scenario 3: You've been working really hard in school, especially in social studies, but you can't seem to get past a C grade. You are talking to your teacher about it.

14. Ask students, "Does anyone know what the word empathy means?" Elicit a definition of **empathy** as the ability to identify with or experience the feelings and thoughts of others.

15. As a way to conclude the lesson, ask students the following questions:

   — Why is it helpful to be in touch with how you are feeling?

   — Why is it helpful to understand different ways to respond to feelings?

   — Why is empathy important?

Extension Activities

■ Have students watch a few scenes from an online video, television program or movie with the sound turned off and have them try to guess what's going on and how the characters are feeling without hearing what they say. Then rewind or play the scene again to see if they got it right. Have them take notes on what the scene was, what they thought with the sound turned off and what actually happened and how the characters felt.

■ Have students use a book they are currently reading from a feelings lens, which means as they read it, they should ask themselves: "How are the different characters feeling about what's going on?" and record that for each chapter and make note of when the characters' feelings change or if they have particularly strong feelings.

FEELINGS SCALE STRIPS TEMPLATE

ANGRY WORDS

- Irritated
- Angry
- Mad
- Furious
- Enraged
- Annoyed

HAPPY WORDS

- Pleased
- Elated
- Cheerful
- Happy
- Joyous
- Thrilled

SAD WORDS

- Down
- Bitter
- Sad
- Sorrowful
- Heartbroken
- Dismal

ASHAMED WORDS

- Ashamed
- Embarrassed
- Mortified
- Disgraced
- Humiliated
- Guilty

NERVOUS WORDS

- Nervous
- Anxious
- Agitated
- Jittery
- Tense
- Stressed

EXUBERANT WORDS

- Eager
- Exuberant
- Zealous
- Enthusiastic
- Passionate
- Avid

SILLY WORDS

- Nonsensical
- Hilarious
- Silly
- Foolish
- Childish
- Playful

CONFUSION WORDS

- Befuddled
- Perplexed
- Confused
- Baffled
- Discombobulated
- Puzzled

EMOJIS AND FEELINGS

Directions: For each emoji, write on the line below it one word that you think describes the feeling of the emoji.

Emojis provided for free by http://emojione.com.

3. COMMUNICATION

TIME
45 minutes

COMMON CORE STANDARDS
Reading, Speaking & Listening,
Language

STRATEGIES AND SKILLS
define terms, turn and talk, large
and small group discussion,
presentation

KEY WORDS AND PHRASES
communication, miscommunication,
nonverbal communication

FLIPPED
CLASSROOM IDEA

Make a short video of you talking
about all the ways in which you
communicated from the evening
before until you walked into school
that day. Include in person, phone
and electronic communication
as part of your discussion. Play
the video then ask the questions
indicated in Procedure #1.

Rationale

The purpose of this lesson is to help students understand the ways in which communication takes place and that it is not exclusively verbal; it also includes nonverbal as well as electronic communication. Effective communication is a critical life skill and helps students understand themselves and each other. This lesson provides an opportunity for students to expand their understanding of communication, understand effective and ineffective communication and work together to explore some of the Do's and Don'ts of different communication strategies.

Objectives

- Students will define communication and reflect on the ways they communicate every day.
- Students will explore the elements of effective and ineffective communication.
- Students will delineate the different ways people communicate and then analyze what are the Do's and Don'ts for each.

What's Needed

Handouts and Resources: The Big Bang Theory 'Please pass the butter' conversation between Amy and Sheldon video (2014, 2 min., www.youtube.com/watch?v=vkSwXL3cGUg)

Other Material: Internet access, screen or LCD projector, speakers

Procedures

1. Play the 2-minute YouTube video, *The Big Bang Theory 'Please pass the butter' conversation between Amy and Sheldon.* This video is a clip from the TV show *The Big Bang Theory,* season 7, episode 19, "The Indecision Amalgamation." After playing the video, ask students, "What

was going on in the scene? Do you think they were communicating?"

2. Ask: *What is communication?* Come to a definition of **communication** as the act of using words, sounds, signs or behaviors to exchange information or express your ideas, thoughts, feelings, etc. to someone else or a group of people.

3. Have students turn and talk with a person sitting next to them and respond to the following question: *Beginning last night after dinner through this morning when you arrived at school, what are all the different ways you communicated?*

   Give students two minutes to do this (one minute per person) and have students take notes for each other on what is said. After the turn and talk is over, ask students to share with the whole class some of what was said. The list might look something like this:

   — Group chat texts with my friends

   — Talked to my family at dinner

   — Sent an email to my teacher

   — Played a video game and direct messaged someone

   — Woke up my little sister

   — Talked on the phone to my grandfather

   — Face timed or skyped someone in class to understand the math homework

4. Ask, "What do you notice about the list?" Elicit from students that there is a lot of communication happening all the time and it takes many forms.

5. Have all students stand up and mill around the room, playing music as they walk around, if possible. Explain that when you stop the music (or call "freeze" if you don't play music), they should stop and answer the question you say out loud with the person standing closest to them. Each student in the pair should come up with one idea each. Then you will move on to the next question.

   Use the following four questions or ones you make up to resonate with your students:

   — If you are doing a class presentation, what should you do to communicate well?

   — If you are asking someone to the dance or prom, what should you do so you don't miscommunicate?

   — If you are asking your parents for an increase in your allowance, what should you do to communicate well?

   — If you are talking to your neighbors about dog sitting for them, what should you not do or say?

6. Have students go back to their desks and engage them in a large group discussion by asking, "Based on what you just discussed, what are some elements of effective or good communication? What are the elements of ineffective or poor communication?" Create a list on the board or smart board that might look something like this:

   — Be clear about what you are communicating and clarify unclear points.

   — Think about the person to whom you are communicating (your audience).

   — Speak for yourself.

   — Communicate your feelings.

   — Be aware of non-verbal communication such as body language and facial expressions (if in person), tone of voice or message (in case of texts, social media), word choice, social space, etc.

— As the person listening or the recipient of communication, pay attention, listen actively and respond when appropriate.

7. With the students, and reflecting on the conversation thus far, create a list of the ways in which we communicate, which should include the following:
   — Phone
   — Texting
   — Direct messages via social media, games, etc.
   — In person (face to face)
   — Video chatting , Facetime or Skype
   — Email/Letters

8. Divide students into six groups and assign each group one of the ways we communicate listed above. Explain that students will have 10–15 minutes to work together and focus on their particular form of communication. For each, they will discuss (1) the various ways their form is used (i.e., phone can include individual phone call, facetime, or 3-way calling), (2) the Do's and Don'ts for each (i.e., when texting, be careful about tone) and (3) how to present their Do's and Don'ts to the rest of the class.

   For the group presentation, you may assign this for homework to allow students to continue working on it, but they should get a start and have a sense of what they will be doing. For the presentation, you can give them a variety of strategies to share their Do's and Don'ts with the class that include:
   — role play or skit
   — poster
   — storyboard
   — written essay
   — video about it
   — photo story on Tumblr or Instagram
   — PowerPoint or Prezi presentation

9. Have each of the groups present their work. As they are illustrating or articulating the Do's and Don'ts, make a general list of Do's and Don'ts that includes all of the different strategies. After all the presentations are completed, engage students in a discussion by asking:
   — Was it easier to come up with the Do's or the Don'ts?
   — Why do you think that is the case?
   — Do you see any patterns among the different ways we communicate? In other words, are there similar things we should and shouldn't do whether it's electronic, phone or in person communication?
   — Are there some Do's and Don'ts that are particular to the form of communication? How so?
   — Reflecting on how you communicate, what might you do differently based on what you heard, discussed and experienced today and these Do's and Don'ts?
   — What gets in the way of effective communication?
   — What makes it easier to communicate?

Extension Activities

▪ Have students practice effective communication by getting them to work in groups of three. Give each triad a topic to discuss and instruct them that one person will be the person talking, the second person will be listening and the third person will be observing and giving feedback. You can also do this with phone and electronic communication and can do several rounds so each person in the triad plays each role.

▪ Have students create and implement a survey about electronic communication (emails, text messages, social media, etc.) among other middle school students that assesses the extent to which students use electronic communication and some of the ways in which miscommunication happens.

4. HANDLING CONFLICT

TIME
45 minutes

COMMON CORE STANDARDS
Reading, Writing, Speaking & Listening, Language

STRATEGIES AND SKILLS
brainstorm, define terms, turn and talk, self-assessment, large group discussion

KEY WORDS AND PHRASES
aggressive, assertive, avoidance, conflict, underlying

Rationale

The purpose of this lesson is to help students understand that conflict is part of life, difficult to avoid and sometimes talking about issues of bias and diversity brings up conflict. It is important that students understand that conflict isn't always negative. It helps to be self-reflective about how we deal with conflict situations and try to improve the way we handle them. This lesson provides an opportunity for students to understand what conflict is, explore the positives and negatives of conflict and reflect on their own conflict styles in order to handle conflict more successfully.

Objectives

- Students will define conflict and reflect on the extent to which conflict is positive and/or negative.
- Students will explore the ways in which they handle conflict situations.
- Students will analyze different strategies for how conflict is handled and the pros and cons for each response.
- Students will understand the difference between wants and needs in a conflict situation.

What's Needed

Handouts and Resources: Conflict Style Self-Assessment (one for each student)

Other Material: Chart paper or board/smart board, markers

Procedures

1. Begin the lesson by brainstorming students' associations with the word conflict. Write the word "conflict" on chart paper or the board (putting a circle around it) and ask students, "What is conflict?" Create a semantic

web by recording students' responses and connecting words and ideas that connect with one other. To elicit as much response as possible, also ask, "What feelings do you associate with conflict? What different kinds of conflict are there?" See sample semantic web below:

2. Ask students, "How would you define conflict?" Come to a definition of **conflict** as an argument, fight, disagreement or struggle over something.  Share an example and ask for a few students to share a conflict they had recently.

3. Ask students: *Is conflict positive or negative?* Have all the students who believe that conflict is positive move to one side of the room and the students who believe conflict is negative should move to the other side of the room. Some students may say they are not sure or it depends on the situation. For the purpose of this activity, have them choose one or the other. After students are situated on their chosen side of the room, students should take 3–5 minutes to share with each other why they are standing in the positive or negative side of the room.

4. After sharing their thoughts, have students go back to their seats, ask some students to share why they feel conflict is positive or negative and ask for examples. Come to a mutual understanding that conflict is usually seen as negative but that there are positive aspects and there can be positive outcomes to conflict.

5. Have students turn and talk to the person sitting next to them and together, come up with at least two things that are negative about conflict and two things that are positive about conflict. Give them five minutes to do this. They should record their ideas on paper. Then have everyone come back together and going around the room, have each pair share what's on their list. If something is shared that another pair has already said, they can pick something else to share until all ideas have been shared. Create a

FLIPPED CLASSROOM IDEA

Make a short video of you talking about a conflict you had recently or a hypothetical conflict situation between two students (make sure it is generic so that it isn't something that happened to students in your class) and share what happened, what caused the conflict and the extent to which it had a positive or negative outcome.

T-chart on the board/smart board that looks something like this and that includes all student responses.

What's Negative about Conflict?	What's Positive about Conflict?
It could lead to a fight	You get to some underlying problems
You feel badly after	Things get better

6. Summarize by saying that conflict can be destructive when it causes more tension between people, makes people feel bad about themselves or each other and causes harm or damage (physical or emotional). On the other hand, conflict can be constructive if it brings more meaning and understanding between people or groups, opens up something that was beneath the surface or brings people together.

7. Distribute a copy of the *Conflict Style Self-Assessment* to each student. Explain that they will have about 10 minutes to complete the self-assessment, which provides conflict situations and asks them to decide how they would handle each. Tell students that it's best if they answer the questions as honestly as possible and that the assessment is "for their eyes only" in order to help them reflect on how they tend to handle conflict situations. Explain to students that for each statement, they should check the box that fits most closely to how they would respond to the conflict situation. If the situation is one they haven't dealt with in the past, they should try to imagine how they would respond, based on past experiences.

8. After students have completed their sheets, engage students in a discussion by asking the following questions:
    — Did you notice any pattern about your responses? (Have them raise their hands if they did see a pattern.)
    — Can someone explain a pattern you noticed?
    — Were some questions more difficult than others to answer?
    — Did you learn anything new about your own responses to conflict? If so, what did you learn?
    — What causes conflict?
    — What else did you learn from doing this?

9. Explain to students that the three choices of responses on their self-assessments represent three general ways people response to conflict. Write on the board these three words: AGGRESSIVE, AVOIDANCE, ASSERTIVE and ask students if they know which of these words represent the different responses on their *Conflict Style Self-Assessment*. It is as follows:

    I would ignore it and hope it just goes away = Avoidance

    I would fight back or do/say something in a mean or angry way = Aggressive

    I would try to talk to the person(s) about what I feel and think = Assertive

10. Engage students in a discussion about the three responses to conflict: aggressive, avoidance and assertive. Elicit the definitions from students and come to a definition as follows:

    Aggressive: Pursue what one wants or needs without regard to the other person, using harsh language, strong resistance or physical force.

    Avoidance: Ignore or delay the problem or conflict, hoping it resolves itself or goes away without confrontation.

    Assertive: Express thoughts and feelings and asking for what you want and need without violating the rights of others.

    After clarifying each of the conflict strategies, share an example of a conflict situation (you can use one of the situations on the sheet or make up a new one) and ask students to share an example of an aggressive response, an avoidance response and an assertive response.

11. Engage students in a discussion by asking the following questions:
    - Which of these conflict strategies is most desirable and why?
    - Does it depend on the situation? Please explain.
    - Do you tend to use one of these strategies more than others?
    - What is lost and what is gained with each of the types of responses?

12. Have a brief discussion with students about the difference between wants and needs. Ask students, "What is a need? What is a want?" Explain that often people say that they want something but there is something else underneath that they feel they need or they may state something as a need but there is something underlying that they really want. Read the following sentence aloud:

    I want to go to bed later than my parents say I should.

13. Ask students, "What do you think is the need that is underneath that?" Have students share and respond to the question and if necessary, add that this person's needs may be social (they want more time to communicate with their friends), school-related (they want more time to do their homework), or maturity-related (all their friends go to bed later and they feel childish). Ask students, "What do you think the parents' needs are in this situation (e.g., want to make sure their child gets enough sleep, they want quiet time, etc.)." Ask, "Knowing both the needs, do you think there's a way to resolve this conflict?"

    Ask, "Why is it helpful to get to the underlying needs in a conflict situation?" Explain that in order for a conflict situation to be resolved, one needs to be aware of their underlying needs in the situation. Often conflicts come about because of competing needs but sometimes they aren't competing if you get to what's underlying.

14. As a closing, have students share something new they learned that will cause them to re-think how they will handle conflict in the future.

Extension Activities

▰ Have students do an analysis of how conflict is portrayed in the media by watching a TV program, video game, movie, video, etc. and respond to the following questions: How do the main characters deal with conflict? Do they avoid it, act aggressive or use assertion? Do you think the response is appropriate given the situation? What makes you think that?

▰ Have students write a story about a conflict they had recently. In the story, the following questions should be answered: What happened? What did you want vs. what did you need? How did you handle it (avoidance, aggressive, assertive)? How did the conflict end? What would you have done differently? What were the positive and negative aspects of the conflict?

CONFLICT STYLE SELF-ASSESSMENT

Directions: For each statement, check the box that fits most closely to how you would respond to the conflict situation. If the situation is one you haven't dealt with in the past, you should try to imagine how you would respond, based on past experiences. The assessment is "for your eyes only" in order to help you reflect on how you tend to handle conflict situations. Thus, it's best if you answer the questions as honestly as possible.

	I would ignore it and hope it just goes away.	I would fight back or do/say something in a mean or angry way.	I would try to talk to the person(s) about what I feel and think.
1. I found out two of my friends said mean things about me in a group text chat.	[ ]	[ ]	[ ]
2. My friend always asks me if s/he can copy my homework, but I don't want to let her/him and get in trouble.	[ ]	[ ]	[ ]
3. I'm embarrassed because my mom won't let me go to my friend's house unless she talks to my friend's mom first, but no one else's mom is calling.	[ ]	[ ]	[ ]
4. I am the best pitcher on the team but the coach always lets this other girl/boy pitch because the coach plays favorites.	[ ]	[ ]	[ ]
5. I got an F on my history project and it's because my teacher hates me; I don't want to tell my parents about the grade.	[ ]	[ ]	[ ]
6. I found out a group of my friends all had a sleepover last weekend and I was the only one not invited.	[ ]	[ ]	[ ]
7. I'm secretly dating someone my best friend likes and I don't want to tell my best friend.	[ ]	[ ]	[ ]
8. I am doing all of the work for my group project.	[ ]	[ ]	[ ]
9. This boy/girl keeps telling people how s/he has a crush on me, but I only like him/her as a friend.	[ ]	[ ]	[ ]
10. A group of kids always makes fun of my little brother and they call him "gay" and "girly."	[ ]	[ ]	[ ]
11. My parents make me go to bed at 9 but all of my friends stay up much later.	[ ]	[ ]	[ ]
12. People call me a loser and a nerd just because I get good grades and am on the debate team.	[ ]	[ ]	[ ]

	I would ignore it and hope it just goes away.	I would fight back or do/say something in a mean or angry way.	I would try to talk to the person(s) about what I feel and think.
13. My male teacher always makes jokes about girls and women but I don't find them funny.	[ ]	[ ]	[ ]
14. My little sister cries to me about how she gets bullied at school by some mean girls but told me not to tell my parents.	[ ]	[ ]	[ ]
15. My sister/brother wore my favorite shirt to a party and stained it.	[ ]	[ ]	[ ]
16. My friend and I got in a fight on an Instagram chat last night and said some pretty horrible things to each other. Now I don't know what to say to her at school tomorrow.	[ ]	[ ]	[ ]
17. My mom won't take me to school until I change my outfit because she says it's "not appropriate." But all my friends wear this kind of stuff.	[ ]	[ ]	[ ]
18. There's a group of girls/boys on my soccer team and they are constantly making fun of how I play.	[ ]	[ ]	[ ]

5. TEAMWORK AND COLLABORATION

TIME
45 minutes

COMMON CORE STANDARDS
Writing, Speaking & Listening

STRATEGIES AND SKILLS
small group problem solving, large group discussion, analyze quotes

KEY WORDS AND PHRASES
collaboration, teamwork

Rationale

The purpose of this lesson is to give students practical skills in collaboration. Teamwork and collaboration are life skills that are essential for success in school, in the workplace and in life and many of the activities in this curriculum include small group discussion and group projects. This lesson provides an opportunity for students to reflect on what makes teamwork successful, complete and reflect on a task that requires collaboration and explore teamwork through a collection of famous quotes.

Objectives

- Students will define teamwork and reflect on the elements of teamwork that make it successful.
- Students will examine how they work together as a team.
- Students will analyze famous quotes about teamwork through writing a short reflection on a quote of their choice.

What's Needed

Handouts and Resources: Quotes about Teamwork (one for each student)

Other Material: Drinking straws (enough for 50 straws per group), one roll of masking tape per group, five paper clips per group

Procedures

1. Begin the lesson by asking students, "What is teamwork?" Define **teamwork** as a cooperative effort in which a group of people work together for a common goal or cause. When does teamwork go well? When does it not go well? Elicit from students that teamwork works well when everyone participates and has a role to play, you reach your goal and everyone feels part of the team (i.e., included.)

2. Ask students, "What are some situations in which you have to work as a team?" Brainstorm a list which might look something like this:
   - sports activity
   - group project at school
   - band—playing together
   - performing a play
   - making something together
   - block party
   - orchestra or chorus
   - a family activity or responsibility/chore

3. Have students turn and talk with a person sitting next to them and respond to the following two questions (two minutes per person):

   Share about a time when teamwork didn't go well.

   Share about a time when teamwork did go well.

4. Have students come back to the large group and engage them in a discussion by asking the following questions:
   - Was it easier to come up with a situation that didn't go well or did go well?
   - Would anyone like to share what they talked about with their partner?
   - What makes teamwork not go well?
   - What makes teamwork go well?

5. Divide students into small groups of 4–5 students each and explain that they will be working together on a group project. Tell them that as a group, they will construct a tower using straws, masking tape and paper clips. Distribute to each small group 50 straws, five paper clips and a roll of masking tape.

6. Explain to students that they will have 15 minutes to build the highest tower they can. They may only use the straws, paper clips and masking tape which were given to them but they do not have to use everything. They will be able to and should interact with each other but cannot interact with other groups or individuals in those groups. Explain that this is somewhat of a competition in that the group with the tallest tower wins. Give students 15 minutes to construct their towers. Circulate around the room to get a sense of how the groups are sharing ideas and communicating, paying attention to both frustration and enthusiasm.

7. After the 15 minutes are up and the towers are constructed, measure the towers, assess which group has the tallest tower and announce the winners. Then, ask each group to share their process for designing and implementing their tower. Do not allow cross talk at this time.

8. Have students come back to the large group and engage them in a discussion by asking the following questions:
   - What was successful in how you built the tower and worked together?
   - What was challenging about working together?
   - Did everyone have a role to play in constructing the tower?
   - Did anyone take a leadership role? Did someone lay back and not contribute as much?
   - How did you work together as a team?

FLIPPED CLASSROOM IDEA

Make a short video of you talking about one of the quotes from the *Quotes About Teamwork* handout, one that particularly resonates for you and discuss whether you agree or disagree with the quote and why and the reason the quote is particularly meaningful for you.

— How was the communication within the team?

— What did you learn about working together?

9.  Distribute to each student the *Quotes About Teamwork* handout. Explain to students that they should read the quotes to themselves and then choose one quote that most resonates with them. It doesn't necessarily have to be a quote with which they agree, just one they find interesting. Their task is to read the quote and then write a short response using these questions:

— Do you agree or disagree with the quote? Why?

— What does the quote mean to you?

— What, if anything, is missing in the quote?

10. Have some students share their quotes and short essays.

Extension Activities

■ Create a game (either electronic, board or activity-based game) that requires cooperation instead of competition. Draw a sketch of the game and write out the rules. If possible, play the game with a group of friends or family members in order to assess its pitfalls and then improve it.

■ Do research about one of the people whose teamwork quote is listed and prepare a short written or oral biography. What were this person's life accomplishments? How did teamwork help them to achieve their accomplishments? What else could we learn about teamwork based on this person's life?

QUOTES ABOUT TEAMWORK

"Talent wins games, but teamwork and intelligence win championships." —Michael Jordan

"I'm not under too much of an illusion of how smart or un-smart I am because filmmaking ultimately is about teamwork." —Guy Ritchie

"Alone we can do so little; together we can do so much." —Helen Keller

"Teamwork is the ability to work together toward a common vision. The ability to direct individual accomplishments toward organizational objectives. It is the fuel that allows common people to attain uncommon results." —Andrew Carnegie

"I never did anything alone. Whatever was accomplished in this country was accomplished collectively." —Golda Meir

"None of us is as smart as all of us." —Ken Blanchard

"It takes two flints to make a fire." —Louisa May Alcott

"So powerful is the light of unity that it can illuminate the whole earth." —Bahaullah (1817-1892); Prophet Founder of The Baha

"Coming together is a beginning, staying together is progress, and working together is success." —Henry Ford

"The way a team plays as a whole determines its success. You may have the greatest bunch of individual stars in the world, but if they don't play together, the club won't be worth a dime." —Babe Ruth

"No individual can win a game by himself." —Pelé

"Individually, we are one drop. Together, we are an ocean." —Ryunosuke Satoro

UNIT II. IDENTITY AND DIFFERENCES

As young people move into middle school and adolescence, understanding their identity and group identification takes on greater importance and meaning. Middle school students are more aware of their skills, interests and abilities, and some of those talents will end up being life-long. In addition, during this time in their lives young people are increasingly able to and interested in understanding identity groups such as race, gender/gender identity, ethnicity, religion, sexual orientation, etc. It is also a time in life when differences tend to divide middle school students; cliques form and identity-based bullying can become more pronounced and challenging. Understanding one's own identity, the groups to which one belongs and reflecting on these are important foundations in understanding and addressing bias.

In Unit II, students will have the opportunity to reflect on aspects of who they are, including identity characteristics that they were born with and those of their choosing. These include interests, skills, family, community, race, gender, culture, ethnicity, religion, etc. Students will explore in some depth their interests, skills and talents and share one with their classmates through the creation of an instructional video. Students will identify the most important groups to which they belong and create a pie chart that reflects the percentages of each part's importance. Middle schoolers will examine the positives and negatives of diversity and reflect on situations in which differences led to conflict or misunderstanding. Finally, students will explore groups, cliques and friendships and how diversity and identity impact those relationships.

6. WHO AM I?
(PART 1)

Rationale

The purpose of this lesson is for students to consider the range of identity groups to which one can belong and to reflect on specific aspects of their own identity. Students' ability to understand and identify groups to which they belong is an important part of understanding and valuing diversity. This lesson provides an opportunity for students to define and name identity characteristics, reflect on their own talents and interests and create an instructional video to share with others.

[**NOTE:** This is the first part of a two-part lesson.]

Objectives

▰ Students will define identity and create a list of identity characteristics.

▰ Students will explore aspects of their identity including interests, skills and talents.

▰ Students will reflect on their own interests, skills and talents and create an instructional video to share those interests/skills with others.

What's Needed

Handouts and Resources: Instructional Video Worksheet (one for each student); *How To Make Ice Cream* video (2012, 2½ mins., www.youtube.com/watch?v=d2OuPIegZgY)

Other Material: Index cards (one per student); *Post-it Notes®* (at least 3 per student); board/smart board; 5–6 brown bags; seven pieces of chart paper; magic markers; Internet access, screen or LCD projector, speakers

Advance Preparation: Write the following letters on separate sheets of chart paper and set aside: (1) A-C, (2) D-F, (3) G-J, (4) K-N, (5) O-R, (6) S-V and (7) W-Z.

TIME
Two 45-minute lessons with time in-between for video creation

COMMON CORE STANDARDS
Writing, Speaking & Listening, Language

STRATEGIES AND SKILLS
define terms, identify groups, create instructional video

KEY WORDS AND PHRASES
identity, interests, skills, talents

Procedures

1. Begin the lesson by dividing students into small groups of 5–6 each. Distribute one bag to each group and one index card to each student and have them write something about themselves that no one in their group knows and they are willing to share. After students in the groups have written on their index cards, have them put them all in the bag and have one person in the group pull out one card at a time, as the other students guess who is who in their small groups.

2. Debrief the small groups quickly by asking, "Were you surprised by what you learned about other people? How did you guess who was who?"

3. Ask students: "What is identity?" Come to a definition of **identity** as the qualities, beliefs, etc. that make a particular person or group different from others.

4. Distribute three *Post-it Notes*® to each student and ask students, "What are all the things that make up one's identity?" Have students jot down at least three aspects of identity and explain they should be general categories such as race or religion rather than specifics such as Latino or Jewish. Give students a few minutes to write them down, one on each post-it.

5. One at a time, have students call out what they came up with and if something has already been shared, the person should share the next one on their list or move on to the next person. As students are sharing, record their responses on chart paper or the board/smart board (and save for next lesson) or put the post-its on the board. If students leave out any important categories, add those after everyone has shared. This list might look something like this:

   — Race
   — Ethnicity
   — Religion
   — Gender
   — Sexual Orientation
   — Hobbies
   — Interests
   — Heritage
   — Where I live
   — Talents
   — Physical Appearance
   — Friends/Peers
   — Personality
   — Gender Identity
   — Gender Expression
   — Skills
   — Ability/Disability
   — Social Relationships
   — Family Structure/Family Roles
   — Nationality
   — Health
   — Education
   — Socioeconomic Status
   — Clothing Style
   — Age
   — Community/Geographic Location
   — Language(s) Spoken

6. Ask students, "What are skills, interests and talents?" Define as follows and if necessary, provide an example for each:

   Skill: An ability to do something well which comes from one's knowledge, practice or aptitude.

   Interest: Something that concerns or arouses the curiosity of a person.

Talent: a special natural ability or aptitude.

7. Explain to students that over the next two lessons, they are going to explore different aspects of their identity and today they are going to focus on skills, talents and interests (the second part of the lesson will focus on race, gender/gender identity, religion, ethnicity, etc.). Have students turn and talk with the person sitting next to them and share something they like to do in their spare time and on the weekend, an aspect of their identity of their own choosing that they have pursued and not necessarily something they were born with.

8. Place the chart paper with letters around the room and a magic marker next to each paper. Tell students that when you say "go," they are going to walk around the room and under each of the group of letters on the paper, they should think of skills, talents and interests that begin with one of those letters. As an example, for the chart with the letters A-C, they might include: acting, bicycling and cooking. Give students 5–7 minutes to do this.

    When the time is up, have a different student read aloud each of the pieces of chart paper, noting the long list and range of skills, interests and talents.

9.  Explain to students that they are going to be working either alone or in pairs to create an instructional video about one of their interests, talents or skills. Ask students, "Has anyone ever seen an instructional video? What are the elements of an instructional video?" Show the following instructional video: *How To Make Ice Cream.* After watching it, ask, "What worked well in the video? What didn't work well or what was missing? What did the instructional video include and not include?"

10. Work with students to figure out what interest, talent or skill they want to choose, using the signs around the room for ideas and inspiration. Distribute the *Instructional Video Worksheet* to each student and go over it, highlighting what questions they need to answer in advance, what the outline for the video is and things they need to think about in planning their video. In class, give students 10–15 minutes to begin planning their video. As a homework assignment, they will finish planning and will shoot their video. Be sure to give them enough time to do this (at least one week is recommended) and offer a "check in" time mid-week for students to give progress reports and ask questions.

11. When students have completed their videos, have them send the video to you via email and upload and share with the class. After each video is viewed, have students talk about their process for creating the video as well as where they learned the skill, interest or talent and why it is important to them. Allow students to ask questions after each video.

FLIPPED CLASSROOM IDEA

Have students watch an instructional video of their choice on something they want to learn how to do (or they can watch the *How To Make Ice Cream* video at www.youtube.com/watch?v=d2OuPIegZgY). While watching the video, they should reflect on the following questions: Was the video effective in teaching you something? What did the video do well? What could have been better? After watching the video, instruct students to write down two things that were done well and two things that could have been done better in the instructional video.

Extension Activities

- Have students create a map of their neighborhood, community or town in which they live. They can include houses, stores, community resources, parks and services. They should include a key with categories and draw in the people where they think they should go. Along with the map, have students identify what is missing in their communities—the services, resources and businesses that do not exist there but that are needed.

- Have students do an "oral history" of someone in their family, ideally someone in their extended family. As a group, generate a list of questions to ask for the interview. Have students record the interview, transcribe it and then turn it into a story or article about the person. Consider posting these online as a blog or web page that can include the written work and/or the recordings of the interviews.

INSTRUCTIONAL VIDEO WORKSHEET

Title of Video	
Overall Subject Matter	Length of Video

OUTLINE

What skill(s) will your video teach? What will viewers have learned after watching it?

VIDEO SHOOT

Dates	Location	Who will shoot?
Initial Shoot: Practice Run: Final Shoot:		

THINGS TO CONSIDER

How you will introduce your subject?

Will you be able to edit the video or will you need to get it right in one take?

What do you want in the background or do you want any "scenery?" What visuals will you use?

Who will narrate the video and who will be "filming?"

Will you need cue cards or notes to remind you what to say?
Do you want music playing in the background?
What props, equipment and other items do you need?

7. WHO AM I?
(PART 2)

Rationale

The purpose of this lesson is for students to delve into aspects of their identity that they were born with or were not of their choosing. Identity characteristics such as race, ethnicity, religion, sexual orientation, etc. are important aspects of identity to understand and explore. This lesson provides an opportunity for students to reflect on the meaning of their names, explore one aspect of their identity that they were born into and share that with their peers and learn about other groups of people by reading youth stories.

[**NOTE:** This is the second part of a two-part lesson.]

Objectives

- Students will reflect on the meaning behind their names.
- Students will identify aspects of identity they were born into or did not choose and will define those terms.
- Students will explore one aspect of their identity and share that with others.
- Students will learn about different groups of people by reading and reflecting on youth essays.

What's Needed

Handouts and Resources: Definitions and *My Identity* (one of each for each student); *Identity Essays by Youth*

Other Material: Chart paper list of identity characteristics from Lesson 6

Advance Preparation: Select one of the eight *Identity Essays by Youth* and make enough copies for all students or evenly distribute several essays among the whole class.

TIME
45 minutes

COMMON CORE STANDARDS
Reading, Writing, Speaking & Listening, Language

STRATEGIES AND SKILLS
turn and talk, large and small group discussion, define terms, essay writing, reading

KEY WORDS AND PHRASES
binary, ethnicity, gender, gender identity, language, nationality, race, religion, sexual orientation, socioeconomic status

Procedures

1. Begin the lesson by asking students to think about their names and what they know about the origin of their names—their first, middle, last names or nicknames. Have students turn and talk with a person sitting next to them and share something about their name that is important or significant to them. It can include something about their family, ancestors, culture, name changes, historical information, etc. Give students two minutes to share with each other and let them know they will be also introducing their partner to the whole class so they should listen carefully to their partner, and also not share anything they don't want everyone to know.

2. After sharing with their partners, have each person in the pair introduce their partner to the whole class with information about that person's name (e.g., "This is Marisol, who got her name because her parents wanted to name her after her Great Grandmother."). After everyone has shared, engage students in a brief discussion by asking the following questions:

    — What did you learn from hearing about other people's names?

    — What are the different ways that people come up with names?

    — To what extent to you think names are important and why?

3. Remind students about the previous lesson, Lesson 6, "Who Am I? (Part 1), in which they did an activity around their interests, skills and talents. Explain that for the most part, interests, skills and talents are those that we choose as we develop over time. In this lesson, students are going to discuss aspects of identity that we do not necessarily choose or those we were born with.

NOTE 4

When you address the category of gender/gender identity, explain that even though people are assigned "male" or "female" at birth, being transgender refers to people whose gender identity differs from the sex they were assigned at birth or whose gender expression does not match society's expectations with regard to gender roles.

4. Remind students about the definition of **identity** (the qualities and beliefs that make a particular person or group different from others) and ask the following question: *What aspects of identity are ones that we are either born into or are not of our choosing?* If you still have it, look back at the list of identity characteristics and make a list of those that we are born into and/or those we do not choose. Your list may look something like this:

    — Race
    — Ethnicity
    — Nationality
    — Religion
    — Gender
    — Gender Identity

    — Sexual Orientation
    — Socioeconomic Status
    — Language
    — Culture
    — Disability

5. For each of the terms above, quickly elicit a definition of each of the words. Distribute the *Definitions* handout and go over it, asking for ideas

and sharing examples of each. Ask if there are any questions before you move on to the next step.

6. Have students choose one of the identity characteristics from the above list that is important to them right now that they want to explore in more depth. For example, if they choose race it could be African American, Latino, Native American, White, Asian, Multiracial, etc. Distribute the *My Identity* handout to each student and explain the following instructions:

   a. First, students should fill in the part that says, "I am" for example: "I am African American. I am Polish. I am Muslim. I am working class." (This is where they will be choosing one of their identity characteristics that is important to them now.)

   b. Next, students will create a symbol that represents that aspect of their identity. Explain that the symbol can be something simple and small like an emoji, a photograph or copy of a photograph, an image they find online or an original drawing. They should draw or paste their symbol into the box.

   c. Finally, they should complete the four sentences on the page that include: (1) I discovered I was____ when, (2) What I like about being ____ is, (3) What is sometimes difficult/ uncomfortable/challenging about being____ is and (4) The messages I received (from family, society, media) about being ____ are ____. Explain that they don't have to complete the sheet in any prescribed order. Give students 10–15 minutes to complete their sheet and if they need to do the symbol at home, assign that part for homework.

7.  When students have completed their *My Identity* handout, divide the class into small groups of four students each. In these groups, students will share their *My Identity* handout with each other. Remind students to be respectful toward one another and if necessary, re-visit the classroom ground rules. Each student will have two minutes to share what they'd like from the sheet. After each student has presented, the other students can ask questions. Then move on to next person.

8. When the small groups are finished talking, bring students back to whole class and engage them in a discussion by asking the following questions:

   — Was it difficult or easy to come up with one aspect of your identity to explore? Why?

   — What was your process for coming up with a symbol?

   — Was it easy or difficult to respond to the four questions? Why?

   — What was the most important of the four questions and why?

   — What did you learn about your own identity?

   — What did you learn about the identity of others?

9. In order to learn about identity groups that are not represented in the class, choose some of the provided *Identity Essays by Youth;* these are

FLIPPED CLASSROOM IDEA

Make a short video of yourself sharing a "My Identity" sheet that you have created in advance. Include everything on the sheet including I Am, the symbol and your response to the four questions.

NOTE 9

Be mindful that the essays provided only tell one young person's experience and by no means represent the experience of most or all of the young people in that identity group. It is important to stress this with your students so they don't make generalizations based on just one essay. In addition, these stories come from a collection of books with a variety of experiences and perspectives from different groups and can be found at Youth Communication's website: www.youthcomm.org.

student written stories about their personal experiences from Youth Communication. You may either distribute one of the essays for all students to read or divide them up and have a small group of students read each one and then report back to the rest of the class about what they read. Give students 15–20 minutes to read their essays. If time permits, have students from each of the essay groups explain the essay they read. Engage students in a class discussion by asking the following questions:

— What was most interesting about the essay you read?

— What did you learn that you didn't know before?

— What was most surprising?

— What aspect of identity was addressed in the essay and what was your biggest takeaway from it?

10. For homework, have students expand upon the sentences they completed on the worksheet and write a 3–5 paragraph essay about this aspect of their identity.

Extension Activities

- Have students interview their parents about these aspects of identity and find out how they identify themselves and ask them the questions. They can also ask the questions from the worksheet. Make a video of this or create it as a podcast interview and make the whole series available online. If you choose to have students write up the interviews, publish them as a class blog on the topic of identity.

- Have students work together to prepare a bulletin board entitled "The United States: A Multicultural Country." Instruct students to use photographs, symbols, Internet images and original drawings of their own as well as others.

DEFINITIONS

Culture
The patterns of daily life learned consciously and unconsciously by a group of people. These patterns can be seen in language, governing practices, arts, customs, holiday celebrations, food, religion, relationships, family roles, clothing, etc.

Disability
A mental or physical condition that restricts an individual's ability to engage in one or more major life activities (e.g., seeing, hearing, speaking, walking, communicating, sensing, breathing, performing manual tasks, learning, working or caring for oneself).

Ethnicity
Refers to a person's identification with a group based on characteristics such as shared history, ancestry, geographic and language origin, and culture.

Gender
The socially-defined "rules" and roles for men and women in a society. Dominant western society generally defines gender as a binary system—men and women—but many cultures define gender as more fluid and existing along a continuum.

Gender Identity
Relates to a person's internal sense of their own gender. Since gender identity is internal, one's gender identity is not necessarily visible to others.

Identity
The qualities, beliefs, etc. that make a particular person or group different from others.

Language
The system of words or signs that people use to express thoughts and feelings to each other. (There are approximately 6000 languages spoken in the world today.)

Nationality
Solely refers to a person s citizenship by origin, birth, or naturalization.

Race
Refers to the categories into which society places individuals on the basis of physical characteristics (such as skin color, hair type, facial form and eye shape).

Religion
An organized system of beliefs, observances, rituals and rules used to worship a god or group of gods.

Sexual Orientation
Determined by one's emotional, physical and/or romantic attractions. Categories of sexual orientation include, but are not limited to, **gay, lesbian** (attracted to some members of the same gender), **bisexual** (attracted to some members of more than one gender) and **heterosexual** (attracted to some members of another gender).

Socioeconomic Status
An individual's or family's economic and social position in relation to others, as measured by factors such as income, wealth and occupation.

MY IDENTITY

I am _____

Draw or paste a symbol that represents the aspect of your identity stated above.

```
┌──────────────────────────────────────────────────────────────────┐
│                                                                    │
│                                                                    │
│                                                                    │
│                                                                    │
│                                                                    │
│                                                                    │
│                                                                    │
│                                                                    │
│                                                                    │
│                                                                    │
│                                                                    │
└──────────────────────────────────────────────────────────────────┘
```

Complete these sentences about this aspect of your identity.

I discovered I was _____ when _____

_____

What I like about being _____ is _____

_____

What is sometimes difficult/uncomfortable/challenging about being _____

_____ is _____

The messages I received (from family, society, media) about being _____

_____ are _____

IDENTITY ESSAY BY YOUTH: AMERICAN ME

"Saying Goodbye"

By Agelta Arqimandriti

I grew up in Tirana, the capital of Albania. It's small, but it looks a little like New York, filled with yelling people, vendors selling things everywhere in the street, and honking cars.

My country, though, was very dangerous when I lived there. In the streets I saw many terrible things. I saw people wearing black masks and carrying machine guns. They would point their weapons at the sky and shoot them to scare everyone.

The people in my country were angry with one another and willing to kill for nothing. Everyone there was poor, too, and when people don't have food, they will sell everything they own to get some.

My family and I were lucky—my parents both had jobs, and eventually we were able to move to New York for a better life. I thought once we moved here, life would be easy. But for my family and me, it has been difficult and disappointing. Life in New York is hard because we have to work so much, and we feel kind of lonely because we don't speak English well.

When I tell people that the life here is difficult, they ask me, "What did you know about America before you came here?" And I don't like to give an answer, but I had been thinking that life would be simple here, because America is a powerful country.

The hardest thing has been losing the friends I had in Albania. Even though life there could be awful, I felt comforted by the people I knew. Now, whenever my friends write me letters, they make me cry because they write about the happy times in our past when we went on trips and had fun. And they write that they miss me so much.

My best friend was Jonila, who I met when I was in the 1st grade. One day we had difficult homework and she asked me if we could do the homework together. After that, she gave me her phone number and we started talking every day. She liked the same things I did, like watching TV, listening to music, reading, and going outside to play.

On her block we had lots of other friends, and I would always go to her block and talk and play with everyone there. She always wanted to have fun and smile, and she didn't ever stay sad. In hard times, she was always telling funny stories. She made other people smile.

Our houses were far apart, so we called each other often. For a while, we both watched a serial movie (like a soap opera) on TV, and each day when it was over, we would call each other and talk about what had happened in the movie. It was a beautiful and romantic story, and we loved to talk about it.

When I left my country, I was in the 8th grade. On my last day of school, my friends and I started to cry. To make fun, one friend told me, "We've had almost our whole lives together, and it's better to go now because I want other friends in my life and not only you." She wanted to make my friends smile. I smiled too, but I felt very sad saying goodbye.

Before I left for the United States, my friends and I had a beautiful Christmas party, where we ate pizza and lollipops and traditional Albanian foods. We danced to the guitar and piano music of my country.

Now, when I listen to this music, I think of our party and feel a little bit sad. Sometimes I lie in my bed, thinking about my past, and I wonder when I can go to my country for a visit. Any time I think about my best friend, I feel far away from everyone, and so alone. We still keep in touch, but we are not as close anymore.

In this country I feel like a stranger, because I don't have any close friends. When I started school here, no one talked to me because I did not speak English. All day at school I was alone, as if no one else was in the room. I felt uncomfortable and sad.

My school has immigrants from many different countries, but I think these people quickly forget what it was like when they first came here, since they didn't try to talk to me or make me feel at home. Instead, they sometimes laughed at me.

My second day of school here, somebody liked my sneakers and she asked me, "What is your size?" I misunderstood what she said and I told her, "I buy that for $60." Everyone who heard me laughed. That day made me hate school, and I didn't want to go anymore.

When I got home, I said to my parents, "I don't want to live here. I am the unluckiest girl in the whole world."

My parents told me, "Don't worry, this will pass. Eventually you will learn English and everything will be fine." Their words made me feel a little bit happier and more relaxed.

They were right, because now that I have worked hard to learn English, I am doing better. Now when I go to school I feel happier because I have made some friends. When I can't understand something, I ask somebody, and they try to help me. I also met a girl from my country, and we understand each other very well.

But so far, I don't have a best friend who I can talk to about the personal things in my life. Maybe when my English is perfect, I will find someone to be close with. But for now, I don't have the connection to anyone here that I used to have with my friends at home.

And in this country, my family life has changed. In my country, my parents had easy work. My father worked in the post office and he enjoyed it. Here, he works long hours in a department store and has to stand up all day. My mom works in a factory here and she is tired, too. They never have free time anymore.

I think my future here will be easier than in Albania, because in my country, many people don't have jobs. They have to struggle for everything. Few people can afford to go to college. Young people who don't go to college have to search for work, which they can't always find, so they end up staying home. Many families don't have enough to eat.

Life here is easier in so many ways. If I get good grades, I can go to college, even if I don't have too much money. Here I have many opportunities, and I feel sure that when I finish college, I can find a good job and have a bright future.

Still, it has been very hard for me and my family to adjust to the big changes in our lives. We didn't expect it. I'm glad to have left the dangers of my country, but we also left the comforts of home. I need to work very hard to be as happy and relaxed as I was in my own country.

I hope that when I finish college, I can go and work in my country for a few years. I would love to leave right now and continue high school there with my old friends, but I can't. Life in my country is too difficult and dangerous. I'm hoping that one day the situation in my country will be good and my family and I can go back.

Reprinted with permission from Agelta Arqimandriti, "Saying Goodbye," in *American Me: Teens Write about the Immigrant Experience,* eds. Marie O'Shea, Laura Longhine and Keith Hefner (New York: Youth Communication, 2010).

IDENTITY ESSAY BY YOUTH: DIFFERENT BUT EQUAL

"Struggling with a Learning Disability"

By Sarah B.

> "You know how to spell it," the teacher yelled. "Sound it out! We just went over this. You're not trying!"

I felt my face get hot, and my hands start shaking. I knew how to spell "hat," but it just wouldn't surface. I didn't even want to try. Not now, not in front of the whole class. "They won't want to be my friends," I thought. "Miss Miller hates me."

That was a typical scene at my elementary school. I was only in 1st grade, and already I knew I was stupid. Everybody was working on spelling harder words, like "because" and "orange," and I couldn't even spell "hat."

At home my younger sister Liza was the cute and funny one. My brother Benji was the overachiever, and I was the shy and stupid one. Ben used to tease me about being stupid and my father would grab him and shake him. "Don't ever talk to your sister like that!" he would yell. That was how I knew Ben was telling the truth. Why else would my dad be so mad?

The school told my parents that I had a learning disability and that I was taking up too much of Miss Miller's time. After 1st grade, I changed schools. Now I was going to a different kind of school in New York City. Central Park East was not a school for children with disabilities, it was just one where teachers had more time. My new school didn't stress correct spelling as much as learning how to think and using creativity. In this school there were no grades or tests and you called teachers by their first names, and all the classrooms were set up like a kindergarten class.

I loved my new teacher, Lucy. She was patient and warm and was always giving hugs around. I loved my new school, but I was still stupid. I couldn't keep up with the rest of the class, but I tried my hardest not to let anybody know it. I didn't want any more attention than the other kids were getting.

And I was smooth. In this new kind of classroom there was lots of independent work. I could sit by myself and pretend to read or write, and nobody would want to interrupt all my hard work. When Lucy came over to see how I was doing, I could fake it really well. I would tell her what the book was about from the cover, or show her a math problem that I had copied off the boy next to me when he wasn't looking.

But soon they caught up with me and that's when the tutors began. First there was Dr. Bloomingthal. She gave me strange exercises to do like copying pictures, or making up a story about a picture. She would show me a shape with lots of sides and then take it away and ask me to draw it from memory. If I got it right I would get an M&M.

All the time she would write things in her notebook. I knew she wanted to know what was wrong with my head. I knew I was being tested, and I hated it. It is a horrible feeling. It feels like everything you do is giving something away. My mom knew how much I hated going, so sometimes she would take me to the ballet afterwards.

After Dr. Bloomingthal I had another tutor, and then another, and another after that. I had horrible parent-teacher conferences where everybody was nice to me. Sometimes I wished that they would get mad at me. I wanted the reason to be that I was bad, that I wasn't trying. But it seemed that some people were smart, and some were slow, and I was one of the slow ones. I wanted to be smart so badly. There were two boys in my class, Wally and Ronald, who always had the answers. I wanted to be like them.

In 4th grade I was left back. I was relieved, because I was terrified of 5th grade. That year I made friends with a girl named Sara who was a year younger than I was. Sara was the kid who always did the best on spelling tests, and was always asked to give the book reports. Sara was nice, funny, and smart, and right away I was drawn to her. Sara made me want to try hard to do better, and I did. Pretty soon I was learning.

I was still far behind, but things were getting better. My tutors were showing me how to take my time, how not to tackle a problem all at once, but to do it piece by piece. It was almost as though I just had to decide when to start trying hard.

I got through 6th grade and found myself in junior high school. By the 7th grade I was getting good grades and I had almost forgotten that I was not supposed to be as quick as everybody else. That year I asked my principal if I could skip a grade and go back with people my own age. She said yes. I was so happy that I walked around smiling for weeks.

By 10th grade I had learned how to deal with my disability. Now I was normal. I wanted to go to a competitive college and have lots of intellectually stimulating ideas to amaze people with.

Then the tests started again. I took the PSAT. I knew it would be hard, but this was ridiculous. During the test I got anxious because of the time. The test was asking me to compare different groups of numbers that didn't seem to have anything to do with each other. There were questions where I knew what they were asking but had no idea how to figure it out. Words were popping up, and I had no clue what they meant. I found myself looking around the room, losing my focus. During the break my friends were talking about different questions, but I couldn't even remember them. That test rolled right over me, and left me for dead.

I didn't know what hit me until I got my score. All of a sudden I was stupid again. I got depressed and started to slack off in school. I figured there was no way I could go to college, and now I was scared. My world was falling apart. I let that one test tear away all the confidence that I had spent years building up.

I didn't tell anybody about my scores. It was too humiliating. Then during the summer I decided to tell my boyfriend. Damian didn't pity me; he didn't make me feel like my parents always had. Damian told me not to let these tests get in my way, that if I tried my hardest I could still do well on the SAT. I didn't want to admit it, but something in what he said got through to me. I held on to those words.

In 11th grade I took it again after taking practice tests over and over. I didn't do much better. That was when I sat down to talk to my parents about it. My dad told me honestly that even if I did much better, it would not be good enough for the competitive colleges I wanted to go to, like Brown and Wesleyan. He gave me a list of colleges that don't require SATs but that wasn't what I wanted. I wanted to try. I thought that if I could learn how to spell "hat," I could learn how to do well on this test. My mother had heard that people with learning disabilities could apply to take the test with more time, so that's what I did.

I had to take a test to find out if my learning disability was strong enough to qualify me for extended time. At the end of the 11th grade I was going through the same sort of evaluation that Dr. Bloomingthal gave me all over again. All the same old feelings came back; it was like being in the 2nd grade again. I would start shaking, and cry on the bus home. It was hard.

Finally, after many sessions, the evaluation was over. I was more sad than happy when I found out that I could take the SAT with extended time. I still had a learning disability. They just don't go away.

I'm determined to make this test work for me. So I've been going to Stanley Kaplan, a school that offers classes to help you improve your SAT scores. According to the practice tests my score has gone up hundreds of points. It hasn't been easy. I've had to work extremely hard but I'm glad I decided to try. Even if those competitive colleges don't take me, after watching that SAT score go up, I feel like I can do anything.

I'm taking the test in two weeks for the last time and I'm scared out of my mind. But whatever happens, I now know that I don't have to let any test take my intelligence away from me. That means much more to me than some number.

Reprinted with permission from Sarah B., "Struggling with a Learning Disability," in *Different But Equal: Teens Write about Living with Disabilities,* eds. Virginia Vitzthum, Laura Longhine and Keith Hefner (New York: Youth Communication, 2010).

IDENTITY ESSAY BY YOUTH: GROWING UP ASIAN

"Dreams of America, Memories of China"

By Chun Lar Tom

I walked slowly through Prospect Park in Brooklyn, New York. It was quiet and peaceful. Little birds flew from one branch to another. The wind hummed. A yellow leaf fell down gently in front of me. Suddenly, I realized time flies and fall was already here. "Oh, I've been here for three years," I thought. I picked up the leaf and stared at it. My memory went back to one day the same season three years ago, when I was 15 years old in China.

I grew up in a small village in southern China called Maoping, surrounded by green hills and huge flat fields. On that beautiful evening, I rode my bike home from school as the setting sun brushed reds and yellows across the western sky. The green fields had turned golden. When I got home, my mother told me that almost all of our family would be going to America in a few months.

For a moment, I couldn't think. Excitement came over me so suddenly and quickly that I felt like an expanded balloon ready to pop. I wanted to run, jump, fly, and tell the world that I was going to America. But instead, I just stood there like a fool with a big smile on my face.

I'd heard people talk about America and had long wondered about it. "They have those extremely tall and big buildings. If you get up to a top floor and put your hand out of the window, you can touch the clouds," my friend Ying told me.

"Also, people there have green eyes and red hair," she added. "They must look like those TV characters in the Japanese cartoons."

"Who told you that?" I asked suspiciously.

"My neighbor. Trust me, he knows a lot."

America seemed like a fairy world to me. I couldn't wait to go there. I imagined myself walking on a clean street with some cartoon-like people, breathing fresh morning air and passing by beautiful buildings.

"Ma, do you know what America looks like?" I asked her one day as we were preparing for the move.

"Well, I don't know," Mom answered. "I'm sure it's very rich. If not, why do so many people want to go there?" Mom was just like me. She knew nothing about America except that it's rich and powerful.

The day before we left, six of my friends came to my house to say goodbye. We talked about the days we'd spent together and wondered when we'd meet again in the future. Then, the room was quiet. Nobody talked. We could hear the clock murmuring in its monotonous tone that time was still going forward. And soon, we'd be separated.

"Hey, don't forget us when you get there," Ling said.

"I'll send you letters and pictures and you have to write me back, OK? You promise?" Bao said. She looked at me seriously and held my hand tightly until I said, "Yes, I will. I swear."

I looked at my friends carefully, from one to another, trying to mark their faces into my brain. I felt so sad. Suddenly, I didn't want to leave my friends and this beautiful familiar village.

We left at midnight the next day. Many of our relatives and neighbors came over to see us off. "Have a safe trip," they said with big smiles on their faces and red eyes from crying. Grandmother and Grandfather, who were staying behind, held me tightly in their arms. "Be a good girl," they said. They gave me a red envelope with money in it, wishing me good luck. I felt the fear and excitement of a new life.

We finally had to get on the bus. I took a last look at my house and my sleeping Maoping. "Goodbye, my dear village," I whispered to myself, and then stepped onto the bus, letting it drive me to my unknown future. I began to cry.

The plane trip was almost a day long. When we got to Brooklyn, New York, we moved in with my aunt, who had immigrated to America when I was a toddler. My cousin took me out to get a look at Manhattan. I was so happy that I was finally going to see the cartoon-like people and the extremely tall buildings. But I didn't see many people with red hair and green eyes. And the buildings didn't reach the clouds. It was just a myth.

I wasn't too disappointed, though, because I was drawn in by diverse new faces. I saw people with light skin, blond hair, and blue eyes. Some people wore long colorful dresses and scarves that covered their heads. Others had dark, healthy-looking skin, braided hair, and long eyelashes like a Barbie doll. Seeing these new looks made me feel like the happiest person in the world.

However, my happiness vanished over the next few days because I couldn't read English signs and maps. I got lost so easily on the subway that I couldn't go anywhere by myself. I became extremely bored and lonely because I had no friends and didn't start school for two months.

I remembered how much I liked being alone when I was in China because being alone meant being relaxed. I used to walk around Maoping by myself and climb up hills to see the sunset. I loved to lie on the grass, watching birds. I forgot time and my worries.

But I felt miserable being alone in the U.S. Being alone here meant sitting home, staring at the walls. My parents had to work late every day and my siblings had already started school.

As time went by, I was eaten up by loneliness. I missed my friends. I wrote to them often. I thought about my village frequently and realized how much I'd left behind. There I had my grandparents. There I had my best friends who grew up with me. There I had a lovely home where I'd lived for 15 years. I'd loved the idea of coming here, but now I hated being here.

When I first started high school, I was lost, confused, and frustrated. I felt like a little tree that was uprooted and transplanted into a huge desert. New cultures, new people, and a new language were like a fierce sun shining on me, making me dizzy. I wanted to escape.

"Ma, can I go back home please?" I asked one day. "I don't know anything here. I don't know how to speak English. I feel so stupid."

"No," she said. "You'll never grow up if you don't try to solve your problems. Escape is not a way to overcome obstacles."

So I had to stay. But gradually, I realized my mother was right. I slowly started to adjust to this new environment. Little by little, I learned the language and culture with help from new friends at school. I no longer felt lonely. They were there for me if I didn't understand anything or needed help. I appreciated them.

Three years passed quickly and I accomplished many things. I learned how to get around the city by myself. I joined the National Honor Society at school and had a chance to visit Washington, D.C.

Coming out of the train station into the warm sunlight during an autumn day, I walked toward Prospect Park. I wandered alone. Yellow leaves flew softly down as the breeze blew. They lay quietly on the ground with the sort of loneliness that I had when I first came here.

"Excuse me!"

A sound suddenly jumped into my head and pulled me back to reality from my memories. I looked up. A stranger was standing in front of me. "Hi. Did you see a red bag somewhere around here?"

"No, no," I said. I looked at my hand; the yellow leaf was still there. I put the leaf down and strode forward.

Reprinted with permission from Chun Lar Tom, "Dreams of America, Memories of China," in *Growing Up Asian: Teens Write about Asian-American Identity,* ed. Maria Tucker (New York: Youth Communication, 2010).

IDENTITY ESSAY BY YOUTH: GROWING UP BLACK

"Coloring Outside the Lines"

By Desiree Bailey

I didn't think much about race until 7th grade, when I joined the gifted class at my school. For the first time, I was the only black person in my class, and I suddenly felt a lot of pressure. I thought that if I didn't do well, my classmates would think it was because I was black. Race suddenly mattered to me, and I felt completely out of place.

It was the first time I'd realized I was a minority. All my life I'd been around a diverse mix of people. On the island of Trinidad, where I was born, the population is mostly of African and Indian descent with a sprinkling of Chinese, Hispanics mainly from Venezuela, Native people (Caribs, Amerindians and Arawaks), and whites. It seemed to me that almost everyone there lived side by side.

In Rosedale, Queens—the New York City neighborhood that I immigrated to when I was 8—almost everyone was black. My elementary school was mostly black, but there were also Indians from the Caribbean. Since my neighbors and classmates in New York were similar to the people I lived around in Trinidad, I still didn't think about race.

At home, race had never been a big issue for my mother. She'd acknowledge racial prejudice but she never dwelled on it. My father, on the other hand, came to America in the 1970s, when black people were struggling for equality and respect. He read a lot about the plight of blacks around the world, and kept us in endless conversations about it. In our kitchen, we even had a beautiful poster depicting all the great kings and queens of Africa's past. But the discussions were all theoretical to me. My real-life encounters with racism were rare.

When I first started 6th grade at a middle school in Bayside, Queens, my class had a mix of black, white, Asian, and Hispanic kids. There were only a few black kids, unlike my elementary school, which was probably 99.9% black. But I still felt at ease because there was such a diverse mix. So when I started 7th grade, being the only black kid in my class caught me by surprise. I couldn't blend in anymore. I was easily recognized as "the black kid," and I was afraid of the attention that I might get.

I felt like I wasn't just representing myself, but all black people. For many of my classmates, I imagined I was the first black person they'd ever had a chance to get to know. I worried for the first time that many people didn't see blacks as individuals, but as a stereotype, a group of people who all acted the same: loud, uneducated, and obnoxious.

I assumed that my classmates had those prejudices, and I couldn't make a fool of myself in front of them. I imagined that one little mistake wouldn't just be mine; it would be the mistake of my race. The pressure I placed on myself made me hesitant to speak. What if I said the wrong thing? What if words flew tangled and contorted out of my nervous mouth? I became quiet. I became even quieter when the topic of black people came up. When we talked about slavery in social studies class, I wanted to disappear. Although I didn't spot any outward signs of racism, I still felt singled out.

My classmates were so cautious around me. When they described black people, they'd pause to search for the best word to use without being offensive. If they described someone white or Asian, I'd never hear that hesitation. Maybe it's because blacks have always had a sensitive position in America. Their self-censorship made me even more uncomfortable and aware of my differences.

Perhaps my insecurities about my people and myself were fueled by negative images of blacks in the media. In the movies I saw, young black men were almost always criminals, blazing a path of destruction wherever they went. In popular music videos, I saw women of all shades of brown exploited by their own black men. I felt like my race was a big show, a huge entertainment session intended to amuse, excite, and instill fear in others.

In my neighborhood, some people reinforced these ideas. It began to bug me that many of the black teenagers I saw on the bus were rude and obnoxious. They'd jump on the bus seats, shout at the top of their lungs and pick fights with each other, bothering innocent people who were minding their own business. Some women would walk around with barely any clothes on while men hooted at them. Many black people I saw seemed to be on edge and angry, or just looking for fun laced with trouble.

I wasn't like that. Instead of wreaking havoc on the bus, I'd quietly read my book. I wasn't rude or a troublemaker, and I didn't want my people to be seen that way. It's true there were many other black kids like me. Instead of hanging around the block, they read books like I did. And they were smart kids with bright futures. But I didn't meet those kids until high school. In 7th grade, I just wanted to fit in with the white and Asian kids in my class.

I decided that it was up to me to show my classmates that not all black people were loud and obnoxious. I'd teach them that black people could be successful and not like the negative characters that they saw on TV. I'd show them that we could enjoy different types of music and be as open-minded and cultured as anyone else.

In my quest to separate myself from the black stereotypes I thought my classmates expected to see in me, I began to reject things I identified as black. I didn't dare pick up a book by Maya Angelou. I avoided listening to hip-hop and r&b. The sounds from my headphones were from bands like Linkin Park, Staind, and System of a Down. If a band played rock, I listened to it. At first, I didn't even enjoy the heavier rock. But I wanted to like it, so I listened to it again and again until it became my love. I thought it would help me be more like my classmates. The confusion and swirls of the drums and guitars eventually came to reflect how I felt.

But no matter how hard I blasted my rock music, it didn't help me to fit in. My physical differences were clearly pointed out by my classmates. One day, a boy with pale skin and brownish-blond hair asked me about my hair. "Why is it like that?" he said. He looked at my neatly braided cornrows with a look more of disgust than curiosity. "It's so stiff and it looks like a bunch of train tracks are stuck to your head." I was extremely hurt by his comments. No one had ever been so rude about my race to my face. How could anyone be so obnoxious and unkind?

When I went to the house of another classmate, I felt even more stigmatized. Her mom was Puerto Rican and her dad was Chinese, and I didn't expect ignorant attitudes from a family with such diversity. But I heard her younger brothers whispering to each other about me. "Why is she so black?" one said. Another said, "Maybe if she scrubs her skin really hard, it'll come off." They walked into another room laughing while I stood there feeling insulted and uncomfortable. My friend acted as if nothing happened. So did I. I didn't want to make a scene.

Situations like that made me feel even more separated from my peers. I sank deeper and deeper into my rock music. But instead of helping me fit in with the white kids, my music separated me from the few black people I knew in other classes. One day, I was on the bus going home with two friends, one black and the other Hispanic. One asked what I was listening to, so I gave him my headphones. When he heard the ear-splitting drums of System of a Down and the monstrous growl of the lead singer, he looked at me like I was a joke.

"What the hell is that?" he asked. "Why are you listening to rock? That's white people music." I felt my face grow hot but I didn't know how to respond, so I just laughed his comments off.

All these conflicts upset me. I felt too black for the kids in my class and too white for my friends in other classes. I'd talk and laugh with people, but inside, I just wanted to get away from everyone. Every chance I got, I isolated myself and delved deeper into my books, my writing, and my music. They were my favorite places to escape.

It was hard to for me to realize who I was becoming until I became friends with Jessica in the 8th grade. She was obsessed with insulting her own dark brown skin. She was devastated because she thought she was hideous and wouldn't be loved by anyone. "I hate myself," she'd say. "I'm so black and ugly."

I didn't pay attention to her at first because I thought she was just fishing for compliments. But it didn't take me long to realize that she meant what she said. She'd look at my friend, Ashley, who was black but light-skinned, and say, "Why can't I be your color?"

Ashley and I worried about her. We told Jessica that skin color and beauty weren't connected, but it was hard to convince her when the media ambushed us with those ideas every day. We couldn't convince her she was wrong about herself, and she eventually withdrew from us.

Seeing how Jessica's negative thoughts destroyed her self-esteem, I began to wonder if I was doing the same thing to myself. When I reexamined my beliefs, I was shocked to realize that all the stereotypes I thought others believed about black people were things I believed. When I saw black people lazing on street corners, or behaving inappropriately in music videos, I shook my head with disgust. I thought back to all the past struggles and achievements of black people and wondered if my generation would flush it all down the drain.

Instead of looking into situations more deeply, I simply pointed my finger and criticized my people. I realized I was stereotyping my own people as rude and ignorant when I was the one who was rude and ignorant. I had poisoned myself against my race just to fit in with my classmates. I began to think that I was a racist—a racist against my own people.

I decided I couldn't let my fears decide my behavior or tastes anymore. I began to work hard to see people as individuals with interesting lives, instead of simplistic stereotypes.

It's taken several years to change my thinking. At times I still feel extremely different from other people, but now I see that as a good thing. My differences showed me the way to writing, playing the flute and guitar, and my interest in anthropology. I still have to deal with ignorance about black people from my white and Asian classmates, and ignorance from black people about my interests. Despite this, I'm committed to being myself instead of trying to represent an entire race. And I'm not going to judge my own race, or any other race, based on stereotypes.

Now I'm in 11th grade and I'm on great terms with myself as a black teenager. It doesn't bother me anymore if I'm seen as "too white" by some and "too black" by others. I know it's impossible to expect everyone to see the world exactly as I do.

My music collection covers Alicia Keys and Kanye West as well as Coldplay and Jimi Hendrix. Books by Maya Angelou, J.K. Rowling, and Pablo Neruda spill off my shelves. My music, my literature, and my perspective don't belong to a particular race. They don't have a specific color. They're just what I love.

Reprinted with permission from Desiree Bailey, "Coloring Outside the Lines," in *Growing Up Black: Teens Write about African-American Identity,* eds. Maria Tucker, Laura Longhine and Keith Hefner (New York: Youth Communication, 2010).

IDENTITY ESSAY BY YOUTH: GROWING UP JEWISH

"There's More Than One Way to be Jewish"

By Yelena Dynnikov

Even though I am Jewish, my family was never very religious as I was growing up. We always chose what appealed to us from the *Torah* (the laws, teachings and divine knowledge of Judaism). I never observed the sabbath (the Jewish day of rest and prayer celebrated on Saturday). I wear pants (which some religious Jews consider inappropriate attire for a woman) and sometimes the food I eat may not be kosher (conform to Jewish dietary laws).

I never saw anything wrong with this until I was sent to an Orthodox Jewish school. (Orthodox Jews follow religious law and tradition much more closely than Conservative or Reformed Jews.) Suddenly, my eyes were opened up.

I was sent to an Orthodox school (yeshiva) in seventh grade because my family thought it would be safer than public school. They also thought it was a way for me to learn more about my identity and what it means to be Jewish. I quickly realized how different my lifestyle was from my new classmates.

No More Mini Skirts

I found out that Orthodox Jews cannot wear clothing like minis and tank tops. Their clothes are more modest: skirts that cover the knees and a shirt or blouse with sleeves up to or covering the elbow.

I started dressing like they did for school, but afterwards I would change into a pair of jeans. As a Conservative Jew, I had always worn whatever I wanted. Suddenly, I found out that the clothes I had been wearing were not right.

Keeping kosher was another big topic. Jewish dietary laws prohibit you from mixing meat and dairy products together. (You can't eat cheeseburgers, for example.) You have to wait six hours after eating meat before you can eat dairy. You can't eat any seafood that doesn't have scales or fins, so shrimp and other shellfish are a no-no. You also can't eat pork or ham.

Conservative Jews don't follow these rules as closely as Orthodox Jews do, so I was used to eating whatever I wanted. Suddenly, someone was telling me that the food I was putting into my body was not right.

A Day of Rest and Prayer

I was also exposed to a real celebration of the sabbath for the first time. It was like nothing I had experienced. On sabbath, you're not allowed to physically create anything which means you can't work. You can't turn on electricity (no watching TV or listening to the stereo) or drive in a car either. Religious Jews celebrate the sabbath by lighting candles, having special meals with their families, and praying. To me, the sabbath had always been just like any other day of the week.

I was confused by all the new things I was learning. There were sharp contradictions between my home life and life at school. I had always considered myself Jewish and now I was being told that I wasn't, really. It's like going through life thinking you're an orange and then being told that you're an apple.

I was frustrated at how one teacher in particular was always trying to get me to become more religious, even though I wasn't sure I wanted to. I enjoyed my life so much that I was afraid to give it up. At the same time, I was starting to feel guilty that I didn't celebrate holidays like Passover (which marks the time the Jews escaped slavery in Egypt) or Yom Kippur (the Day of Atonement) correctly.

I had also grown to love the traditional shabat (sabbath) celebration. Teachers would invite me and other students to their houses to sleep over and experience the sabbath. We'd talk, sing songs, go for walks in the evening, and eat a lot at meals. The teachers would try to stay up the whole night learning *Torah,* but the rest of us would be out by midnight. I began to see the sabbath as a time of tranquility, purity, and holiness.

Putting Others First

In many ways, going to an Orthodox school has made me a better person. At school, we contribute to charity, take food and old clothes to the poor, visit nursing homes, and help women who can't afford babysitters take care of their children. We contribute money to buy presents for orphans during the holidays. These activities have taught me to think of others, especially those who are not as well off as me.

I often feel torn between Orthodoxy and Conservatism. These days, I consider myself Conservative but with Orthodox influences. I sometimes doubt that Orthodoxy is right for me, since the laws regarding the holidays, keeping kosher, and observing the sabbath are so hard to follow. I'm still trying to find my way. But my experiences at school have made me realize more than ever what a beautiful religion Judaism is.

Reprinted with permission from Yelena Dynnikov, "There's More Than One Way to be Jewish," in *YCteen,* 1993.

IDENTITY ESSAY BY YOUTH: GROWING UP LATINO

"Showin' off My Flag All Proud"

By Omar Morales

A couple of years ago, I bought a beaded necklace of the Puerto Rican flag, and once or twice a week I wear the beads around my neck. When I do, I feel more connected with my roots. I feel like I'm a part of something bigger than myself.

When I see other Puerto Ricans showing off the flag, I say to myself, "Yeah, represent." I guess I feel a connection.

But I think I also wear the Puerto Rican beads because in some ways I feel disconnected from my roots. I only know little pieces of our culture.

I've never been to Puerto Rico, and I can't speak Spanish. It would be good to know how to speak the language that my family speaks. Wearing the flag reminds me who I am and where my family came from.

Sometimes, teenagers I've never met pass by me and say things like, "No doubt, kid, showin' off your flag all proud." I just say, "Yeah;" and smile for a minute and keep on walking.

In my old neighborhood, in Williamsburg, Brooklyn, where I lived until I was 5, most of the families were Puerto Rican. People were close. They spoke the same language and went to the same small church at the end of my block.

Even after I moved, I went back to visit often because a lot of my family still lived there. It was always fun. I saw the other kids in the street who I'd known for a long time. And every time my family threw a party, whether it was in one of my aunts' houses or a small club, they would start blasting out salsa, merengue or Latin reggae and they would dance all night long. I felt at home there.

But a couple of years ago, after my grandfather died, most of my family who lived in Williamsburg moved out and they live all over the place now.

I've lived in my current neighborhood, which is in between Bensonhurst and Midwood in Brooklyn, for years. There are people from different races and religions, which is good because I get to see how people from different nationalities celebrate their cultures.

It helps to communicate with other people so that there won't be misunderstandings, which is how racism gets started. And at the same time, I see how we are all similar.

But having the people I know move out of Williamsburg also made me feel a little disconnected from Puerto Ricans. So I try my best to learn whatever I can about Puerto Rico.

I listen to some Latin music, and I also listen to a lot of Latin artists who perform songs in English. And any time they are showing a program about Puerto Rico on TV, I watch so I can learn and know all about it.

I've learned about how the indigenous (native) Puerto Ricans lost their land to Spain and then were given to the United States. And I've learned how many Puerto Ricans are also of African descent.

But the main way I know about Puerto Rico is through the stories my mother told me, about when she lived on the island as a teenager for a couple of years.

She told me that inside the house, they put nets over the bed whenever it was time to go to sleep to keep insects and other small animals away. She described how frogs and small lizards would run around the house. Having a bunch of frogs and lizards running through the living room sounded fun to me.

My mother also told me about the small bridge that she and my uncles used to cross. The bridge was very thin and only two people could cross at a time because it couldn't hold too much weight.

Stories like that fascinated me and made me more interested in visiting the island. I'm not sure I'd want to live there permanently. I'm already used to living in New York with the crowded streets and trains. But in the future, I hope to visit the island and see how it really is.

Until I do, wearing the beads gives me some kind of bond with other Puerto Ricans. Wearing them makes me feel like I'm part of a family.

_____

Reprinted with permission from Omar Morales, "Showin' Off My Flag All Proud ," in *Growing Up Latino: Teens Write about Hispanic-American Identity,* eds. Keith Hefner and Laura Longhine (New York: Youth Communication, 2009).

IDENTITY ESSAY BY YOUTH: GROWING UP MUSLIM

"Walking while Arab"

By Sara Said

Some names have been changed.

As a devout Muslim, I wear a scarf that covers my hair and neck. After the September 11 attacks, I became an object of attention.

Walking to school in New York City about a week and a half after the attacks, a man in his 30s or 40s riding his bike saw me and yelled, "I will kill all Arabs and I will show you!"

He yelled so hard I thought my eardrums would break. I felt like bursting into tears and running home. If he hadn't kept riding past, I would've been running like crazy.

But when strangers heard and saw the man screaming those terrifying words, they asked me, "Are you OK?" or said, "Just ignore him." Some smiled and tried to make me feel safe, which helped a little.

I felt relieved that they didn't act against me, and happy and thankful that they understood how I felt at that moment. I couldn't look up at their faces because I was trying to keep myself from crying. Still, I really appreciated their kindness.

At school that day, I felt that my mind was somewhere else. The man's screaming kept bothering me when I was in class. I was shaken, but I wasn't shocked by his hateful message. From the time September 11 happened, it was hard to avoid feeling hated because I am a Muslim.

Then and in the months that followed, many Muslims and Arabs all over the United States were discriminated against and attacked. Some were kicked off airplanes because other passengers didn't like the way they looked or dressed. At least six people were even murdered because their killers wanted to strike back at a Muslim or an Arab. Hundreds of other violent incidents were reported.

In school, I heard about people in New York City who were attacked both physically and verbally while going to their mosques, or who had their stores or cars attacked and damaged. And many, like me, were verbally harassed.

After that man's threats and the looks that people gave me after the tragedy, I wanted to go back to my home country, Yemen, where people accepted me as a Muslim and an Arab. I didn't want to be in a place where people saw me as a terrorist. I didn't want to live someplace where every day I walked in the streets feeling like an alien in fear of being attacked.

I was afraid to go to school and leave the house wearing my veil. All my friends who wear veils had a hard time deciding whether we should continue wearing our veils in the streets, or keep them off until we got to school. On our first day back to school after the attacks, I decided to wear my veil—but I made my brother come with me. And in case my father couldn't pick me up at the end of the day, I kept jeans and a hat in my backpack to change into so people wouldn't realize that I'm a Muslim.

When we weren't in school, my Muslim friends and I locked ourselves in our homes, and the Arabs and Muslims that I knew in my neighborhood deserted the streets. But after a few days, my friends and I came to the conclusion that we were wrong to fear anyone but God. That helped us conquer our fears. However, our parents were strict about the time we came home. We had to be home exactly at 4 or they'd be ready to call the cops, because they'd worry something had happened to us. It was like living in a 24-hour fear movie.

After I got screamed at, I decided to tell my mom what had happened. But I didn't come right out and say it; first, I told her like it was a joke.

"You know what, Mom? Today, right, I heard this as a joke, right," I said. "There was this man who screamed at a Muslim and told her—ha ha—that he would kill all Arabs. Isn't that stupid?" Telling her that way helped me keep myself from crying. Then I said, in a low voice, "To tell you the truth, it happened to me."

My mom looked at me as if she wanted to know if I was for real. When she saw that I was, she prayed for our safety. "Ahmudi Rabic ineik ahsan min kahric," she said, meaning, "Be thankful to God you are in a better position than others." She meant I should be thankful that I wasn't physically hurt like others have been. My mom said to have faith in God, for he is the Protector.

My friends who wear the veil were also harassed around the same time. Lamya, 19, said two people gave her the finger, including a woman in a car who opened the car door to gesture at her. "I felt really bad when they did that," Lamya said, but it didn't surprise her.

Similarly, Khadija, 18, went out with her friends in the first week after the tragedy and saw three teenage guys. One said, "Oh, check this out, a terrorist is living in this neighborhood too."

"It hurt me," Khadija said. She also felt that she'd been harassed in school. On her locker, she'd had a sticker that said, "I love Allah." One day, she walked out of science class and saw that her sticker was torn and thrown on the floor.

"I went to my teacher, and before I'd finished telling her what happened, I was crying and screaming, 'Why did they do it?' I was so disheartened," Khadija said.

In one of her classes, a discussion on a poem about the World Trade Center led to religion. Khadija's teacher mentioned that she'd been to Arab countries. One of the students said, "Oh, my God, how could you go to such countries?" The teacher ignored him. Then another student said something like, "Oh yeah, Muslims believe in killing, and their religion teaches them that." Khadija was angry, but she didn't say anything. The teacher just gave the student a disapproving look.

Later, Khadija found a way to respond. Along with the president of the Bengali Society at our high school and me, she organized a meeting where we talked about what Islam really is. We explained that Islam in Arabic means peace and submission to God. Islam is based on the teachings of God as revealed to his last prophet, Mohammad, and teaches only peace, justice, and righteousness.

We organized the conference because we believe that education is the enemy of discrimination. When you know about other people's cultures and religions, you don't depend on stereotypes, which are often negative, to form your opinion of that particular group.

Teachers and students who came to the meeting said they were glad we'd organized it. It helped them understand what we were going through, and why we felt the media was playing a big role in creating hatred against us by focusing so much on Arabs and Muslims who are terrorists.

These days, people still stare at me on the street, but not as much, and I'm no longer feeling scared. The fear that was caught in my heart has faded because I learned I must never allow fear to rule my life or conquer my dreams.

I keep in mind the nice people who supported me, helped me think more positively, and made me believe that there is more good in the world than there is bad. I will not let some people's ignorant hate become an obstacle and a barrier to living my life the way I want—as a Muslim, in the U.S.

Reprinted with permission from Sara Saidy, "Walking While Arab," in *Growing Up Muslim in America: Stories by Muslim Youth,* eds. Maria O'Shea, Laura Longhine and Keith Hefner (New York: Youth Communication, 2010).

IDENTITY ESSAY BY YOUTH: OUT WITH IT

"Mom, Dad, I Have Something to Tell You"

By José Miguel Jimenez

When I realized that I was gay, I knew that I couldn't tell everyone my self-discovery. If I did, I might face serious consequences, like getting homophobic comments hurled at me and getting into fistfights. But I didn't want to keep my revelation all to myself either. I wanted to share my enlightenment with some of my friends and teachers. And I wanted to eventually tell my parents. I didn't want there to be any big secrets between us.

Yet I didn't feel like I could tell them right away. Though I'd never heard them make homophobic comments, I didn't know how they'd handle my sexuality. I didn't expect anything too bad from my mother, since she's a lot more modern than my father. He's tough and can be really old-fashioned about how things should be done in the house, how children should behave, and how to discipline them. My father is quicker to argue and fight than talk things out with his kids. I thought he'd get angry with me for being gay. I didn't think he'd approve of guys liking other guys.

So instead of telling my parents, I selectively told people I felt I could trust and who would accept me. Telling them was like setting up a safety net for when I chose to tell my parents—I'd be able to turn to them for support if my parents rejected me.

I decided to tell my friends Oscarina, Vanessa, and Belinda first. I knew that they'd be OK with it. Vanessa had helped me realize that I was gay, and Oscarina had told me before that she didn't have a problem with gay people. I knew Belinda would be surprised by the news, which she was, but she dealt with it well.

My English teacher, Ms. Somerville, was the first adult I decided to tell. We'd talked before about what was going on in my life. She was also in charge of the poetry club, where I got to see her as more as a friend than as just a teacher. A few days after figuring out that I was gay, I waited to talk to her after class.

"I'm gay," I blurted out, looking away for a fraction of a second.

"That's great," she said, smiling and giving me a hug. She said it was perfectly normal. She immediately made me feel more confident about who I am.

It felt great to be supported, but I still didn't feel up to telling my parents. After some careful thought I decided to tell my sister Katherine, who's a year older than me. We'd grown close since we were kids, and I occasionally confided in her about my life. My sister has adopted a lot of my parents' viewpoints, so I figured telling her would be a good way to measure how they might react.

"I'm gay," I said one morning in our bathroom as Katherine used the mouthwash. I got extremely anxious as I waited for a response.

"Hmmm."

Silence.

"I'm not surprised," she finally said after a few seconds. She said she thought I might be and that it was fine. I told her my concerns about our father and she agreed that I should hold off on telling him.

It was a relief to have told someone in my family. There was one less person I had to keep a big secret from. Maybe I'd even be able to talk to her about guys.

I was slowly gaining more confidence about telling my parents. But I was still very worried about how my father would react. So I decided to tell my Aunt Maritza. She's open-minded, and I trusted her to tell my parents for me in a sympathetic way.

When I told her she smiled. She said that she already knew and would handle telling my parents. But this didn't fully solve my problems. While my aunt did indeed tell my parents, I knew that they wouldn't talk about my sexuality with me unless I brought it up first.

I wanted everything to be openly discussed between us, so there wouldn't be any tension. I wanted to be honest about the things I was doing, like working with a gay-related organization.

I chose to speak to my mother first. One day we sat on her bed to talk. I was beating around the subject of my sexuality throughout the entire conversation.

"If you're going to say it, then just say it," she suddenly said. So I told her and she said she wasn't too surprised. I felt relaxed now that I'd told one of my parents. But then she said she wanted me to tell my father.

"You've got to be kidding," I said.

"It won't be as bad as you think," she replied.

I wanted to avoid a hostile confrontation, but my mother insisted.

I held back. But a few days later, while I was getting ready for summer school, I walked into my parents' room to get some lotion. My mother was sitting on their bed. My father was ironing a shirt.

"Tell him," my mother said. I looked at her, surprised and annoyed that she chose this moment to have me do it. I had to leave for school in a few minutes.

"Tell him," she repeated.

I turned to my father, wishing that I could hide. He looked at me expectantly. It didn't seem to matter that he already knew.

"I have to tell you something," I said.

"What? You have a girlfriend?" he said jokingly.

"No, I don't," I answered, only half looking at him. "And you know that I'm not going to have one."

His face grew very serious. I was tense. Time stopped. I thought that I would be stuck forever in that moment, stuck with that feeling of dread. I watched his face closely, waiting for an explosion. Was this the calm before the storm?

But he didn't freak out. We talked for the next five minutes. He was calm and didn't say anything about how it was bad to be gay. He told me how I had to be careful, that there are not only people who wouldn't accept me, but diseases like HIV/AIDS.

I nodded that I already knew all this because I wanted the conversation to end as quickly as possible. Now that I'd spoken to him about it, I didn't want to talk about it anymore. All my feelings about being open had flown away. It felt too weird talking to him about my gayness.

My mother dismissed me, saying that I needed to leave or I'd be late for school. I left happy, knowing that everything had been cleared. I think that my father was so calm because he'd talked to my aunt. He had time to digest the news.

But despite what I'd hoped for, things are far from open in my house. I only talk to my sister Katherine about being gay. It feels too odd to talk about guys with my parents, particularly since my father can be so overprotective. I went to a park the other day just to chill. Because he'd heard that gay men have sex there, he freaked out and started lecturing me. At times like these, I try to zone him out. While he may be trying to protect me, it also shows how he has a lot to learn about me since I don't do sex in parks.

Coming out to my parents was one of the most difficult experiences in my life, but that was partially because I'd expected the worst. I'm pleased with how I went about telling them and thankful I had the support of other people. Still, I'm glad that it's over, and hope I never have to go through something like that again.

José Miguel Jimenez graduated from SUNY-Purchase College in New York.

Reprinted with permission from José Miguel Jimenez, "Mom, Dad, I Having Something to Tell You," in *Out With It: Gay and Straight Teens Write about Homosexuality,* eds. Al Desetta (New York: Youth Communication, 2008).

8. GROUPS I BELONG TO

TIME
45 minutes

COMMON CORE STANDARDS
Writing, Speaking & Listening, Language

STRATEGIES AND SKILLS
brainstorm, create pie chart, large group discussion, turn and talk, essay writing

KEY WORDS AND PHRASES
pie chart, proportion

Rationale

The purpose of this lesson is for students to combine what they learned in the previous two lessons and identify several aspects of their identity that are most important to them. Reflecting upon groups to which they belong builds self-esteem and helps students understand similarities and differences. This lesson provides an opportunity for students to explore the groups to which they belong, reflect on the relative importance of each and learn about similarities and differences among their classmates.

Objectives

- Students will explore identity groups and compare and contrast their group memberships to those of their peers/classmates.
- Students will identify groups to which they belong and chart them on a pie graph.
- Students will reflect on the groups to which they belong.

What's Needed

Handouts and Resources: I Belong to Many Groups Pie Chart (one for each student)

Other Material: Several rulers

Procedures

1. Begin the lesson by having students think about identity groups to which they belong, reflecting on the previous two lessons (Lessons 6 & 7, "Who Am I," Parts 1 & 2). Remind them that groups can include those they are born into, groups of their choosing or groups they did not choose. Provide examples such as Jamaican, Latino, seventh graders, guitar player, same-sex household family, Jehovah's Witness, dancer, person with a hearing disability, etc. Give students five minutes to write down their list of groups, encouraging them to list as many as possible.

2. After they have created their lists, have students call out the groups one at a time, giving each student the opportunity to name one group, then start over and do not repeat when a group is named. Record these on the board/smart board as students say the name of the group.

3. Have students stand in a straight line along the length or width of the classroom. Tell students that you are going to say the names of several groups. If students see themselves as part of the group named, they should move forward one step. If they don't see themselves as part of the group, they should remain standing where they are. After naming each group, encourage students to observe who is stepping forward with them, how often the whole class steps forward or if they, or anyone else, ever steps forward with just a few people or alone.

4. Call several groups one by one. Some of the groups should be ones that all or many students will belong to (e.g., seventh grader or whatever grade students are in, girls, Iowans or whatever state you live in) and some groups should be ones that involve fewer students stepping forward (e.g., only child, Spanish speakers). Be mindful that if you call out a group for which only one student will step forward, be reasonably certain the student will be comfortable stepping forward by themselves. After calling several groups, briefly ask students, "What do you observe so far?" Then continue the exercise by naming other groups.

5. Have students return to their seats and explain that they are each going to identify the groups that they belong to by completing a pie chart. Ask students, "What is a pie chart?" Explain that a **pie chart** is a circular graph which is divided into slices (like a pie) to illustrate proportion. For example, a small pizza pie is usually divided into six equal slices. They will be deciding if their pieces are all the same size or different sizes (based on the importance of the group to their identity). You can show students a picture of a pie chart if you think they need it to understand.

6.  Distribute the handout, *I Belong to Many Groups Pie Chart,* to each student. Ask students to think about groups to which they belong. In addition to those they named at the beginning of the lesson, they can also consider any groups they heard during the stepping forward activity. Explain that each of the groups is like a "piece" of who they are.

   Refer back to the list of identity characteristics generated in Lesson 6 such as race (white, African American, Asian), family (number of siblings, single parent, interracial family), gender (male, female, transgender) and religion (Catholic, Jewish, Sikh). Once students have determined the groups that they will identify on the pie chart, have them consider the size of each "piece of the pie," helping them to understand that the groups that they belong to may not be equal in importance and they can factor that into their pie chart, either by dividing some of the six pieces in half or creating a whole new pie chart).

FLIPPED CLASSROOM IDEA

Make a short video of you talking about your *I Belong to Many Groups Pie Chart* that you prepare in advance. Share the pie graph and talk about how you selected the groups and the size of each piece of the pie.

7. Provide students with rulers and give them 10–15 minutes to complete their pie charts. After completing their pie charts, have students talk with a person sitting next to them, explaining their pie chart and comparing and contrasting their pie charts, noticing similarities and differences.

8. Have students come back to the large group and time permitting, invite those students who want to share with the whole class their pie chart. Engage them in a class discussion by asking the following questions:
   — What was your process for determining your groups?
   — Was it easy or difficult to come up with groups and/or to narrow the groups down?
   — Did you notice whether there were any groups to which many students identified? How about few or no students identified?
   — What are some reasons why people don't belong to all of the same exact groups?
   — Can the groups to which people belong change? Please share examples of those.
   — What are some of the positive aspects of our similarities and differences? What are some of the challenges of our similarities and differences?
   — What did you learn by doing this activity?

Extension Activities

▪ Provide a list of well-known people (historical, writers, celebrities, etc.), both living and dead, from many walks of life and who represent different groups—race, ethnicity, gender identity, sexual orientation, religion, etc. Have students choose a person from the list and then work alone or in small groups to research more about the person, identify the groups to which the person belonged and reflect on their identity and the contribution they made/are making to our society.

▪ Have students explore census data for the United States, their state and their city or town, looking at available data on race, ethnicity, gender, and socioeconomic status, etc. Have them create an anonymous survey for their school that asks people about different aspects of identity (race, languages spoken, etc.) and then create charts and a summary of what they learned.

I BELONG TO MANY GROUPS PIE CHART

Name: _____

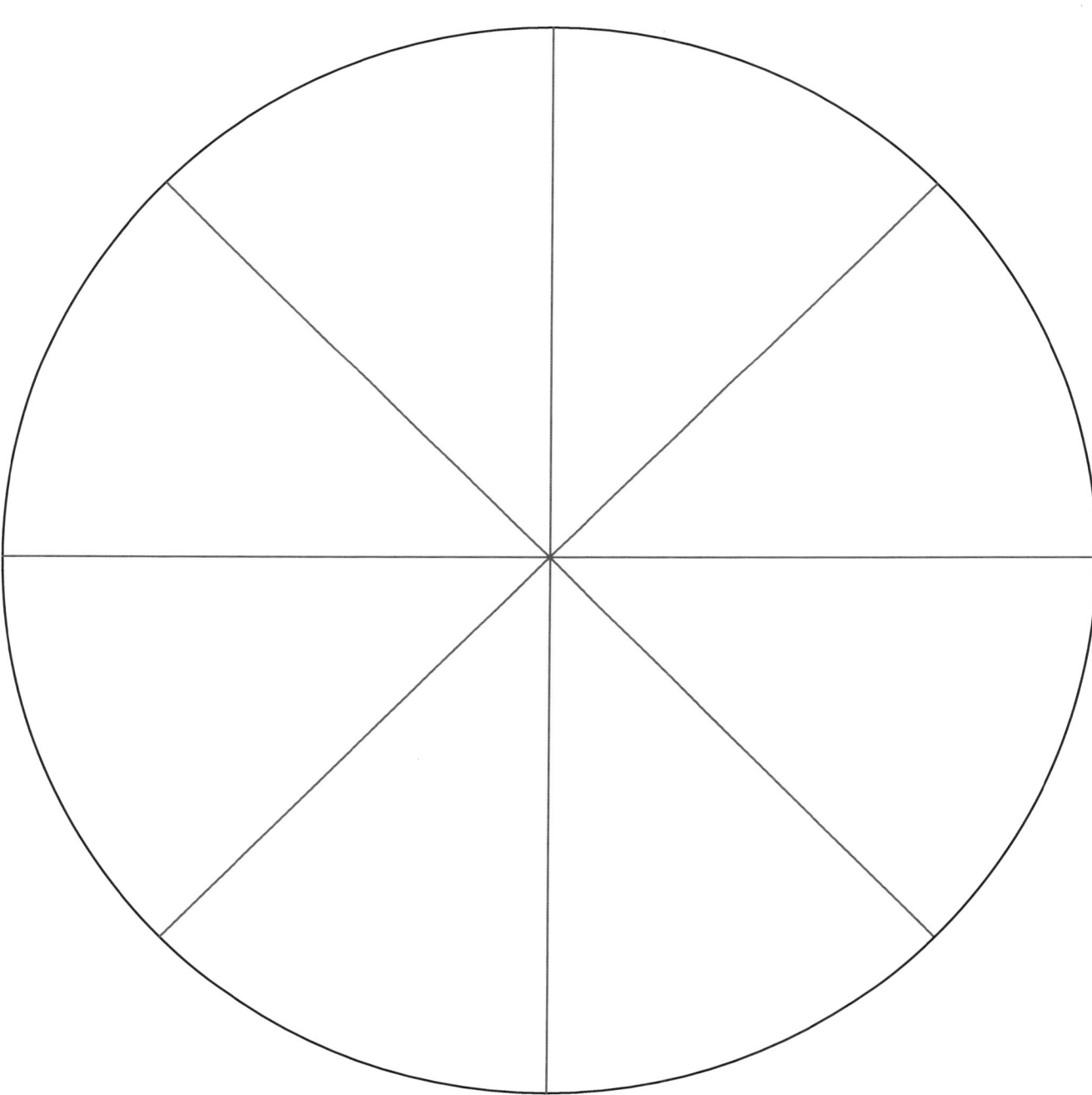

9. UNDERSTANDING AND ADDRESSING DIFFERENCES

TIME
45–50 minutes

COMMON CORE STANDARDS
Writing, Speaking & Listening

STRATEGIES AND SKILLS
define terms, turn and talk, large and small group discussion, fishbowl

KEY WORDS AND PHRASES
diversity, miscommunication, tension

FLIPPED
CLASSROOM IDEA

Have students watch the *Lunch Box Moment* video and jot down some thoughts and feelings about it.

Rationale

The purpose of this lesson is for students to reflect on the differences among and between them in order to discover what is both positive and challenging about diversity. Understanding and addressing differences is helpful in being able to examine and confront bias. This lesson provides an opportunity for students to explore what's positive and negative about diversity and reflect on situations where differences between people cause conflict or miscommunication.

Objectives

- Students will explore the meaning of diversity and what's positive and negative about it.
- Students will create a list of examples that include the aspect of diversity (i.e., differences) they see in their lives.
- Students will reflect on situations where differences were challenging and/or negative and how they dealt with those.

What's Needed

Handouts and Resources: Intergroup Miscommunication (one for each small group); "Lunch Box Moment" video (2016, 3 mins., NBC Asian America, www.nbcnews.com/news/asian-america/voices-have-you-ever-had-lunch-box-moment-n566411)

Other Material: Internet access, screen or LCD projector, speakers; 13 sheets of chart paper; markers

Advance Preparation: Write 7–10 of the identity characteristics listed in Procedure #4, each on a separate sheet of chart paper and post them around the room.

Procedures

1. [📷] Begin the lesson by showing the video *Lunch Box Moment.* This

video is part of a five-episode series, "Jubilee Project: Voices," from NBC Asian American. Engage in a group discussion by asking the following questions:

- What's happening in the video?
- What is a lunchbox moment?
- How do you think the people in the video felt during their lunchbox moments and how do they feel now?
- Have you ever had a lunchbox moment or witnessed one?
- What did you learn from the video?

2. Briefly review the previous lessons in this unit. Explain that now that they have talked about their own identities and the groups to which they belong, they are going to discuss differences and diversity. Ask, "What is diversity?" Elicit from students that **diversity** means different and varied and that we often say the United States is diverse because it is made up of people belonging to diverse groups characterized by culture, race, ethnicity, nationality, gender, sexual orientation, ability, etc.

3. Ask students, "What is good or positive about diversity and what is challenging or negative about diversity?" Have students turn and talk to the person sitting next to them and come up with 2–3 things that are good or positive about diversity and 2–3 things that are challenging or negative about diversity. Have students come back to the large group and share their ideas and record them on the board like this:

What's Good/Positive about Diversity?	What's Challenging/Negative about Diversity?

4. Ask students, "Where do we see diversity in our lives?" Record students' responses on the board. Add to the list by asking them, "Going back to your identity groups, in which groups are there differences between people?" Create a list that may look something like this and add any categories that are important that are not initially included:

- Appearance
- Race
- Income/Socioeconomic Status
- Religion
- Nationality
- Language

- Age
- Ethnicity
- Gender
- Sexual Orientation
- Opinions and Perspective
- Political Affiliation
- Disability

5. Explain to students that there are signs up around the room with the different categories of identity groups. They are going to spend a few minutes walking around the room listing all of the differences they can think of. For example under "appearance," you might include: body size, height, complexion, eye color and shape, complexion, birthmarks, facial appliances (glasses/braces), etc. To give everyone the opportunity to add something, tell students they should only list one or two items on each sheet and then move on. After the lists are complete, briefly have students read aloud all of the words on each page.

6. Explain to students that they each are now going to choose one of the groups (e.g., age, appearance, race, etc.) that interest them the most and move to that sign. When students gather in front of their signs, they should add anything that wasn't included in the initial listing of ideas. If Internet access is available in your classroom, students can do additional online research to make sure their lists are complete but they should not begin with that. Give students five minutes to add anything that is missing.

   Still sitting with their small groups, distribute to each group the *Intergroup Miscommunication* handout. Instruct students to complete the handout as a group as they discuss what happens when there is conflict, tension, miscommunication or misunderstanding that involves an aspect of diversity or identity. (For example, a person goes into a store to buy something and the storekeeper only speaks Chinese so they have trouble communicating.)

7. Have students come back to the whole class and share what they came up with in their small groups. Start to create a growing list of what gets in the way of communication and what can be done to remedy this challenge.

8. Tell students that they are going to do a "fishbowl" activity. Ask, "What is a fishbowl?" Explain that this activity is like a fishbowl in that we will make a circle and some students will be inside the circle (i.e., in a fishbowl) and the rest of the students will be observers outside of it.

9. Ask for 4–6 volunteers who are willing to sit inside the circle and talk about experiences with differences (or volunteers to talk about the anonymous essays that the teacher will read). Create a small circle with chairs for those sitting inside the circle. Arrange the other chairs to sit outside this smaller circle. Before discussing the specific ground rules for the fishbowl, review your classroom guidelines, as past experiences and strong feelings may emerge from the fishbowl.

10. Explain the ground rules for the fishbowl:

    a. The observers are not allowed to speak. Their job is to listen and learn from the fishbowl students. The observers will have an opportunity to discuss any issues that emerge later.

    b. You (the teacher) will facilitate the fishbowl discussion and you will make sure everyone has the opportunity to talk.

       Optional: Once the fishbowl discussion has happened for at least 10 minutes and you sense that others want to speak, you can allow a time where, if someone in the observer groups wants to join the fishbowl, they can tap the shoulder of someone in the fishbowl and take their place. Use this step at your discretion.

    c. If real situations are being shared, students should maintain confidentiality by not mentioning names or other revealing characteristics that would identify individuals in the story.

NOTE 8

You may choose to do this fishbowl activity in a variety of ways. You can either have students who are inside the fishbowl talk about their own experience with differences or a situation that they witnessed or observed. Another option is to have students write about experiences with differences (which will be anonymous) and some of those essays can be shared anonymously in the fishbowl for students to discuss.

11. Use the following questions to guide the fishbowl and at the same time, allow it to move in the natural direction that the conversation is moving.

   — Share about a time when you experienced something negative, challenging or difficult due to differences between you and another person or group of people. What happened? (This can be substituted with students' writing.)

   — How did you (or the person) feel?

   — What did you (or the person) do or want to do?

   — What did other people do that helped or made the situation worse?

12. After the fishbowl, engage the students in a discussion by asking the following questions:

   — **To the observers:** Was it difficult to not respond to the comments made during the fishbowl? Why?

   — **To the fishbowl students:** How did it feel to share your thoughts and feelings about differences?

   — **To everyone:** Did you hear anything from the fishbowl that surprised you? What did you learn from the experience? What came out from the discussion about how it feels to deal with differences?

Extension Activities

◾ Have students work in small groups to create role plays/skits that illustrate conflict or miscommunication because of differences/diversity. Remind students not to use the names of students or teachers in the class or act out situations that will reveal a recent situation that everyone knows about and it is clear who specifically it is about.

◾ Have students write realistic fiction stories where the main characters and plot focus on a conflict or disagreement that takes places because of certain differences between people. Use the writing process to have students write and revise their stories, getting feedback from their classmates and refining the stories as needed. When completed, publish a class blog with all the stories.

INTERGROUP MISCOMMUNICATION

Names of our group members: _____

Differences within our group: _____

_____

_____

Directions: Discuss what happens when there is conflict, tension, miscommunication or misunderstanding that involves an aspect of diversity or identity and answer the questions below.

1. What are some examples of conflict, tension or miscommunication between people who are different (in this group)?

2. What are some of the underlying reasons for the conflict, tension or miscommunication?

3. What are some ways to address the problem(s)?

10. GROUPS, CLIQUES AND FRIENDSHIP

Rationale

The purpose of this lesson is for students to reflect on friendships, groups and cliques. Friendship and social dynamics are an important aspect of middle school students' lives. In addition, identity and diversity are sometimes factors in how students form friendships and/or exclude others. This lesson provides an opportunity for students to reflect on past and present friendships, identify what's important to their friendships and explore their experiences with cliques.

Objectives

- Students will explore their friendships past and present.
- Students will identify the "cliques" at their school.
- Students will reflect on their positive and negative experiences with and feelings about cliques.
- Students will understand the role identity plays in being included or excluded from cliques.

What's Needed

Material: *Post-it® Notes* (10 per student, ideally half one color, half another color), chart paper, board/smart board, markers

Advance Preparation: On two separate sheets of chart paper, write at the top "Positive Qualities" and "Negative Qualities" and set aside.

Procedures

1.  Begin the lesson by asking students to think about their friendships. Ask some or all of the following questions while students think, jot down notes and/or sketch. Explain that their notes and thoughts are for their eyes only. You may want to play some quiet music in the background.

TIME
45 minutes

COMMON CORE STANDARDS
Writing, Speaking & Listening, Language

STRATEGIES AND SKILLS
large and small group discussion, brainstorm, writing

KEY WORDS AND PHRASES
clique, excluded, included

FLIPPED CLASSROOM IDEA

Make a short video of you asking the questions above while students write down notes or drawings at home while listening to the questions.

- Do you remember your first friend and how you became friends?
- What did you like about that person? What didn't you like?
- When you got to elementary school, did you make a new friend or friends?
- Was it sometimes difficult to make friends?
- Did your friendship(s) change and if so, how?
- What did you do when someone wanted to be friends but you didn't?
- Do you have a new friend or friends in middle school?
- Was it hard to make new friends?
- If you have new or different friends, how are they similar to and different from your friend(s) in elementary school?
- How does technology impact your friendship(s)?
- Do you wish you had more or fewer friends?
- Do you notice you have more friends who are similar in some ways? How so?
- What do you like and appreciate about your friend(s)?
- Do you ever feel bad or uncomfortable around your friend(s)?
- Do you wish you could be friends with someone but can't?

2. Engage students in a discussion by asking the following questions:
   - What came up for you when you thought about past and present friendships?
   - Why do you think it is important to have friends?

3. Distribute *Post-it® Notes* to students (6–10 each, ideally half one color, half another color). On one color, have students write qualities that they look for in friends, what is important to them about their friendships. Using the other color, have students write down qualities that make them not want to be friends with someone or cause them to end the friendship.

4. Hang the two pieces of chart paper previously prepared on opposite sides of the board/smart board. Call students up one row or table at a time (in groups of 5–7) to post their post-its on each chart or side of the board. When all are finished, ask a student to read aloud each chart.

5. Engage students in a discussion by asking the following questions:
   - What do you notice about the charts?
   - Are there any patterns that you notice?
   - What are positive qualities of friends and what are negative qualities?
   - Do you have anything to add after reading the charts?

6. Ask students, "What is a clique?" Engage students in a brief discussion about this, eliciting a definition of **clique** as a small group of people who spend time together and who are not friendly to other people. Ask, "What other qualities do cliques have?" Explain that when you are in a particular clique, the members of it sometimes/ often don't want you to be friends with other people outside the group and there are often unwritten rules about how the members of the clique should behave, dress and with whom they can be friendly. In addition, cliques sometimes (or often) form around an aspect of identity and then exclude others who are not part of that group (e.g., all white girls, all kids who live in a certain neighborhood).

7. Have students turn and talk to a person sitting next to them and brainstorm a list of cliques that exist in their school. One person should take notes. They should take five minutes to do this and not name specific people but identify the group either by name (i.e., "jocks") or description ("the kids who work hard in school"). After the pairs complete their task, have the whole group come together and list all of the cliques they came up with, having each pair share one at a time until all the cliques are listed. Ask students, "What do all the cliques have in common? Why do you think these cliques exist? What purpose do they serve?"

8. Have students explore cliques in more depth by having them write a short essay by choosing one of the following prompts (A or B). They should write about the main question and use the bulleted questions below as prompts to help them craft their essay. Have them spend 15 minutes; this can also be assigned as a homework assignment to complete. Remind students not to name specific people or incidents that will make it clear they are talking about specific people.

   A. Write about a time (present or past) that you were part of a clique.
      — What is it like to be part of a clique?
      — How does it make you feel?
      — Are the members of the clique similar in certain ways?
      — Are the members of the clique similar in terms of certain identity groups (i.e., race, gender, religion, socioeconomic status, etc.)?
      — Are certain individuals or groups of people excluded from the clique?
      — What are some of the unwritten rules about how to behave, what to be interested in, dress and act towards other people?
      — Do you feel pressure to keep out certain people and not talk to or be friends with certain people? Please explain.

   B. Write about a time (present or past) that you wanted to be part of a clique but weren't "allowed" or were excluded.
      — What is it like to be excluded from the clique?
      — How does it make you feel?
      — Are the members of the clique similar in certain ways?
      — Are the members of the clique similar in terms of certain identity groups (i.e., race, gender, religion, socioeconomic status, etc.)?
      — Are certain individuals or groups of people excluded from the clique?
      — What is your perception of the unwritten rules about how that clique is supposed to behave, what to be interested in, dress and act towards other people?
      — Do you ever feel ignored or snubbed by cliques and what is that like?

9. After writing, ask if any students would like to share their essays aloud. Be mindful that students may not feel comfortable reading them aloud or some essays may not be appropriate to read aloud. You should read the essays in advance to make sure that there isn't anything inappropriate, personal or potentially embarrassing for another student in them. You may also offer to read some of the essays aloud without identifying who wrote the essay.

10. Engage students in a discussion by asking the following questions:
    — What did you learn from what you heard?

- What came out from the discussion about cliques?
- What's positive about cliques?
- What is negative and potentially hurtful/painful about cliques?
- How does identity impact cliques and inclusion/exclusion?
- Are some identity groups (race, gender, religion, socioeconomic status, etc.) included or excluded more than others?
- Are cliques defined by similarities and differences? How so?
- What happens to those kids who are not in a clique or group (or "squad")?
- How can we find a balance between having friends of our choosing but not excluding people?

11. Summarize the lesson by explaining that while we don't have to be friends with everyone, it is important not to exclude people and make others feel hurt or sad. In addition, explain that we are part of a community and have a responsibility to help people feel respected and included even if we are not friends with particular people. Try to elicit that it is also helpful to talk to different people and be open because sometimes there are people who we think we might not be friends with who we might actually have a connection with and we are missing out if we don't even talk to people outside our groups and cliques.

Extension Activities

- Have students identify a favorite movie or television program and explore how friendships are portrayed. They can reflect on some of the topics explored in the lesson such as identity, differences, cliques and exclusion and write an analysis (or create a short video "TED Talk") on what they learned by watching with this lens.

- Have students create a presentation on how friendships are strengthened and weakened with technology and social media. They can include smartphones, texting, gaming, social media, etc. as examples of how friendships can be formed, hurt and helped by using technology. They can include survey data or interviews they do with young people on the topic.

UNIT III. ANALYZING WHERE WE GET INFORMATION

We live in a time where information comes to us at high speed, in different ways and at all times of the day and night. Young people, especially tweens and teens, also receive constant information through their smartphones, tablets, social media channels, news and overheard conversations among adults. Information comes from a variety of sources—from news and social media to people in our lives to what we learn from teachers and peers in school. Taking in all of this information is not the same as understanding it. Therefore, young people need to be able to distinguish between facts and opinions, think critically about the information they absorb, expand their understanding of how information informs perspective and be able to see and understand the bias and stereotypes that are sometimes embedded in this information.

In Unit III of this curriculum, students will have the opportunity to differentiate between facts and opinions, think about what shapes their opinions and hear other people's points of view. To help them explore perspective, middle schoolers will engage in and reflect upon an activity where their perspective differs from someone else's. Young people will consider the variety of ways in which they receive information and will develop critical thinking skills for assessing and analyzing online information. Rumors, gossip and misinformation take place a great deal in middle school and students will reflect on their own experiences with it and consider what can be done with realistic scenarios. Finally, students will learn more about advertising and propaganda—other forms of information that are particular to "selling" and manipulating, and will learn how to understand and deconstruct those forms.

11. FACTS VS. OPINIONS

Rationale

The purpose of this lesson is for students to understand that people have different opinions about a variety of topics and issues. Understanding the difference between facts and opinions and learning how to share your opinions with others and hear other points of view is an important part of seeing and accepting differences. This lesson provides an opportunity for students to distinguish between fact and opinion, reflect on their own opinions and write an essay on one of those opinions.

Objectives

▰ Students will be able to differentiate between facts and opinions.

▰ Students will identify their own opinions and understand the opinions of others on a variety of topics.

▰ Students will organize their thoughts and "evidence" for an opinion they hold by writing a persuasive letter.

What's Needed

Handouts and Resources: *Persuasive Letter Organizer* (one for each student)

Other Material: Five 8½" x 11" sheets of paper, markers

Advance Preparation: Create five signs by writing the following phrases on separate sheets of paper to be placed around the room: (1) STRONGLY AGREE, (2) AGREE, (3) NOT SURE/IN BETWEEN, (4) DISAGREE, and (5) STRONGLY DISAGREE.

Procedures

1. Begin the lesson by asking students, "What is the difference between a fact and an opinion?" Elicit from students that **facts** are absolutely true statements (something that truly exists or happened) and **opinions** are

TIME
45 minutes

COMMON CORE STANDARDS
Reading, Writing, Speaking and Listening, Language

STRATEGIES AND SKILLS
Here I Stand, persuasive letter writing

KEY WORDS AND PHRASES
controversial, fact, opinion

FLIPPED CLASSROOM IDEA

Make a short video of you reading aloud the statements indicated in Procedure #2 and have students jot them down and note which of them are facts and which are opinions.

what people feel, think and believe; there can be a wide range of opinions or points of view about something.

2. 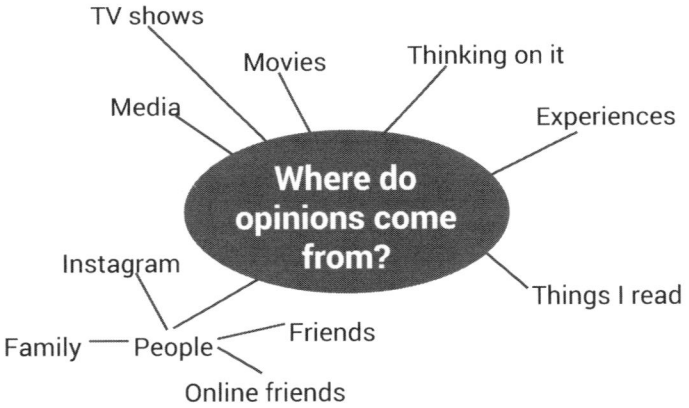 Explain to students that you are going to call out a list of facts and opinions and ask students to say whether each of the statements is a fact or an opinion. You can do that by having them raise hands (hands up for fact, down for opinion) move to one side of the room or another if you have the space, or jot it down on a sheet of paper.

   — The 44th President of the United States was Barack Obama.

   — Instagram is a form of social media.

   — Dogs are better pets than cats.

   — Coffee is bad for your health.

   — Christmas is on December 25.

   — Doing the laundry is a lot of work.

   — Facebook is the best social media site.

3. After going through each of the statements, ask students to share their own examples of facts and opinions. Then ask, "How can you tell the difference between a fact and an opinion? What differentiates facts from opinions?"

4. Ask students to think about an opinion they have about something, particularly something that is important to them. Ask them to think about where that opinion or point of view comes from. Create a semantic web with the words: "Where do opinions come from?" Then ask, "What are the different sources for our opinions?" Brainstorm a list using a semantic web, which may look something like this:

TV shows
Movies
Thinking on it
Media
Experiences
Where do opinions come from?
Instagram
Things I read
Family — People
Friends
Online friends

5. Explain to students that they are going to do an activity called "Here I Stand" which helps them explore their own opinions and the opinions of others. Tell them that they will listen to some statements and decide to what extent they agree or disagree with the statement. They will be indicating their opinion about each topic by positioning themselves along an imaginary line, depending upon how strongly they agree or disagree with a statement.

6. Select a large open space and indicate the position of an imaginary line with the farthest right point representing a STRONGLY AGREE response and the farthest left point a STRONGLY DISAGREE ; in between, place AGREE, NOT SURE/IN BETWEEN, AND DISAGREE along the continuum (using the signs you created in advance). Then, read each statement below, one-at-a-time, requesting students to take a few minutes to decide where they stand on the continuum and have them walk silently to that place and observe where others choose to stand.

7. After everyone has chosen their spot for the first statement, have students spend 2–3 minutes talking among themselves about why they are standing where they are. Then have a few students briefly share aloud with the class why they're standing where they are. Then pause and ask, "After hearing everyone's thoughts, does anyone wish to move to a different place on the continuum?" Then move on to the next statement, using the same process.

   Use the following statements (you can make up statements of your own but be sure that they are opinions, not facts):

   — The iPhone is better than the Samsung.

   — Money can buy you happiness.

   — Kids our age should be able to set our own bedtimes.

   — Playing violent video games makes you more aggressive and violent.

   — Students should be able to grade their teachers.

   — If you see someone being bullied, you should do something about it.

   — Technology is making us less social.

   — Teenagers should be able to vote when they are 16.

   — Children under 10 years old should not have smartphones.

8. After all of the statements have been read, engage students in a whole class discussion using some or all of the following questions:

   — Was it easy or difficult to decide where to stand?

   — Were some statements easier to decide and some more difficult?

   — How did it feel when most people had the same response as you?

   — How about when most people had different responses than you? What was it like to stand alone or with only a few people?

   — How did it feel when your friend(s) were standing in a different spot than you?

   — Did you ever feel you needed to explain where you chose to stand? If so, why did you feel this way?

   — Did you ever decide to change your position when you saw you did not agree with a majority of the group? How about after hearing others' points of view?

   — What happens when we have different opinions about things?

   — What is the value in differences of opinion?

   — How can we make it easier or more comfortable to disagree with each other?

9. Explain to students that they are going to write persuasive letters about one of the topics discussed in the "Here I Stand" activity or they may also select another controversial topic that they care about to address in a letter. First they will decide their topic, their opinion on the topic and to whom the letter should go (i.e., the

letter about bedtimes could go to their parents, the letter about voting could go to their local elected official or the President). Then they will need to provide some background about the topic, at least three reasons for their opinion backed up with quotes, facts, statistics or examples, and what a person with a different point of view might say and what they would say in response. This can be started in class using the *Persuasive Letter Organizer* handout and completed at home for homework.

10. When the assignment is due, have students read their persuasive letters aloud and then have them mail or email the letters to the appropriate person, organization or company.

Extension Activities

◼ Have students select a topic or controversial issue and then read 2–3 op-eds with different points of view on the same issue. After reading and analyzing the different op-eds, they can write an essay or develop a PowerPoint presentation that reflects the different points of view about the topic.

◼ Brainstorm a variety of controversial topics that are current in the news and together select one in which to hold a debate. Have students research different positions on the issues and then form teams in which to debate. Hold a debate in class.

PERSUASIVE LETTER ORGANIZER

Student Name: _____

Directions: Use this organizer to outline your persuasive letter before writing.

State your opinion/position about the issue you chose.
Provide background information about the issue.
List 2–3 main reasons that would convince someone of your position (use examples, statistics, quotes, etc.).

Indicate what those who have a different point of view might say.

Indicate what you might say in response.

12. PERSPECTIVE

Rationale

The purpose of this lesson is for students to understand what perspective is and reflect on how one's perspective is formed. Understanding that people have different perspectives on things and situations is an important aspect of understanding diversity. This lesson provides an opportunity for students to understand and explore perspective, reflect on what shapes perspective and engage in an experience where they may have a different perspective than someone else.

Objectives

- Students will explore the concept of perspective and what shapes one's perspective.
- Students will reflect on what specific factors impact their perspective.
- Students will create stories and perspectives based on photographs and compare/contrast them with others.

What's Needed

Handouts and Resources: The True Story of the Three Little Pigs video (2012, 5½ mins., www.youtube.com/watch?v=m75aEhm-BYw); *Glasses Cut-Out* (one for each student); *Photographs #1–10* (one for each pair of students)

Other Material: Paper and pencils/pens; Internet access, screen or LCD projector, speakers

Advance Preparation: Duplicate and cut out enough glasses, using the *Glasses Cut-Out,* to distribute to each student.

Procedures

1. Begin the lesson by briefly re-telling the story of "The Three Little Pigs" or ask a student to tell it. Then show *The True Story of the Three Little Pigs*

TIME
45 minutes

COMMON CORE STANDARDS
Reading, Writing, Speaking and Listening

STRATEGIES AND SKILLS
brainstorm, large group discussion, work in pairs

KEY WORDS AND PHRASES
lens, perspective

video or if you are unable to show videos, briefly re-tell the story from the wolf's point of view. Engage students in a brief discussion by asking: *How was this surprising to you? What was the wolf's point of view?*

2. Ask students, "What does the re-telling of the story have to do with perspective? What is perspective?" Come to a definition of **perspective** as a way of looking or thinking about facts and/or situations or a point of view.

3. Explain that perspective is like a pair of glasses or sunglasses and is like the lens with which we look through the glasses. Not everyone looks at the same thing the same way. Ask students, "What shapes how you look at things? What factors impact how you view facts and situations?" Brainstorm a list that includes:

   — identity (refer to Lesson 6 & 7)

   — experiences

   — beliefs

   — values

   — media

   — people—friends, family, peers, acquaintances

   — context of a situation

4. Distribute a cut-out of a pair of glasses to each student. Have them think silently about what things shape their perspective, using the brainstormed list (above) and getting more specific about the details; they can get specific about identity (e.g., I'm Korean), experiences (e.g., "I have 6 brothers and sisters") and/or beliefs and values (e.g., "God and religion are an important part of my life."). Have students spend 5–7 minutes writing on the glasses those things that shape their perspective. When finished, have some students come to the front of the room and share their glasses and what shapes their perspective.

5. Engage in a brief group discussion by asking the following questions:

   — What did you notice about our different "lenses" or perspectives?

   — What shapes our perspective?

   — Can you think of a time when you had a different perspective than someone? What happened?

6.  Divide students into pairs and distribute one of the *Photographs* provided to each pair. Explain to students that using the photograph, they are going to explore perspective in more depth.

7. After each pair has received their photograph, explain that they should look at the photograph together but keep their thoughts and ideas to themselves (for now). Instruct them to first create a story in their minds as to what is going on with the person or people in the photo. Next, they should write a caption for the photo on a piece of paper, again silently

NOTE 6

You can use the photographs provided, use some of your own or access and use free photos at www. unsplash.com or www.pexels.com/ search/people.

FLIPPED CLASSROOM IDEA

Make a short video of you discussing a photograph (use one of the photos provided or one you like) and creating a caption for the photo as well as the story behind it which captures the perspective of the person or people in it. Respond to some of the questions in #7.

and to themselves so their partner doesn't see it. Then, they will write a 4–5 sentence paragraph about the perspective of the person(s) in the photo by responding to the following questions:

— What's going on in the picture?

— Who is the person/people?

— How are they feeling?

— What are they thinking about?

— What's their story?

— What is their perspective in the situation and what makes you think that (identity, experiences, values, beliefs)?

The best way to approach this would be to answer the questions first and then construct their paragraph. This writing activity should be done individually. Give students 10 minutes to do this.

8. When students have completed their paragraphs, they should read them aloud to their partner. After reading aloud, have them discuss the ways in which each of their perspectives is both different and similar and how each of them came up with the perspective reflected in the photos.

9. Ask if any of the pairs would like to share their paragraphs and what they discussed with the whole class. Then engage students in a class discussion by asking the following questions:

— How did you come up with your story?

— How did you determine the perspective of the person? What factors did you consider?

— What did you notice about the paragraph and perspective your partner wrote about?

— What was similar? What was different?

— How is perspective shaped by our identities?

Extension Activities

■ Using *The New York Times'* Room for Debate (www.nytimes.com/roomfordebate), have students identify a topic of interest to them in their comprehensive list of topics and read all of the different perspectives on the issue that are reflected. Have them choose one they agree with and one they disagree with and write an essay explaining why they agree/disagree, including the perspective of the writer and what they think may shape the writer's and their own perspectives.

■ Have students create one scene from a play or a short skit (to be acted out) that happens when people have different perspectives on the same situation. They should conceptualize the idea, write the script, assign parts and then either act it out for the class or create a video of it.

GLASSES CUT-OUT

Directions: Cut along the dashed-line leaving the lens intact.

PHOTOGRAPH #1

PHOTOGRAPH #2

PHOTOGRAPH #3

PHOTOGRAPH #4

PHOTOGRAPH #5

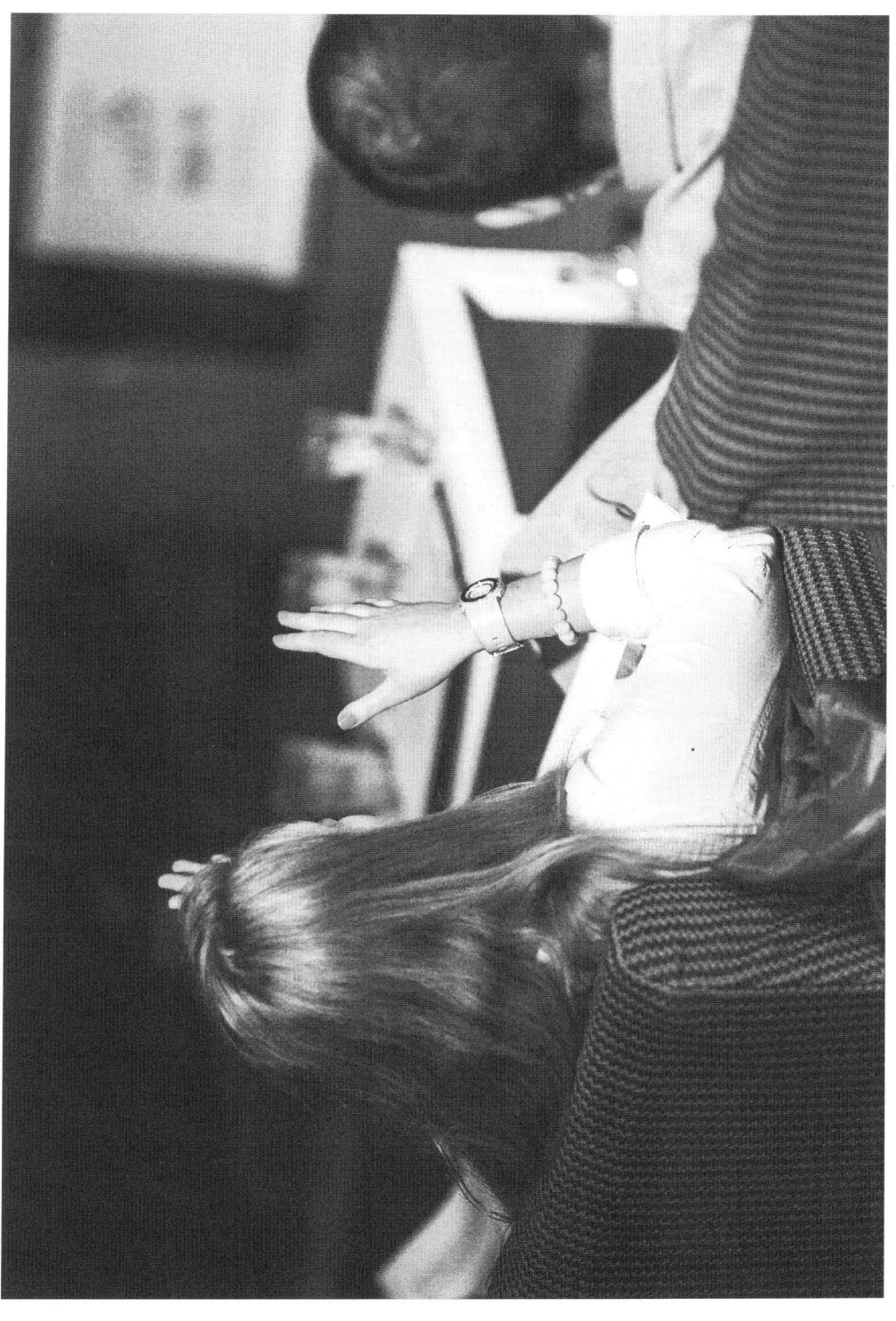

PHOTOGRAPH #6

PHOTOGRAPH #7

PHOTOGRAPH #8

PHOTOGRAPH #9

PHOTOGRAPH #10

13. SOURCES OF INFORMATION

Rationale

The purpose of this lesson is for students to reflect on the wide range of information sources available to them and reflect on each source's reliability, perspective and potential bias. Understanding that different sources of information have different degrees of credibility is important in understanding perspective and in reflecting on what sources to use. This lesson provides an opportunity for students to explore different sources of information, assess them and engage in a small group experience that exposes them to different information sources.

Objectives

- Students will be able to understand different ways we get information and that they may convey different perspectives.

- Students will understand that there are a variety of ways you can find one piece of information.

- Students will engage in and reflect upon a small group project in which they use different sources of information.

What's Needed

Handouts and Resources: Information Source Group Activity (one for each student)

Other Material: Sheets of paper with different information sources (see Procedure #5), board/smart board, markers

Procedures

1. Define **bias** as an inclination or preference either for or against an individual or group that interferes with impartial judgment.

   Explain that while we will do a more thorough exploration of bias later, we define it here because it is used in this lesson.

TIME
Two 45-minute sessions and time in between for homework

COMMON CORE STANDARDS
Writing, Speaking and Listening

STRATEGIES AND SKILLS
large and small group discussion, turn and talk, brainstorm, free writing

KEY WORDS AND PHRASES
bias, reliability, sources

2. Ask students to think about one thing they know a lot about. It can be one of their skills, talents or interests from Lesson 6, historical information, a video game or movie they love or someone they know. Explain that they are going to be doing some "free writing" about the topic, which means that they will have a set amount of time to write about the topic (in this case, five minutes) and they cannot stop writing until time is called. Explain that they should not worry about punctuation or grammar and they can use paragraph form or bulleted points, as long as they do not stop writing for the full five minutes.

3. After the five minutes of writing are up, have students turn and talk with a partner, either reading aloud their writing or summarizing it with their partner.

4. Have students come back to the large group and ask, "Reflecting on what you wrote about, what are the various ways you learned what you know? Where did you get the information?" Have a few students respond. Then ask more generally, "What are all the different ways we get information?" Brainstorm a list and record it on the board/smart board and allow as many possible sources as possible. The list may look like the following:

- Websites*
- Newspapers/Magazines*
- People in our lives (friends, family, acquaintances, classmates)*
- Government Reports and Legal Documents
- Press Releases and Advertising
- Books*
- Videos*
- Television

- Music, songs
- Flyers, Pamphlets, Leaflets
- Art: paintings,
- Diaries
- Patents
- Surveys*
- Social Media
- School

5. Take 5–7 of the most common "information sources" of your choice (or the ones marked with an asterisk) and write each of them on a large piece of paper and post the sheets around the room. Add one additional paper that says "another source."

6. Explain to students that you are going to read a list of things you want to know and for each, have students identify where they think they could find the information (what information source) and go to that spot in the room. For each item on the list, give at least one additional opportunity for students to choose another information source for that item by moving to that section of the room. Below are suggested topics but you can substitute or add others.

- How many grams of fat there are in a glass of milk.
- The 24th President of the United States and their most important accomplishments.
- The best place to get burritos in Austin, Texas.
- The place where your great grandparents were born.
- How people in the United States feel about marriage equality.
- The plot of the movie, *Mission Impossible 5.*
- The history of social media, when different social media platforms started being used and how they became popular.
- The rules of soccer.

- How to make the "butterfly stitch" with lanyard.
- The history of the Voting Rights Act and what events led to it.

7. After this activity is completed, engage students in a class discussion by asking the following questions:
   - How did you decide where to stand?
   - For what topics did you move to a second possible source?
   - Which of the items are facts? Which are opinions? How do you know?
   - Was it easier to find sources for facts or opinions?
   - How did you decide in your mind which would be the best source?
   - Are any of these sources more reliable than others?
   - Is there a particular perspective or potential bias in any of these sources?

8.  Divide students into small groups, with each group assigned to one of the topics above. Give the small groups a few minutes to get together and begin to brainstorm specific sources, places to find out the answer to the question and then begin to rank the sources for reliability. The goal of the small group work is for students to think of as many sources as possible and also begin to rank the sources. Also, make students aware that there could be some variation in the answer to the question and it could be answered in a few ways, even if it is seemingly a fact (e.g., a glass of milk has a different amount of fat depending on whether it's whole, skim, soy, 2%, etc.).

   For homework, each student in their small group should be assigned to a different source and using that source, come up with information, facts, statistics and/or quotes to share what they found out about their topic. After getting the information, as a group they will go through all the information they have and find a way to present it to the rest of the class. The possible forms of presentation could include: PowerPoint or Prezi presentation, skit, written essay, drawing, infographic, speech, video, etc.

9. Have students present their small group work to the rest of the class. Then engage students in a discussion by asking the following questions:
   - Were you easily able to find the answers to the questions?
   - Did different sources have different information?
   - How did you assess each source's reliability?
   - What perspective or bias may be present in some or all of the sources?
   - What did you learn by doing this activity?

FLIPPED CLASSROOM IDEA

Make a short video of you talking about one specific fact or opinion about something and then delineate all of the ways in which you can find that information—use props (books, people, Internet, etc.) if possible to illustrate your main points.

Extension Activities

- Have students create a timeline or infographic about sources of information over the last 50 or 100 years, starting with 1965 or 1915 and coming to the present, noting when new sources of information were introduced.

- Have students interview their parents, grandparents and great-grandparents about what sources of information they had when they were growing up, what sources were added when they were adults and how they adjusted or haven't adjusted to new sources of information. Students can then present what they learned by writing a paper or creating a PowerPoint or poster presentation of their findings.

INFORMATION SOURCE GROUP ACTIVITY

GROUP TOPIC:	
GROUP MEMBERS:	

POSSIBLE SOURCES OF INFORMATION	
(List all and next to each write who will be assigned to each information source)	
Information Source:	Person Assigned:

Information Source:	Person Assigned:

How we will present our information:

14. ASSESSING AND ANALYZING ONLINE INFORMATION

Rationale

The purpose of this lesson is for students to learn to think critically about the information they receive digitally. Being able to assess and analyze online information is not only an important life skill as a student and adult, it is also part of being able to critically assess information sources and bias in online information. This lesson provides an opportunity for students to reflect on how they use digital information, consider how to assess the reliability of Internet sources and evaluate online information for credibility.

Objectives

- Students will reflect on the extent to which they use the Internet as an information source.

- Students will analyze the difference between a reliable Internet source and an unreliable one.

- Students will consider the important factors in evaluating the validity and use of an Internet source.

- Students will assess a few specific online sources for reliability and usefulness.

What's Needed

Handouts and Resources: *Evaluating Online Information* and *Website Evaluation Form* (one of each for each student)

Other Material: Websites www.theflatearthsociety.org/cms, www. ourhollowearth.com, www.who.int/docstore/tobacco/ntday/ntday96/ or another one of your choosing; board/smart board; markers

Advance Preparation: If you are unable to access the Internet at school, take a few screen shots of the three websites listed above and show these instead or have students look at them the previous night for homework.

TIME
Two 45-minute classes (one for small group presentations)

COMMON CORE STANDARDS
Reading, Writing, Speaking and Listening, Language

STRATEGIES AND SKILLS
large group discussion, small group work, Internet research

KEY WORDS AND PHRASES
accurate, analyze, bigotry, cyberhate, evaluate, recommend

Procedures

1. Begin the lesson by reminding students that in the previous lesson, sources of information were discussed and that the Internet—or online information—came up a great deal as a source of information we all use regularly. Explain that in today's lesson we will discuss how to evaluate and assess online information.

NOTE 2

Be mindful that some or many students may not have Internet access at home or smartphones in which they can get online. If that is the case, instead of having students do this activity in a public way, you may choose to have students write down the responses on the piece of paper while seated.

2. Instruct students to stand at the back of room and explain that you are going to read aloud six statements. For each statement that they answer "yes," they will move up one step. If their answer is "no," they should stay where they are.

   — I use the Internet/mobile apps to do research for school.

   — I use the Internet/mobile apps to shop.

   — I use the Internet/mobile apps to play games.

   — I use the Internet/mobile apps to communicate with my friends.

   — I use the Internet/mobile apps to learn something about one of my interests or hobbies.

   — I use the Internet/mobile apps to find things for my parents or family members.

   — I use the Internet/mobile apps to watch movies or TV programs.

3. Have students return to their seats and engage in a class discussion by asking the following questions:

   — What do you notice about your own use of online sources?

   — What do you notice about our class as a whole?

   — Does anything surprise you and if so, what?

   — When you read something online, do you automatically think it's true or false?

   — How can you tell if something is accurate or not?

   — What's an example of something you read online that wasn't true? How did you know?

 FLIPPED CLASSROOM IDEA

Make a short video of yourself talking about websites that you have visited (one that is reputable and one that is unreliable) and indicate briefly a few elements that gave each that quality, using some of the items from the *Evaluating Online Information* handout.

4.  On the board/smart board, project an example of a poorly designed and/or unreliable website (Three possibilities are www.theflatearthsociety.org/cms or www.ourhollowearth.com, www.who.int/docstore/tobacco/ntday/ntday96/ or one of your own choosing.) After projecting it, click to a few different places on the website, asking students the following questions:

   — What is the perspective of the website?

   — In what ways is the website set up well and not set up well?

   — Is the information reliable?

- Is there bias?

- Is it useful? How do you know?

Next, show a reliable and useful website (choose one based on something you're studying in class or a topic you know would interest your students). As you did with the other website, project or show screenshots of this one and click to a few different places on the website and ask the following questions:

- What is the perspective of the website?

- In what ways is the website set up well and not set up well?

- Is the information reliable?

- Is there bias?

- Is it useful? How do you know?

5. Explain to students that they are going to spend some time exploring how they can determine whether online sources are good ones—whether they are organized well, reliable and useful. Explain that anyone can publish on the Internet and in addition, there are many groups online that have a presence for the sole purpose of spreading hate and bigotry, commonly referred to as "cyberhate."

6. Distribute the *Evaluating Online Information* handout to each student and read it aloud as a class. After each section is read aloud, ask for an example of a website where some or most of those features are present. Ask if there are any questions or additions.

7. Go back to the two websites you looked at in Procedure #4. Go through the handout with the two websites and have students name what is there and what isn't there in each of the websites that helps to determine whether it's good and reputable or not.

8. Explain that students will work together in small groups to evaluate websites. First, as a class, brainstorm a list of 6–7 possible topics that the students want to learn more about using websites. The list may look something like this:

- Candidates for upcoming local or presidential election

- Learning how to cook

- Redecorating my room

- *Go Set a Watchman* vs. *To Kill a Mockingbird*

- History of social media

- Where to buy a good skateboard

- Climate change

9. Have students either choose which group they want to participate in or assign random small groups of 5–6 students each and have them pick a topic as a group from the brainstormed list. As a group, they will then look for relevant websites and narrow the list down to 2–3 websites that they will evaluate as a group. Evaluating the websites can be assigned for homework or worked on in class, depending on how much time you have and whether you have access to computers/tablets.

10. In small groups, students should use their copies of *Evaluating Online Information* and together will complete the *Website Evaluation Form* to compile their results.

11. Have each small group share their findings with the rest of the class, showing their website(s), what they determined about their use and reliability and how they worked together as a group. After all the groups have

presented their websites, engage students in a class discussion by asking the following questions:

- — What did you discover as you looked at and evaluated websites?
- — What did you learn about the usefulness and reliability of websites?
- — How does perspective and bias play a role in websites?
- — How did you determine what is reliable and not reliable?
- — How does what you learned influence how you will look for online sources of information in the future?

Extension Activities

- Using programs like Word Press, etc. have students create a class website that integrates what they learned about the elements of usefulness and reliability to create a class website that is useful, reliable and user-friendly. You can divide students into small groups and divide up all the aspects of web creation among the groups (visuals, writing content, research, tech set-up, etc.).

- Have students write a letter to a younger brother/sister, friend or someone in school giving them advice about what to look for in websites. They should use what they learned in class with tips and examples as a basis for their letter.

EVALUATING ONLINE INFORMATION

WHO

- Who (person, company, organization) is responsible for the website?
- Is the person, company or organization an expert and reputable in the field? How do you know?
- Who writes materials on the website?
- Can you tell which sources the author used in obtaining the info?
- If this is a blog or social media site, does this person cite reputable sources?

WHAT

- What is the purpose and goal of the website or page?
- Is the purpose or mission clear and easy to find?
- What sources of information are cited?
- What is the point of view of the website? What are their biases?
- Does the site cover the content or topic comprehensively?
- Is the website easy to use?

WHERE

- Where does the information come from?
- Can I find that information elsewhere on the web from another source?
- Where did you find this website—did you find it through a search engine (e.g., Google) or was it recommended?
- Is there contact information for someone on the website?

WHY

- Why was this site created?
- Why is this page or site better than another one?
- Why is this information useful for my purpose?

WHEN

- When was the site created?
- How old is the information?
- When was the last update of the website? Is it outdated?
- Is there updated information somewhere else?

WEBSITE EVALUATION FORM

Directions: Obtain several copies of this form. Using the *Evaluating Online Information* handout as a guide, complete this form for each website you evaluate.

GROUP MEMBERS:

Topic: _____

Name of website and web address: _____

_____

Is the information useful or not? How do you know? _____

_____

_____

_____

Is the information reliable or not? How do you know? _____

_____

_____

_____

What are the overall strengths of the website? _____

_____

_____

What are the overall weaknesses of the website? _____

_____

_____

Would you recommend this website to others—why or why not? _____

_____

_____

15. MISINFORMATION, RUMORS AND GOSSIP

Rationale

The purpose of this lesson is for students to understand and think critically about misinformation, rumors and gossip. Misinformation, rumors and gossip are strong social forces in middle schools and ones in which many kids engage, on purpose or unwittingly. This lesson provides an opportunity for students to learn more about misinformation, rumors and gossip, reflect on their own experience and behavior and analyze scenarios in which this social information is being transmitted.

Objectives

- Students will be able to define miscommunication, rumors and gossip and explore the similarities and differences among them.

- Students will reflect on their own experience with miscommunication, gossip and rumors.

- Students will critically analyze a realistic scenario involving misinformation, rumors and/or gossip.

What's Needed

Handouts and Resources: Misinformation, Rumors and Gossip Scenarios #1–6

Procedures

1. Begin the lesson by asking students, "What is misinformation? What is gossip? What are rumors?" Elicit and come to the following definitions:

    Misinformation: False or misleading information.

    Gossip: Information that is shared about the behavior and personal lives of other people.

    Rumor: Information or a story about someone that is spread that has not been proven to be true.

TIME
45 minutes

COMMON CORE STANDARDS
Reading, Writing, Speaking and Listening, Language

STRATEGIES AND SKILLS
define terms, large and small group discussion

KEY WORDS AND PHRASES
gossip, intent, misinformation, rumor, transmitted

 **FLIPPED CLASSROOM IDEA**

Make a short video of you defining miscommunication, gossip and rumor, providing an example for each and asking students to think about their own recent experiences with miscommunication, gossip and rumors.

2. Have students reflect silently on the following questions, giving a few seconds to think after asking each question.

   — When was the last time you heard or shared misinformation?

   — When was the last time you heard or spread a rumor?

   — When was the last time you heard or spread gossip?

   — What feels good about sharing misinformation, rumors and gossip?

   — What feels badly about sharing misinformation, rumors and gossip?

   This is a silent self-reflection activity. However, after giving students a few minutes to silently consider each question, ask if anyone would like to share and provide an opportunity to do so.

3. Ask students, "What is different about misinformation, gossip and rumors? What is similar?" In large group discussion, come up with a chart as follows and together with the students, fill in the blanks.

	Misinformation	Gossip	Rumors
Intent			
How it's transmitted (verbal, texting, social media, etc.)			
Possible topics			
Number of people involved			
Where does it take place (in school, after school activities, sports practice, school dance, party, clubs, sleepover)?			

4. Explain to students that they are going to work together in small groups to discuss scenarios that involve misinformation, gossip and rumors. Divide students into groups of 4–5 students each. Distribute a different *Misinformation, Rumors and Gossip Scenario* to each small group, giving a copy of the scenario to each student in their group. Students in each group should read their scenario silently, discuss the scenario using the discussion questions on their worksheet (although they can discuss beyond the questions) and then as a group, write a summary paragraph about their scenario that responds to some or all of the questions.

5. Each scenario includes some specific questions and each of them also asks the following:

   — What's happening and why?

   — Is there a certain identity group(s) impacted; how does diversity and/or bias play a role?

   — Which of the three (misinformation, gossip, rumors) takes place in the scenario?

   — What are the possible negative consequences in this scenario?

   — What could some of the characters portrayed in the scenario realistically do differently in the future to prevent this from happening again?

6. Give students 15–20 minutes to complete this task. Circulate around the room to make sure students understand the task and stay focused. After writing their paragraph together, they should decide as a group who will read the scenario and their paragraph aloud or if everyone will read part of it (i.e., a few sentences each).

7. Have each group present their small group work to the class by reading both their scenario and the paragraph essay they wrote together. After each presentation, ask if anyone else has something new to add to what the group came up with in their essay.

8. Engage students in a class discussion by asking the following questions:
   — What have you learned about miscommunication, gossip and rumors?
   — Are they prevalent in your lives? Why do you think they are or are not?
   — In what ways does identity and diversity play a role in miscommunication, gossip and rumors?
   — Do you think miscommunication, gossip and rumors happen more in middle school than in elementary or high school? Why or why not?
   — What do you think should be done to prevent miscommunication, gossip and rumors from hurting people?
   — What could you do as an individual?

Extension Activities

■ Have students write their own realistic fiction stories about misinformation, rumors and/or gossip, either using the scenarios as a springboard or creating new ones. The stories should not include names of classmates or other people in school or scenarios that closely replicate something that recently happened.

■ Have students brainstorm what can be done about misinformation, rumors and gossip. Consider organizing a school forum on the topic in order to help students understand more about it and brainstorm ideas about what can be done to address it.

MISINFORMATION, RUMORS AND GOSSIP SCENARIO #1

Directions: Read the following scenario silently. As a whole group, discuss and write a paragraph summarizing your discussion around the questions for discussion below.

Julia and Lena have been friends for years. They met when they were five and were best friends all through elementary school. Now they're in seventh grade and Lena has made some new friends who all live on the more wealthy side of town. In trying to impress this new group of girls, Lena tells them that she doesn't like Julia anymore, although in reality, she does still like her. Some of these new friends told other people about how Lena claims she feels about Julia and it got back to Julia.

Questions for Discussion:

▰ What's happening and why?

▰ Is there a certain identity group(s) impacted; how does diversity and/or bias play a role?

▰ Which of the three (misinformation, gossip, rumors) takes place in the scenario?

▰ What are the possible negative consequences of this scenario?

▰ What should Julia do?

▰ What should Lena do?

▰ What should the friends do?

▰ What could some/all of them realistically do differently in the future to prevent this from happening again?

Our summary paragraph:

_____

_____

_____

_____

_____

MISINFORMATION, RUMORS AND GOSSIP SCENARIO #2

Directions: Read the following scenario silently. As a whole group, discuss and write a paragraph summarizing your discussion around the questions for discussion below.

The eighth grade students are getting ready to go on an overnight trip to Washington, DC. They don't know what their room assignments are yet and will find out a few days before the trip. Everyone is anxiously talking about it. Alex stops by a teacher's classroom to ask a question about the homework. While talking to the teacher, he sees one of the room assignments for a few girls. Later on, he tells his good friend casually with no intent of spreading any rumors. His friend tells more people about this and soon everyone is saying that Alex knows all of the room assignments. In the hallway, people keep asking Alex who they are rooming with. Alex doesn't know what to do so he goes along with it and makes up room assignments.

Questions for Discussion:

- What's happening and why?

- Is there a certain identity group(s) impacted; how does diversity and/or bias play a role?

- Which of the three (misinformation, gossip, rumors) takes place in the scenario?

- What are the possible negative consequences of this scenario?

- What should Alex do?

- What should his friend do?

- What could some/all of them realistically do differently in the future to prevent this from happening again?

Our summary paragraph:

_____

_____

_____

_____

_____

MISINFORMATION, RUMORS AND GOSSIP SCENARIO #3

Directions: Read the following scenario silently. As a whole group, discuss and write a paragraph summarizing your discussion around the questions for discussion below.

In the middle of sixth grade, Gaby switches middle schools within the same town. She had told only her small group of friends about the move. A day after Gaby left, some kids quickly began telling other people different stories as to why she had switched schools because they wanted to appear as if they were "in the know." Some of the reasons they shared included: she got kicked out of her old school because of her grades, she was getting bullied because of her special needs and dropped out, or that she never wanted to go to the old school (this was the actual reason). Gaby heard about what people were saying and was really upset.

Questions for Discussion:

◼ What's happening and why?

◼ Is there a certain identity group(s) impacted; how does diversity and/or bias play a role?

◼ Which of the three (misinformation, gossip, rumors) takes place in the scenario?

◼ What are the possible negative consequences of this scenario?

◼ What should Gaby do?

◼ What should her friends do?

◼ What could some/all of them realistically do differently in the future to prevent this from happening again?

Our summary paragraph:

_____

_____

_____

_____

_____

MISINFORMATION, RUMORS AND GOSSIP SCENARIO #4

Directions: Read the following scenario silently. As a whole group, discuss and write a paragraph summarizing your discussion around the questions for discussion below.

Kayla tried out for the lead role in the school play this year. The listing of who got what parts was posted outside the auditorium at the end of the day. Right after school, Kayla looked at the paper and then left the school, excited to tell her family that she got the lead role. Back at school, a group of kids were huddled around the paper looking at who got what part. Sally and Daniel were talking about the roles while standing in front of the paper. "Oh, Kayla got the lead," Daniel says. "Yeah, did you know her dad is the head of the PTA?" Sally asks. Daniel: "Yes, my mom told me he donated money for the school play." Then Sally jokes, "I bet that's why she got the lead role." Several kids overhear this and take it seriously. They tell other students, who tell other people who spread it around the school that the only reason Kayla got the part was because of her father.

Questions for Discussion:

- What's happening and why?

- Is there a certain identity group(s) impacted; how does diversity and/or bias play a role?

- Which of the three (misinformation, gossip, rumors) takes place in the scenario?

- What are the possible negative consequences of this scenario?

- What should Sally do?

- What should Daniel do?

- What could some/all of them realistically do differently in the future to prevent this from happening again?

Our summary paragraph:

_____

_____

_____

_____

MISINFORMATION, RUMORS AND GOSSIP SCENARIO #5

Directions: Read the following scenario silently. As a whole group, discuss and write a paragraph summarizing your discussion around the questions for discussion below.

Anthony and his friends are comparing scores from their math test. Anthony got a 96%, while all his friends got 70's and 80's. They start teasing Anthony, saying he's the "teacher's pet," a "nerd," and that the teacher favors him because he's Latino and she is also Latina. Anthony feels uncomfortable and therefore lies and says he copied someone's answers; that's how he did so well. His friends start to tell other people that he cheated. Then people start approaching Anthony asking him "how did you cheat?" as if wanting advice for their own benefit.

Questions for Discussion:

◼ What's happening and why?

◼ Is there a certain identity group(s) impacted; how does diversity and/or bias play a role?

◼ Which of the three (misinformation, gossip, rumors) takes place in the scenario?

◼ What are the possible negative consequences of this scenario?

◼ What should Anthony do?

◼ What should his friends do?

◼ What could some/all of them realistically do differently in the future to prevent this from happening again?

Our summary paragraph:

_____

_____

_____

_____

_____

_____

MISINFORMATION, RUMORS AND GOSSIP SCENARIO #6

Directions: Read the following scenario silently. As a whole group, discuss and write a paragraph summarizing your discussion around the questions for discussion below.

Carlos likes a guy named Matt. Only Carlos' closest friends know that he likes Matt but he made them promise not to tell anyone. One of them named Molly tells another friend of hers and tells her not to tell anyone. Before you know it, several other people have been spreading it around on a group text and Matt finally finds out. Matt isn't gay and doesn't want anyone to think he is so he asks Molly out on a date so that everyone knows he likes girls.

Questions for Discussion:

- What's happening and why?

- Is there a certain identity group(s) impacted; how does diversity and/or bias play a role?

- Which of the three (misinformation, gossip, rumors) takes place in the scenario?

- What are the possible negative consequences of this scenario?

- What should Carlos do?

- What should Matt do?

- What should Molly do?

- What should Carlos' friends do?

- What could some/all of them realistically do differently in the future to prevent this from happening again?

Our summary paragraph:

_____

_____

_____

_____

16. ADVERTISING AND PROPAGANDA

TIME
45 minutes

COMMON CORE STANDARDS
Reading, Writing, Speaking and Listening, Language

STRATEGIES AND SKILLS
define terms, turn and talk, create advertisement, large group discussion

KEY WORDS AND PHRASES
advertising, manipulate, persuasive, political, propaganda

Rationale

The purpose of this lesson is for students to learn more about advertising and propaganda as ways of accessing information that shapes our perspective and that young people need to learn how to deconstruct. Advertising and propaganda are both forms of media information used to persuade people to either purchase products (advertising) or believe or do something (propaganda). This lesson provides an opportunity for students to learn about advertising and propaganda and create their own advertisements in order for them to reflect on the process.

Objectives

- Students will understand that advertising and propaganda are forms of media information.
- Students will explore the motivations for both advertising and propaganda.
- Students will create their own advertisements in order to deconstruct how advertisers think and what motivates them.

What's Needed

Handouts and Resources: Advertisement Creation Worksheet (one for each student); *Share a Coke USA Commercial* video (2016, 1 ½ mins., www.youtube.com/watch?v=5-ahnFYzMp8) or a commercial of your choosing; *Daisy Ad* video (1964, 1 min., www.youtube.com/watch?v=2cwqHB6QeUw); *Examples of Propaganda*

Other Material: Paper, pencils/pens, art supplies (chart or cardboard paper and markers, crayons, colored pencils, etc.); Internet access, screen or LCD; *Elements of Propaganda* (see Extension Activities)

Procedures

1.  Begin the lesson by showing this commercial "Share a Coke" (or another one of your choosing). After watching the video, engage students in a discussion by asking the following questions:
   - What happened in the video?
   - How did you feel while watching it?
   - What is the overall message of it?
   - How do the feelings it is meant to evoke connect with the product?
   - Are certain groups of people highlighted in their ad and if so, what kinds of people?

2. If students do not suggest this themselves, explain that the commercial is a form of advertising. Ask students, "What is advertising?" Come to a definition of **advertising** as speech, writing, pictures or films/video meant to persuade people to buy something.

3. Have students turn and talk with a person sitting next to them and take a few minutes to come up with a list of other forms of advertising besides commercials, having students write down their ideas on a piece of paper. Give the pairs five minutes to come up with their list.

4. Have each pair share one of their responses and then move onto the next pair (reminding them not to repeat anything that was already said) until all their ideas have been recorded. The list may look something like this:
   - Television commercials
   - Online video commercials
   - Billboards and other outdoors advertising (in stadiums, etc.)
   - Magazine and newspaper ads
   - "Product placement" on television shows and videos
   - Online banner ads
   - Text ads on cell phones
   - Email advertisements
   - Ads on radio
   - Celebrities and athletes' sponsorship of products (sneakers, shirts, etc.)
   - Ads on social networks
   - Ads before movies

5. Engage students in a discussion by asking the following questions:
   - How do you assess the information you receive from advertisements?
   - How do you know if the product is good or not?

FLIPPED CLASSROOM IDEA

Have students watch the *Share a Coke USA Commercial* video and think about the following questions: What happened in the video? How did you feel while watching it? What is the overall message of it? How do the feelings it is meant to evoke connect with the product?

— How do you know whether the advertisement is truthful or not?

— Have you ever seen bias or stereotypes about groups of people in advertisements?

— How would you assess the *Share a Coke USA* commercial you watched?

Explain that some people say commercials and other forms of advertising are a form of manipulation. Ask, "What happens when you watch a commercial?"

6. Divide students into small groups of 4–5 students each. Explain that each small group is going to create their own advertisement. When they are situated in their groups, explain that they will have 20 minutes to make decisions together about the ad and then create their own picture/print advertisements, like a billboard or ad in a magazine. (As an extension activity, students can spend more time and create a video commercial.)

7. Distribute to each group the *Advertisement Creation Worksheet.* Instruct them to complete this handout as a guide to creating their advertisement. Give 20 minutes or additional class time to complete their advertisements.

8. When students have completed their advertisements, have each group share their advertisement with the class. Then, engage students in a class discussion by asking the following questions:

    — How did you work together as a group?

    — What was it like to create an advertisement?

    — Did anything surprise you about the process?

    — What was your main goal in creating the ad?

    — How did you think about "selling" your product to your audience?

    — What did you learn about advertising by creating your own advertisement?

9. Explain to students that we are now going to discuss another form of persuasive media information, which is propaganda. Ask students, "What is propaganda?" Elicit from students a definition of **propaganda** as information that is shared and spread in order to influence public opinion and to manipulate other people's beliefs, often to promote or publicize a particular political cause or point of view.

    Ask students if they have ever read or seen anything that they think of as propaganda. Share one or both of the *Examples of Propaganda.*

10. After showing one or both of the *Examples of Propaganda,* engage students in a discussion by asking the following question:

    — What's going on?

    — What are they trying to convey?

    — Is this propaganda and if so, how do you know?

    — What strategies did they use to influence and/or persuade you to believe something?

    — Is there any bias or stereotypes about groups of people in this propaganda or others you have seen?

    — How is this propaganda similar to or different from propaganda you have seen?

11. Follow up on the last question by explaining that advertising and propaganda are both media tools used to convey something. Propaganda is similar to **advertising** in that it uses similar media formats in order to spread its message. However, unlike advertising, propaganda does not try to encourage the sale of a product, service or idea. **Propaganda** is a verbal and visual presentation used to change public attitudes about a particular person or subject.

Extension Activities

- Have students explore in depth some of the common elements in propaganda using the *Elements of Propaganda handout*. Then have them find examples of propaganda (on television, print ads, Internet ads, etc.) and categorize them according to the elements, explaining that propaganda often includes more than one of the elements.

- Have students watch at least an hour of television without using a DVR so that they see the commercials, which may include advertisements for products and political ads which are a form of propaganda. Have them do a content analysis of all the commercials they see which can include what products are being sold, how they are being sold, other propaganda they might see on television and the nature of it. They can then write up what they learned in a written essay or a PowerPoint.

ADVERTISEMENT CREATION WORKSHEET

GROUP MEMBERS:	

What form of advertisement will you create (billboard, magazine ad, etc.)?

What product will you create an ad for? It should be something for which you are familiar.

Who is the intended audience?

What is your strategy for "selling" (persuading) the product to your audience?

What materials will you need to create the ad (art materials, props, people, etc.)?

EXAMPLES OF PROPAGANDA

Example 1

Daisy Ad video at www.youtube.com/watch?v=2cwqHB6QeUw

Description: **"Daisy",** sometimes known as **"Daisy Girl"** or **"Peace, Little Girl,"** was a controversial political advertisement aired on television for Lyndon B. Johnson who was running against Barry Goldwater for President in 1964. Though only aired once (by the campaign), it is considered an important factor in Johnson's landslide victory over Barry Goldwater and an important turning point in political and advertising history.

Example 2

"Rosie the Riveter"

Description: This poster was designed to boost the morale of women who were encouraged to work during World War II (while men were at war) including making airplanes and ships for the war effort. (To view this poster in color, visit https://en.wikipedia.org/wiki/Rosie_the_Riveter#/media/File:We_Can_Do_It!.jpg.)

ELEMENTS OF PROPAGANDA

Almost all propaganda shares one element in common: It presents a little true information surrounded by a lot of misleading or untrue information. People see the true information and so may believe that everything the propaganda piece says is also true. Most elements of propaganda are different ways of using true information to be misleading.

1. **Bandwagon:** Conveying to the audience through an advertisement that since everyone is doing it, so should you, or in other words, if it is good enough for the people in the propaganda, it is good enough for you.

   Example: All of these great people agree that their cause is right and that everyone else is wrong. Who are you to disagree with them?

2. **Scapegoating:** Assigning blame to a group or individual, when that group or individual is really not the cause of the problem. This takes away the blame from responsible parties.

   Example: The Nazis used scapegoating against the Jews. They blamed the Jews for their bad economy.

3. **Assertion:** An enthusiastic statement that is presented as fact, but may not actually be true.

   Examples: If an advertiser claims that their product is the best, but doesn't include any evidence.

   Stating that people don't have jobs because they are taken by immigrants, even though research proves that immigration creates more jobs.

4. **Omission:** Not presenting the whole truth. This leads people to jump to conclusions about the evidence being presented.

   Example: Showing the hijacked planes hitting the twin towers on 9/11 conveys a message of revenge and anger, but only showing the aftermath conveys a message of sorrow.

5. **Plain folk:** Using a prominent person to convince the audience that this person and his ideas are "of the people."

   Example: Showing an actor buying groceries or paying taxes or showing an important politician eating at a fast food restaurant.

6. **Fear:** Use fear to convince the audience that if they do not take a particular course of action, like getting home insurance, something bad will happen, like flooding.

   Example: This was used in the Holocaust as well. The Germans became convinced that the Jews were going to take over the government, and they needed to do something to prevent this from happening.

7. **Half the information:** Convincing the audience to choose one option by presenting it as the best of the worse options. Alternatively, making predictions based on the future that are based only on a few facts or allowing the audience to come to false conclusions by only presenting some facts, but not all of them.

   Example: There are some real problems in society, including poverty and high divorce rates. The only way to escape these problems is to join our group.

UNIT IV. UNDERSTANDING BULLYING, BIAS AND INJUSTICE

We are surrounded by incidents of bias and injustice reported in the news as well as mistrust, fear and misunderstanding in our schools, communities and world. The potential for conflict, bullying and discrimination is high when bias and stereotyping go unchecked or are ignored. Biased attitudes can lead to biased behaviors which have the potential to escalate into discrimination, violent acts and systemic injustice. Teaching students what bias is, where it comes from, what forms it takes and how it manifests itself into all aspects of society is the first step in being able to do something and reverse this trajectory. At their age, middle school students are becoming keenly aware of the injustices in their world and educators can create an opening for them to broaden their understanding of bias and what can be done about it.

In Unit IV, students will have the opportunity to define and explore bias, discrimination, prejudice and implicit bias. They will explore what stereotypes are, how they come about and how to decrease stereotypical thinking. Young people will learn the various forms that bias and discrimination take and reflect on their own experiences as well as current day examples. Students will understand more about bullying and how the intersection of bias and bullying leads to identity-based bullying. Middle schoolers will reflect on their experiences with technology and differentiate between mean online behavior and cyberbullying, especially where bias is present. Students will examine different forms of media and explore how bias gets perpetuated through media. Finally, young people will understand how hate escalates and in particular, how the seeds of hate like bias can quickly lead to hate-filled violence.

17. WHAT IS BIAS?

Rationale

The purpose of this lesson is for students to understand what bias is and how it can be personal or structural in nature. Being able to understand and differentiate between bias, prejudice, discrimination and implicit bias is helpful in identifying different manifestations of bias and will set the foundation for subsequent lessons. This lesson provides an opportunity for students to learn what bias is, dig deeper into the topic and reflect on their own experiences with bias by sharing with others and writing.

Objectives

- Students will be able to define bias, prejudice, discrimination and implicit bias.

- Students will reflect on either their own experiences of bias or what they have witnessed of others' experiences of bias.

- Students will explore in more depth their experience with bias by writing an essay.

What's Needed

Handouts and Resources: *Types of Bias: Terms & Definitions* (one copy for each student); *The Oscars and learning the craft of being good* video (2015, 5 mins., Jay Smooth, www.youtube.com/watch?v=E7c9CIHm09M)

Other Material: Index cards (at least one per student); board/smart board; pens/pencils; Internet access, screen or LCD projector, speakers

Procedures

1. Begin the lesson by having students line up (in one line) at the widest part of the classroom. Explain that you are going to read a few statements and if the statement is true for them, they should step forward one step. Step forward if you agree with or have experienced the following:

TIME
45 minutes

COMMON CORE STANDARDS
Reading, Writing, Speaking and Listening, Language

STRATEGIES AND SKILLS
semantic web, brainstorm, define terms, turn and talk, write

KEY WORDS AND PHRASES
bias, discrimination, impartial, implicit bias, institution, interpersonal, prejudice

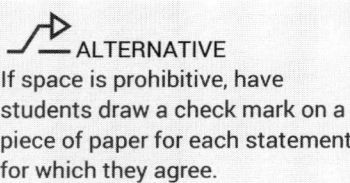

ALTERNATIVE
If space is prohibitive, have students draw a check mark on a piece of paper for each statement for which they agree.

- People don't ask for or respect my opinion because I'm a teenager.
- I have to be supervised everywhere I go.
- I have been asked to leave a store, restaurant or public transportation (i.e., the bus) because I was with friends and laughing and/or talking loudly.
- I have been paid less for a job that was done by someone older just because of my age.
- I don't have a say about things that are important to me.

Have students go back to their seats and engage them in a discussion by asking the following questions:

- Did you answer yes for some, most or all of the questions?
- Why do you think I asked you these questions?
- What about your age makes people treat you this way?

If it doesn't come up in the discussion, explain that **ageism** is a form of bias and both older people and young people experience age-related bias.

2. Have students brainstorm their associations with the word bias. Write the word bias on the board/smart board and ask students, "When you hear the word bias, what words, phrases and feelings come to mind?" Using a semantic web, chart student responses.

ALTERNATIVE
Use the words that students share to create a word cloud using wordle (www.wordle.net).

3. After creating the web, ask students the following questions:
   - What patterns do you notice on the web?
   - Is bias positive or negative?
   - How does bias play out (racism, sexism, antisemitism, heterosexism, ageism, etc.) that you have seen?
   - How do you feel looking at the web?

4. Ask students, "What is bias?" Come to a definition of **bias** as an inclination or preference either for or against an individual or group that interferes with impartial judgment.

5. Explain that bias can take place in a number of ways. Ask students, "What is prejudice?" Define **prejudice** as a premature judgment or belief formed about a person, group or concept before gaining sufficient knowledge or by selectively disregarding facts. Ask for an example and if students are unable to come up with one, share the following: "Women are not good at sports."

   Then, ask, "What is discrimination?" Come to a definition of **discrimination** as the denial of justice, resources and fair treatment of individuals and groups (often based on social identity), through employment, education, housing, banking, political rights, etc. Discrimination is an action that can follow prejudicial thinking.

   Ask for an example and if students are unable to come up with one, share the following example from the opening activity: You are followed around a store or not allowed to shop in a certain store because you are a teenager.

6. Ask, "What is the difference between prejudice and discrimination?" Explain that **discrimination** involves actions whereas bias and **prejudice** describe attitudes, thoughts or feelings. Explain that we will be discussing discrimination later in the unit.

7. Finally, ask, "What is implicit bias?" Explain to students that it is also sometimes referred to as "unconscious bias." Students may need to define implicit first, which is understood though not put clearly into words. Share the definition of implicit bias as follows:

   Implicit bias: The unconscious attitudes, stereotypes and unintentional actions (positive or negative) towards members of a group merely because of their membership in that group. These associations develop over the course of a lifetime beginning at a very early age through exposure to direct and indirect messages. When people are acting out of their implicit bias, they are not even aware that their actions are biased. In fact, those biases may be in direct conflict with a person's explicit beliefs and values.

8.  As an example, share that in the Academy Awards (awards for movies held annually), in 87 years (1927–2015), only one person of color (1% of total) won an Academy Award for Best Actress and only seven people (8% of total) of color won an Academy Award for Best Actor. To explain more about this, show the following video: *The Oscars and learning the craft of being good* by Jay Smooth.

   FLIPPED CLASSROOM IDEA

   Have students watch the Jay Smooth video, *The Oscars and learning the craft of being good* and reflect on the following questions: What is Jay Smooth trying to say? Do you agree or disagree with his point of view and why?

9. Engage students in a discussion by asking the following questions:

   — What was Jay Smooth saying?

   — Do you agree or disagree with his point of view and why?

   — What is the "contradiction" Jay Smooth refers to?

   — Are the academy awards an example of implicit or unconscious bias? Please explain.

   — What other examples did Jay Smooth use about implicit bias?

   — How does implicit bias work?

10. Ask for other examples of implicit bias. Because this may be a topic students have not yet studied or addressed, share the following examples:

    Example 1: There was a study where thousands of resumes were sent to employers with job openings. Before sending them out, the researchers randomly assigned stereotypically African American names ("Jamal") on some and stereotypically white names ("Brendan") on others. The same resume was 50% more likely to get a callback for an interview if it had a "white" name (*Source:* Marianne Bertrand and Sendhil Mullainathan, "Are Emily and Greg More Employable Than Lakisha and Jamal? A Field

Experiment on Labor Market Discrimination," *American Economic Review* 94(September 2004), 991–1013).

Example 2: Researchers asked students to rate teachers of an online course (the students never saw the teachers). To some of the students, a male teacher claimed to be female and vice versa. When students took a class from someone they believed to be male, they rated the teacher more highly. The very same teacher, when believed to be female, was rated significantly lower (*Source:* Lillian MacNell and Matt Shipman, "Online Students Give Instructors Higher Marks If They Think Instructors Are Men" (Raleigh: NC State University), https://news.ncsu.edu/2014/12/macnell-gender-2014/).

11. Distribute one index card to each student. Have them think about bias, including the different types of bias discussed during the lesson. Instruct students to think about an incident of bias that they either experienced themselves, witnessed by others, heard about in the news, saw on TV or a movie, or read about in a book. They should describe that bias incident in 2–3 sentences on their note card.

12. Collect the note cards, mix them up and redistribute them, giving one to each student and making sure that no student gets their own. Have students turn and talk with someone sitting next to them. They should read their card, respond to whether they have ever heard of something like that happening, and identify whether it is an example of bias, discrimination and/or implicit bias.

13. Depending on how much time you have, ask several of the pairs to share with the rest of the class what was written on their cards. Then the pairs will describe what form of bias is involved in the incident and see if the rest of the class agrees or disagrees.

14. Have students write an essay that describes a bias incident in more depth. They can use the same incident they shared on their index card or another one. As with the cards, it can be something they experienced themselves, witnessed by others, heard about in the news, saw on TV or a movie or something they read in a book. The essay should include (1) what happened with some detail, (2) how others responded or did not, (3) how you or the person felt who was the target of bias and (4) what you think could be done about it. The essays can be completed for homework or if time permits, students can conference with each other in order to get feedback and make edits. Share some of them the next day in class.

Extension Activities

■ Have students watch a television program or movie and record bias incidents, taking notes on (1) the details of what happened (2) the type of bias and (3) how the target of the bias responded and what other people said or did. Students can either write up their results or find another way to share their results.

■ Have students conduct a survey with their class, their whole grade or the school as a whole about bias they have experienced or witnessed. They can create the survey, distribute it electronically or on paper, organize the results and then find a way to share what they found out with their class, grade or school.

TYPES OF BIAS: TERMS & DEFINITIONS

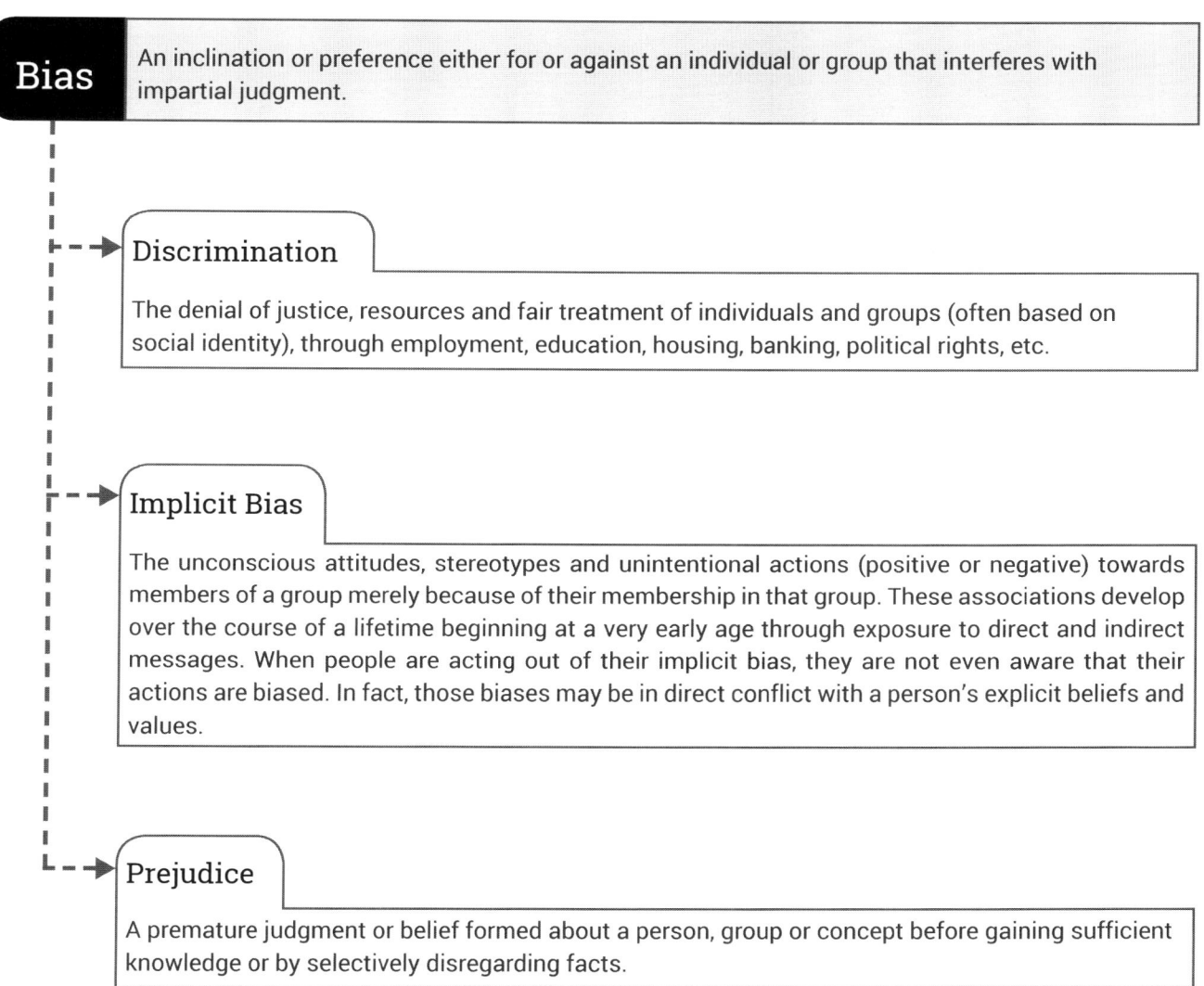

Bias
An inclination or preference either for or against an individual or group that interferes with impartial judgment.

Discrimination

The denial of justice, resources and fair treatment of individuals and groups (often based on social identity), through employment, education, housing, banking, political rights, etc.

Implicit Bias

The unconscious attitudes, stereotypes and unintentional actions (positive or negative) towards members of a group merely because of their membership in that group. These associations develop over the course of a lifetime beginning at a very early age through exposure to direct and indirect messages. When people are acting out of their implicit bias, they are not even aware that their actions are biased. In fact, those biases may be in direct conflict with a person's explicit beliefs and values.

Prejudice

A premature judgment or belief formed about a person, group or concept before gaining sufficient knowledge or by selectively disregarding facts.

18. STEREOTYPES

TIME
60 minutes

COMMON CORE STANDARDS
Reading, Writing, Speaking and
Listening

STRATEGIES AND SKILLS
define terms, large and small group
discussion

KEY WORDS AND PHRASES
assumption, stereotype

Rationale

The purpose of this lesson is for students to understand what stereotypes are and where they come from. Stereotypical thinking often leads to bias and discrimination. Therefore, it is important that students understand what stereotypes are, how they are formed, the harm they cause and what can be done to counteract them. This lesson provides an opportunity for students to explore and reflect upon stereotypes they have heard and seen in their lives and ways to diminish stereotypical thinking.

Objectives

- Students will be able to define stereotypes.
- Students will reflect on their own experiences with stereotypes.
- Students will identify stereotypes by looking at photographs and focusing on a particular group and the stereotypes surrounding that identity group.

What's Needed

Handouts and Resources: Photographs #1–4; *The Danger of a Single Story* video (2009, 19 mins., TED Talks, www.youtube.com/ watch?v=D9Ihs241zeg)

Other Material: Board/smart board; eight sheets of chart paper; markers; Internet access, screen or LCD projector; paper and pens/pencils

Advance Preparation:
- On separate sheets of chart paper, write the following words in the center or at the top of the page: (1) Age, (2) Race/Ethnicity, (3) Gender/ Gender Identity, (4) Religion, (5) Ability/Disability, (6) Sexual Orientation, (7) Socioeconomic Status and (8) Appearance/Size.

  [**NOTE:** Choose the identity areas that will most resonate with your students so add or subtract categories as you see fit.]

- Write the following quote by Chimamanda Ngozi Adichie on chart paper and set aside:

  "The single story creates stereotypes, and the problem with stereotypes is not that they are untrue, but that they are incomplete. They make one story become the only story."

- Read through the lesson, particularly Procedure #6 and decide whether you will (1) assign the groups in advance, (2) assign the groups randomly by having students count off 1–8 or (3) allow students to work in the groups for which they are most interested.

Procedures

1. Begin the lesson by asking students, "Has anyone ever made an assumption about you?" Then ask, "Has anyone ever made an assumption about you because of an aspect of your identity (race, gender or gender identity, sexual orientation, physical or mental ability, religion)?" Have students raise their hands if yes and keep them down if no. Ask, "Have you ever made an assumption about someone based on an aspect of their identity?" Have them raise their hands if yes and keep them down if no. Then ask students, "What are these assumptions called?"

2. Explain that these are stereotypes. Ask if anyone can define stereotype and elicit/explain the definition as follows:

   Stereotype: An oversimplified generalization about a person or group of people without regard for individual differences. Even seemingly positive stereotypes that link a person or group to a specific positive trait can have negative consequences.

   Explain that stereotypes are ingrained in all of us because we are part of society and we take in those messages and generalizations in a variety of ways. Today we will be exploring stereotypes and what we can do to combat them.

3. Explain to students that they are now are going to reflect on specific stereotypes by looking at some photographs and writing down their first thoughts about the person in the photograph.

4. ⤴ One at a time, project the photographs on the board/smart board, pause and ask, "What are your first thoughts about that person? Write down a few words to describe who you think that person is." Then move onto the next one.

   Have students write down the first words or ideas about that person in the photograph that comes into their heads. Tell them to be as honest with themselves as possible and that the papers will not be shared with anyone else.

⤴ **ALTERNATIVE**
Post the photographs on the wall around the room, number them and have students record their notes on a piece of paper.

NOTE 5

You can also have students respond to the questions in writing instead of verbally if you think they may be reluctant to share their responses out loud.

NOTE 6

It is important to convey to students that while stereotypes are hurtful and often lead to bias and discrimination, we all have some stereotypes in our minds because we live in a society that includes stereotypes and we learn them just by being exposed to them. Stereotypes are often transmitted in a variety of ways—media, parents, institutions—and we are all susceptible to them in some ways.

FLIPPED CLASSROOM IDEA

Have students watch MTV News Decoded video *Why Do You Think Stereotypes Are True?* at www.youtube.com/watch?v=D1-aSIUP4wM and jot down any notes and/or quotes they want to remember.

5. After completing all the photos, engage students in a discussion about the activity by asking the following questions:
   — Without sharing what you wrote down (unless you choose to), what did you notice about your first thoughts and reflections?
   — Did you make assumptions about some and not others?
   — What kind of assumptions did you make?
   — Did you notice that some stereotypes came up for you? How so?
   — What did you learn about yourself by doing this activity?

6. Divide students into eight small groups. Each group will have a category for which they will list stereotypes they have seen or heard. The groups are as follows (answer any clarifying questions about the groups before getting into them).
   — Age
   — Race/Ethnicity
   — Gender or Gender Identity
   — Religion
   — Ability/Disability
   — Sexual Orientation
   — Socioeconomic Status (i.e., rich, poor, middle class, working class)
   — Appearance/Size

7. Have students work in small groups and come up with a list of stereotypes for that category by recording them on a piece of paper. Each category may include more than one group. For example, in the group on "Age," students can come up with stereotypes about children, teenagers, elderly people, middle age people, etc. or for the Race/Ethnicity group, this may include White, African-American, Latino, Native-American or Asian. Give small groups 10 minutes for this task.

8. When the groups have completed their work, have the groups share with the rest of the class what they came up with and invite others in the class to add to the list. If time is limited, have each group share 2–3 stereotypes.

9. Engage students in a discussion by asking the following questions:
   — Where do stereotypes come from?
   — What are the harmful effects of stereotyping?
   — Can stereotypes sometimes appear to be positive? In what ways are these harmful?
   — In what ways do stereotypes lead to bias and discrimination?
   — How can people challenge and fight against stereotypes?

10. 📷 If students watched the *Why Do You Think Stereotypes Are True?*

video, engage them in a brief discussion by having a few students share the notes they jotted down while watching. Ask, "What was your reaction to the video?"

11. Show the video *The Danger of a Single Story* by Chimamanda Ngozi Adichie in which she explores stereotypes. Make sure students have paper and pen available to jot down any thoughts or quotes they want to remember from the talk. Remind them to think about the concept of stereotypes as they are watching it.

12. After watching the video, have students turn and talk to the person sitting next to them and share some reflections with each other, taking one minute per person to do so.

13. Engage students in a class discussion by asking the following questions:

    — What was Chimamanda Ngozi Adichie saying?

    — Why do you think the talk is titled "The danger of a single story?"

    — What assumptions were made about her?

    — What assumptions did she make about others?

    — Do you think she made her case well? Why or why not?

    — What did you learn about stereotypes?

14. Post the quote by Chimamanda Ngozi Adichie and ask students to reflect on what it means (either verbally or a "quick write" about it).

15. Invite volunteers to share aloud their quick write about the quote.

Extension Activities

■ Have students apply what they learned from the video, *The Danger of a Single Story,* to their own experience by having them either (1) write a story from their experience that formed a stereotype they have about others or (2) write a story about themselves that challenges stereotypes about a group with whom they identify.

■ Have students choose one form of media (movie, video game, website, advertisements) and do an analysis of stereotypes in that form of media. If they uncover any stereotypes, have them write a letter to the producer/company that shares their concern about the stereotypes present. If it was stereotype-free, have them write a letter congratulating the company.

PHOTOGRAPH #1

David Dennis/CC BY-SA 2.0 (B-W modification)

PHOTOGRAPH #2

Ed Yourdon/CC BY-NC-SA 2.0

PHOTOGRAPH #3

Gilabrand/CC BY 3.0

PHOTOGRAPH #4

Bigstock

19. FORMS OF BIAS AND DISCRIMINATION

TIME
90 minutes (two 45 minute class periods)

COMMON CORE STANDARDS
Reading, Speaking and Listening, Language

STRATEGIES AND SKILLS
define terms, fishbowl

KEY WORDS AND PHRASES
ableism, ageism, anti-immigrant bias, anti-Muslim bias, antisemitism, anti-Trans bias, bigotry, classism, disproportionately, favorable, heterosexism, racism, religious bias, sexism, unfavorable, weightism

Rationale

The purpose of this lesson is for students to understand that bias and discrimination manifest themselves in a variety of ways and take different forms. It is important that students understand the different forms of bias and discrimination so they can work to combat them. This lesson provides an opportunity for students to understand the different forms that bias and discrimination takes, reflect on personal and institutional bias and analyze current day examples of discrimination.

Objectives

◾ Students will understand and be able to provide examples for the different forms of bias and discrimination.

◾ Students will explore the differences between individual and systemic bias.

◾ Students will reflect on current day examples and statistics about bias and discrimination in the United States.

What's Needed

Handouts and Resources: Forms of Bias and Definitions and *Bias and Discrimination In Our Lives* (one for each student); *Being 12: 'People Think I'm Supposed to Talk Ghetto, Whatever That Is'* video (2015, 4½ mins., WNYC Radio, www.wnyc.org/story/people-sometimes-think-im-supposed-talk-ghetto-whatever-kids-race/)

Other Material: Internet access, screen or LCD projector

Advance Preparation: Make at least two copies of the *Forms of Bias and Definitions*. Cut out a set of terms and definitions so that you will have 24 strips of paper with a term and a matching definition. Repeat this process based on the size of class if you need more than 24 (see Procedure #2).

Procedures

1. Begin the lesson by reminding students briefly what they learned about bias and discrimination in the previous lessons and review the definitions on page 155 if there is confusion. Explain that in today's lesson they will explore the different forms bias and discrimination can take and what groups are targeted.

   Ask students, "Who have you seen bias and discrimination directed towards?" Have students jot down a quick list (without names, using only identifying features) of the kinds of people and groups who are targeted for bias and discrimination. Then ask students to share those thoughts aloud and record on board.

2. Distribute the strips of terms and definitions prepared in advance, making sure that each student gets one. Some will receive a term strip and others will receive a definition strip; depending on class size, there may be multiples. Make sure that each term strip has a corresponding definition strip. If there is an uneven number of students, participate by taking a strip yourself.

3. Explain to students that half the class has a word on their strip of paper and the other half has a definition on their strip. They will have five minutes to find each other and make a match between their word and its corresponding definition. Explain that there could be more than one pairing so if there is more than one pair with the same word/definition, they all should find each other. After the time is up and everyone is situated with their group, go around the room to make sure they have accurately matched up words and definitions and are in the correct place.

4. Have students sit together in their pairs or groups and respond to the questions below. One person should take notes on what is said because they will be reporting back to the rest of the class. Give students 10 minutes to complete this task and remind them of the definitions of stereotypes, prejudice, bias, discrimination and implicit bias.

   — Have you ever heard this term?

   — Does the definition match what you thought the word means?

   — What are some examples (at least two) of where you have seen this form of bias/discrimination play out in real life? If you haven't seen it in real life, share an example from television, movies, social media, books, ads, etc.

   — What are some examples (at least two) of when this form of bias/discrimination has taken place in history or in current events news stories? (For this last question, they may need more time and/or Internet access so you may assign for homework.)

5. Staying in their small groups, have each group briefly share what they discussed and ask the rest of the class if they have any other different examples to share.

6. After all of the groups have presented, ask students, "What is the difference between individual bias/discrimination and systemic bias/discrimination?" Have them brainstorm their thoughts and elicit/explain the difference as follows (writing this on the board/smart board):

   Individual: includes individual acts of bias, meanness or exclusion.

   Systemic: includes policies and practices that are supported by power and authority (in institutions) and that benefits some and disadvantages others.

7. Ask students to share an example of individual bias/discrimination and an example of systemic bias/discrimination. If needed, you can share the following examples:

   Sexism can be *individual* when someone tells a joke about girls being bad at sports.

Sexism can be *systemic* when a school has certain sports teams for boys but not for girls (basketball/soccer).

8. In their pairs or groups, have students share again their examples of bias/discrimination but this time they should identify if the example is personal or institutional. You can record on the board like the chart below, which lists examples but those examples should come from the students sharing out.

What happened?	Form of bias/ discrimination	Individual	Systemic
Make a joke about girls being bad at sports	Sexism	X	
My school only has basketball and soccer team for boys.	Sexism		X

FLIPPED CLASSROOM IDEA

Have students watch the video *Being 12: 'People Think I'm Supposed to Talk Ghetto, Whatever That Is'* and take notes on their thoughts, feelings and quotes they want to remember, preparing themselves to have a class discussion about it.

9. Show the video *Being 12: 'People Think I'm Supposed to Talk Ghetto, Whatever That Is'*. Instruct students to take notes on their thoughts, feeling and quotes they want to remember. After watching the video, engage students in a discussion by asking the following questions:

— How did you feel while watching the video?

— How did the students identify themselves?

— What categories of identity did they mention?

— What were the young people talking about?

— What examples of bias and discrimination did they talk about?

— What feelings did they express?

— What is privilege?

— Did anything resonate with you and if so, what?

— In the examples of bias they shared, which were personal and which were institutional?

10. Explain to students that as discussed, there are different ways that bias takes place in real life and has throughout history. Sometimes it will be stereotypes which can lead to bias. Sometimes it is overt discrimination. And sometimes it is more subtle and is more in the category of implicit bias.

11. Explain that over the last 50 years, many laws have been put in place to protect people's rights, but laws are still broken every day and people and institutions sometimes find ways around them. Provide an example such as voting rights, explaining to students that although sweeping legislation was passed in 1965 securing voting rights for people regardless of race, serious problems remain. Explain that over the past few years, many states have enacted specific voting laws that restrict

voting which include (1) requiring voter ID and/or proof of citizenship, (2) restricting early in-person voting and (3) making voter registration more difficult. These laws disenfranchise eligible voters, and disproportionately affect people of color, the elderly, young voters, and those who live in poverty.

12. Divide students into small groups of 4–5 students each and distribute the *Bias and Discrimination In Our Lives* handout to each student. Working in groups, have students read each bullet point, discuss it and identify which form(s) of bias/discrimination it illustrates and whether it is prejudice, discrimination, stereotypes or implicit bias.

13. After working in their small groups, engage students in a discussion by asking the following questions:

    — What did you learn?

    — In what ways are laws helpful?

    — In what ways are laws not enough to eliminate discrimination?

    — What else needs to be in place to reduce or eliminate bias and discrimination?

Extension Activities

■ Using a fishbowl style strategy, select a small group of students (4–6) who volunteer to come into the fishbowl and discuss an experience they have personally had with bias/discrimination. Have students on the inside circle describe what happened, how they felt, and what, if anything, was done or if anyone intervened. Have students on the outside circle listen actively and reflect on their thoughts and feelings.

■ Create a group poem about bias and discrimination by having each student write one sentence about a form of bias/discrimination: the sentence should include something that used to happen and something that still does take place. For example, "Women used to not be able to vote... But now women earn 75% of what men get paid." Put them all together to create the group poem.

FORMS OF BIAS AND DEFINITIONS

Ableism	Prejudice and/or discrimination against people who have disabilities, including temporary, developmental, physical, psychiatric and/or intellectual disabilities.
Ageism	Prejudice and/or discrimination against older people based on the belief that older people are inferior, incapable or irrelevant. Ageism also describes the Prejudice and/or discrimination of people who are too young to have social independence.
Anti-Immigrant Bias	Prejudice and/or discrimination against people who are of immigrant origin, transnational or outside the dominant national identity or culture.
Anti-Muslim Bias	Prejudice and/or discrimination against people who are Muslim based on the belief in stereotypes and myths about Muslim people, Islam and countries with predominantly Muslim populations.
Antisemitism	Prejudice and/or discrimination against people who are Jewish based on the belief in stereotypes and myths about Jewish people, Judaism and Israel.
Anti-Trans Bias	Prejudice and/or discrimination against people who are transgender and/or non-binary (identifying as neither a man nor a woman) based on the belief that cisgender (gender identity that corresponds with the sex one was assigned at birth) is the norm.

FORMS OF BIAS AND DEFINITIONS

Classism	Prejudice and/or discrimination against people who are from low-income or working-class households based on a social hierarchy in which people are ranked according to socioeconomic status.
Heterosexism	Prejudice and/or discriination against people who are lesbian, gay, bisexual, queer and/or asexual, based on the belief that heterosexuality is the norm.
Racism	Prejudice and/or discrimination against people of color based on a socially constructed racial hierarchy that privileges white people. Differences in physical characteristics (e.g., skin color, hair texture, eye shape) are used to support a system of inequities.
Religious Bias	Prejudice and/or discrimination against people who belong to one or more religious groups or no religious group based on the belief in a correct or sanctioned faith system.
Sexism	Prejudice and/or discrimination against women, based on the belief in a natural order based on sex that privileges men.
Weightism	Prejudice and/or discrimination against people who are larger than the socially constructed norm for body size.

BIAS AND DISCRIMINATION IN OUR LIVES

- In 2015, women working full-time in the United States typically were paid 80% of what men were paid overall for a comparable job. During the same time period, Latina women were paid only 54% of what white men were paid and African-American women were paid 63% of what white men were paid. (*Source:* Catherine Hill, *The Simple Truth about the Gender Pay Gap* (Washington, DC: American Association of University Women, 2016), www.aauw.org/research/the-simple-truth-about-the-gender-pay-gap/)

- A 2015 report revealed that almost 85.2% of LGBTQ students were verbally harassed (e.g., called names or threatened) in the past year based on a personal characteristic, most commonly sexual orientation and gender expression. (*Source: The 2015 School Climate Survey* Executive Summary (New York: GLSEN, 2016), www.glsen.org/sites/default/files/2019-10/GLSEN%202015%20National%20School%20Climate%20Survey%20%28NSCS%29%20-%20Executive%20Summary.pdf)

- African-American people make up 13% of the general U.S. population yet they constitute 28% of all arrests, 40% of all inmates held in prisons and jails and 42% of the population on death row. The rate of arrests for African Americans is 2.5 times higher than for whites. African Americans are more likely to be sentenced to prison and less likely to be sentenced to probation than whites. (*Source:* Christopher Hartney and Linh Vuong, *Created Equal* (Oakland: National Council on Crime & Delinquency, 2009), www.nccdglobal.org/sites/default/files/publication_pdf/created-equal.pdf)

- In 2013 the Anti-Defamation League (ADL) commissioned a study to research the attitudes and opinions of the general public towards Jewish people in over 100 countries around the world. The data is captured in an online index called Global 100™: An Index of Antisemitism. ADL interviewed 53,100 adults in 102 countries and territories in an effort to establish a comprehensive data-based research survey of the level and intensity of anti-Jewish sentiment around the world. It explores how widespread the negative attitudes and stereotypes are of Jewish people around the world at this point in time. The survey found that 26% of people around the world harbor antisemitic attitudes and beliefs. (*Sources:* First International Resources, ADL Global 100™ (New York: Anti-Defamation League, 2015), http://global100.adl.org; and Rick Gladstone, "26 Percent of World's Adults Are Antisemitic, Survey Finds," *The New York Times,* May 13, 2014, www.nytimes.com/2014/05/14/world/26-percent-of-worlds-adults-are-anti-semitic-survey-finds.html)

- More than 20 years after passage of the Americans with Disabilities Act (ADA) in 1990, transportation choices for people with disabilities are still extremely limited. The ADA has led to major improvements in transit systems across the United States; however, there continue to be barriers for people with disabilities. Of the nearly 2 million people with disabilities who never leave their homes, 560,000 never leave home because of transportation difficulties. Because many people with disabilities do not have the option to drive cars, lack of access to other modes of transportation disproportionately harms them. The lack of transportation options in many communities is a major barrier to being able to get a job. (*Source:* "Equity in Transportation for People with Disabilities" (Washington, DC: The Leadership Conference Education Fund), www.civilrightsdocs.info/pdf/transportation/final-transportation-equity-disability.pdf)

- In a survey about people's opinions of different religious groups, Muslims and Arabs had the lowest favorable/highest unfavorable ratings among the religious groups covered, and one in four Americans were either unfamiliar with or not sure of their attitudes toward these two communities. A significant number of Americans (42%) support the use of profiling by law enforcement against Arab Americans and American Muslims. A growing percentage of Americans say that they lack confidence in the ability of individuals from either community to perform their duties as Americans should they be appointed to an important government position. (*Source: American Attitudes Toward Arabs and Muslims* (Washington, DC: Arab American Institute, 2014), www.aaiusa.org/american-attitudes-toward-arabs-and-muslims-2014)

- In 2016, employers created hundreds of thousands of new jobs but millions of older workers who want a job cannot find work. Age discrimination is illegal under the Age Discrimination in Employment Act of 1967 but most of the complaints filed with the U.S. Equal Employment Opportunity Commission focus on age-bias terminations rather than hiring—simply because hiring discrimination is so difficult to prove. Two-thirds of older workers believe age discrimination occurs in the workplace, according to a 2013 survey by AARP. Older job seekers need much more time to find a job than older workers - 36 weeks in 2015, compared with 26 weeks for younger workers. A recent study found strong evidence of age discrimination in hiring, particularly for older women. The researchers sent out 40,000 dummy job applications that included signals on the job-seekers' ages, and then watched the response rates. They measured callback rates for various occupations; workers age 49-51 applying for administrative positions had a callback rate 29% lower than younger workers, and it was 47% lower for workers over age 64. (*Source:* Mark Miller, "Column: Older and jobless - the U.S. recovery's forgotten story" (Reuters, 2017), www.reuters.com/article/us-column-miller-unemployment-idUSKCN11E297)

20. BULLYING AND IDENTITY-BASED BULLYING

TIME
45 minutes

COMMON CORE STANDARDS
Reading, Writing, Speaking and Listening, Language

STRATEGIES AND SKILLS
define terms, large group discussion, create PSA

KEY WORDS AND PHRASES
bullying, distress, identity, identity-based bullying, status

Rationale

The purpose of this lesson is for students to understand and explore bullying and identity-based bullying. Bullying, especially identity-based bullying, takes place in schools and among young people and impacts all the members of the school community. Identity-based bullying is the intersection of bias and bullying that targets aspects of a person's identity. This lesson provides an opportunity for students to understand bullying and identity-based bullying and reflect on what they wish teachers knew and would do about it.

Objectives

- Students will define bullying and will identify the elements present in bullying.
- Students will explore the extent to which bullying takes place at their school.
- Students will consider what they wish teachers knew about their feelings about bullying.
- Students will understand what identity-based bullying is and create a PSA about it.

What's Needed

Handouts and Resources: Ten Things Students Wish Teachers Knew (one for each student); *Identity-Based Bullying* video (2015, 2½ mins., International Bullying Prevention Association, www.youtube.com/watch?v=u54bg43-D9I)

Other Material: Index cards (one per student); chart paper; magic markers (at least 10); Internet access, screen or LCD projector

Advance Preparation: Write the following questions on chart paper, one question per sheet and set aside:

- How often does bullying happen in this school?

- What kind of bullying takes place among students?
- Are there certain types of students that get bullied more than others?
- What can you do when you see bullying?

Procedures

1. Begin the lesson by asking, "What is bullying?" Come to a definition as follows:

    Bullying is the repeated actions or threats of action directed toward a person by one or more people who have (or are perceived to have) more power or status than their target in order to cause fear, distress or harm.

2. With the students, create a chart that looks like this, together filling in the left side of what bullying is and what mean behavior that isn't bullying may include:

What Bullying Is	What Mean Behavior Is
Repeated actions or threats of actions	Once or intermittent
Instigated by one or more people who have or are perceived to have more power/status than their target	Between people who have similar amounts of power
Causes fear, distress or harm	Can cause fear, distress or harm

3. Place the four pieces of chart paper with questions, prepared in advance, around the room with a few markers at each station. Have students walk around the room and write responses to the questions on the pieces of chart paper. Give students 10 minutes to do this and a few minutes at the end to walk around and look at the comments.

4. Engage students in a brief class discussion by asking the following questions:
    — What do you notice about what is written on the sheets of paper?
    — Are there similarities and patterns?
    — What differences do you notice in the responses?

5. Acknowledge with students that you know bullying is discussed a lot in school (and to different degrees depending on the class). You may want to say something about what you are doing in your school about bullying that you know to be the case. Explain to students that sometimes adults don't know or understand what goes on between students around bullying because it often happens when teachers, parents and other adults are not around and young people often do not report bullying.

6. Explain that in this lesson, there will be an opportunity for students to share what they wish teachers knew about bullying and what they wish teachers would do or say about bullying.

7. Distribute one index card to each student. Explain to students that they are going to write their responses to the following two questions—one on each side:

    Question 1: What do I wish teachers knew about bullying?

    Question 2 (side 2 of card): What do I wish teachers would say or do about bullying?

8. Collect the cards, mix them up and then distribute them to the class so that everyone gets a new card, not the one they filled out. Ask each student to read aloud both sides of their new cards. Then engage students in a class discussion by asking the questions below:

   — What did you hear?

   — Were there any patterns or repeated responses?

   — What do you think about what you heard?

   — Did anything you heard particularly resonate for you?

9. Distribute the *10 Things Students Wish Teachers Knew* handout to each student. Have students take 5–10 minutes to read it silently. Then engage students in a discussion by asking:

   — What on the list is similar to what we read on the index cards?

   — What is on the list that is different?

   — Does anything resonate with you? If so, what?

   — In your opinion, what are the most important things teachers should know about bullying?

   — In your opinion, what are the most important things teachers should do about bullying?

10. Thinking back to "Who Am I?" activity in Lesson 6, remind students about aspects of identity including race, ethnicity, gender, sexual orientation, etc. Read aloud the following scenario:

    Rajeev is an Indian student who is new to the school. A number of students in your class have been calling him an Arab when he walks by them in the hallway. They say it in a mean way and laugh at him. He tries to correct them that he isn't Arab and is Indian but this makes them laugh harder and begin to call him a terrorist instead. At lunch, he often sits by himself and as kids walk by him and see what he's eating, they hold their noses to indicate disgust.

11. Engage students in a discussion by asking the questions below:

    — What's happening here?

    — How do you think Rajeev is feeling?

    — How do you think the kids who are teasing/bullying him feel?

    — Have you ever seen anything like this happen? Please explain.

    — What can/would you do if you see something like this happening?

    — Why do you think it's especially hurtful to Rajeev?

12. Explain to students that this is an example of identity-based bullying. Ask, "How would you define identity-based bullying?" Come to a definition of **identity-based bullying** as referring to any form of bullying related to the characteristics considered unique to a person's identity, such as their race, religion, sexual orientation or physical appearance.

13. Engage students in a discussion by asking the following questions:

    — Does identity-based bullying take place at this school? Please explain.

    — Have you ever seen or experienced identity-based bullying? If so, please explain.

    — What about identity-based bullying makes it especially hurtful?

    — What do you think we can do about identity-based bullying?

14.  Then show the *Identity-Based Bullying* video and ask students, "What more did you learn about identity-based bullying?"

15. Have students create a project that expresses how they feel about identity-based bullying and what they think can be done about it. This could be similar to a Public Service Announcement (PSA). Have them first develop a focus for their PSA which should include a "slogan" or succinct statement they want to convey. They could then write a few sentences about what message they want to get across. The PSA could be in the form of a short skit, video, social media campaign using Instagram, blog with student stories or an infographic blog with student stories. Allow students to work on these individually or with a partner and you may assign it for homework over the next few days or week.

16. Have students present their projects to the class.

Extension Activities

- Have students write their own stories about identity-based bullying. Caution them to not use names or specific situations that would identify particular students in their class or school, but their stories can be based in part on situations they have seen and heard. The stories should highlight what aspects of the person's identity was targeted (it could be more than one), what happened, how the target felt and dealt with it and if anyone else got involved.

- Have students conduct research about identity-based bullying nationwide. They should look at different studies that have been done (use resources in this link www.pacer.org/bullying/about/media-kit/stats.asp) and present what they find out in a PowerPoint presentation to their class or school.

10 THINGS STUDENTS WISH TEACHERS KNEW

1. **Take the issue of name-calling and teasing seriously.** Rethink statements like, "Kids will be kids..." or "He didn't mean anything by that comment; he was just kidding."

2. **Let students know that you are available to talk to them.** If possible, set aside ten minutes of class time each week to discuss issues that students want to bring up. Get to know students as individuals.

3. **Take time to listen.** Don't try to "fix" a situation before you have taken time to listen carefully. Avoid making the situation worse by blaming the targeted student. Make sure your actions don't discourage students' honesty.

4. **Don't harp on what should have been done in the past; focus on the present.** Saying, "Why didn't you tell me sooner?" is not helpful.

5. **Be a role model.** If students observe you gossiping or exhibiting other bullying behaviors toward students, their families or colleagues, they will interpret it as permission to behave similarly. Remember that everyone, including yourself, has biases that can influence behavior, and that your words can have a strong impact.

6. **Do not belittle, tear down or publicly embarrass students.** Although these strategies are common in competitive sports, they are ineffective in motivating students to do better.

7. **Help students learn how to become effective allies.** Provide time for them to learn the range of behaviors practiced by good allies. Do not communicate the expectation that students should always directly intervene when bias incidents occur. Discuss safety concerns and brainstorm effective alternative strategies with students.

8. **Acknowledge that name-calling and teasing are occurring and that being the target of these incidents can be painful.** Do not downplay what a student says he or she is feeling or experiencing.

9. **Be proactive.** Prepare your students to respond effectively to bias incidents and become a partner to their families. Discuss name-calling and bullying and school policies that outline how these situations will be handled. Explore the different roles students can take in bias incidents—target, perpetrator, bystander and ally, and help students strategize responses to situations from the perspectives of each of these roles.

10. **Be discreet and whenever possible, maintain confidentiality.** Some teachers announce to the class when a student is having a problem with name-calling, bullying or harassment. Whenever possible, help each student privately.

21. ONLINE BEHAVIOR AND CYBERBULLYING

Rationale

The purpose of this lesson is for students to reflect on their own technology experience and differentiate between mean digital behavior and cyberbullying. Tweens and teens spend a lot of time using technology, much of it positive, but it can move into cyberbullying and other online mean behavior. Students will have the opportunity to understand their own personal technology use, understand how technology negatively and positively impacts relationships and analyze scenarios that involve mean online behavior and cyberbullying.

Objectives

- Students will reflect on their personal technology use.
- Students will explore teens' use of technology and how it impacts relationships.
- Students will continue to reflect on what bullying is and is not.
- Students will differentiate between cyberbullying and mean behavior and analyze scenarios.

What's Needed

Handouts and Resources: *Teens, Technology and Friendships Report Summary* (Pew Research Center, Washington DC (August, 2015), www.pewinternet. org/2015/08/06/teens-technology-and-friendships/); *Scenario Worksheet* and *Navigating a Digital World: Tips for Youth* (one of each for each student); *#JustStandUp* video (2016, 2 mins., Hampton Creek, www.youtube.com/watch?v=p9i2RQ5PxaA)

Other Material: *My Technology Use* (optional)

Advance Preparation: Print the *Teens, Technology and Friendships* Report Summary and distribute to each student to read as a homework assignment the night before so students are prepared to discuss it. Remind them to bring the report summary with them to class.

TIME
45 minutes

COMMON CORE STANDARDS
Reading, Speaking and Listening, Language

STRATEGIES AND SKILLS
large and small group discussion, turn and talk

KEY WORDS AND PHRASES
cyberbullying, imply, social media

Procedures

 ALTERNATIVE

Use the *My Technology Use* handout as an alternative to the standing up strategy to have more privacy if you think that is needed.

1. Begin the lesson by doing a brief survey about students' technology use. You will read each of the statements below and students will note which statements are true for them (during the past week) by standing up and if the statement is not true for them, they will remain seated.

2. Read each statement one at a time and have students stand up if the statement is true for them during the past week. Allow a few seconds for standing up and then have everyone sit back down.

   - I spent more than two hours at one time on a social networking site like Instagram, Twitter or Snapchat.

   - I spent more than an hour at one time texting with a friend.

   - I watched a video on YouTube.

   - I participated in a group texting chat.

   - I made a new friend through an online game.

   - I unfriended, unfollowed or blocked someone I used to be friends with.

   - I sent or received a picture of someone without their permission.

   - I took a screen shot of a private text conversation and sent it to someone.

   - I received or sent, or know someone who received or sent, a hurtful, mean or hate motivated text or text message.

   - I felt threatened or know someone else who has felt threatened, by something online.

   - I was supportive to someone who experienced cyberbullying.

3. After going through all the statements, have students turn and talk with a person sitting near them and share what they experienced as they stood up/sat down or what they recorded on their sheets.

4. Engage students in a class discussion by asking the questions below:

   - Were you surprised by how many times you or others stood up (or made a check mark)?

   - How do you feel about your use of technology?

   - What's positive about being so connected digitally?

   - What's difficult or challenging about being so connected digitally?

5. Explain to students they will now discuss the *Teens, Technology and Friendships* Report Summary they read for homework. Engage students in a class discussion by asking the following questions:

   - What did you learn that you didn't know before?

   - What was surprising in the report?

   - What did you already know about teens, technology and friendship?

 NOTE 5

If students haven't read the report summary, give them 10–15 minutes to read the report silently.

- What about this report can you relate to?

- What is something in the report that does not resonate with your experience?

6. Explain to students that there are both positive and negative things about teens and technology use. Ask, "What are some positive things you have seen or experienced using technology?" Then ask, "What are some negative and/or mean things you have seen involving technology?"

7. Ask students if they remember the definition of bullying from the previous lesson and apply that to cyberbullying. Define **cyberbullying** as the intentional and repeated mistreatment of others through the use of technology, such as computers, cell phones and other electronic devices.

8. Ask students, "What are some of the differences between mean behavior and cyberbullying?"

9. Show the 2-minute video *#JustStandUp*.

10. Engage students in a discussion by asking the following questions:

- What happens in the video?

- How does cyberbullying impact the girl?

- What behavior did you observe among the other young people?

- What do you think motivated the person who engaged in ally behavior (the girl in the top left corner) to take action?

- Do you think her actions were effective? Why or why not?

- Can you relate to anyone in the video? If so, who and why?

- What are your reactions to the video?

11. After the discussion, explain that the video was produced as part of a hashtag campaign to raise awareness about the harmful effects of cyberbullying and to encourage young people to stand up against it.

12. Explain to students that they will now have the opportunity to explore cyberbullying and mean online behavior. Divide students into groups of 4–5 students each. Explain that they will be given three scenarios and they will discuss them as a group and answer a few questions about them using the *Scenario Worksheet* handout. They will discuss the scenario and then (1) determine if it is mean behavior or cyberbullying, (2) identify the reasons for the behavior, (3) discuss the impact of the behavior and (4) come up with ideas about what could have been done or could be in the future. Give students 10–15 minutes for this task.

13. After students discuss the scenarios in their small groups, have them share in the larger group what they came up with for each scenario. Discuss one scenario at a time, first asking whether it was cyberbullying or mean behavior and why and then going through the other questions and having them share their responses.

 FLIPPED CLASSROOM IDEA

Make a short video of you reading aloud some of the key points from the *Navigating a Digital World: Tips for Youth* handout.

14.  Ask students, "What can we do to be safe and responsible with our

NOTE

(Optional) Download and reproduce the color version of *Navigating a Digital World: Tips for Youth* at www.adl.org/education/resources/tools-and-strategies/navigating-a-digital-world-tips-for-youth-en-espanol. Available in English and Spanish

technology use?" Brainstorm a list and then distribute the *Navigating a Digital World: Tips for Youth* handout to each student. Read aloud and engage students in a brief discussion by asking the following questions:

— Do these make sense for you?

— Which of these have you used?

— Which of these will you try to use in the future?

— Are there any other strategies that you would add? Please explain.

Extension Activities

■ Have students take one point from the *Navigating a Digital World: Tips for Youth* handout and create a poster about it, using the language itself or a slogan that is catchy, and creating an illustration that goes along with it. As a class, think together how these posters may be useful, either gaining permission to hang them around the school building or having an information assembly about Internet safety strategies.

■ Use some of the questions from the *Teens, Technology and Friendship Report* and have students create a survey for the school that has students respond to some of the same questions and then use the data to compare their school to the United States as a whole.

MY TECHNOLOGY USE

Directions: Please check *yes* if you have done this in the past week and *no* if you have not.

1. I spent more than two hours at one time on a social networking site like Instagram, Twitter or Snapchat. ☐ Yes ☐ No

2. I spent more than an hour at one time texting with a friend. ☐ Yes ☐ No

3. I watched a video on YouTube. ☐ Yes ☐ No

4. I participated in a group texting chat. ☐ Yes ☐ No

5. I made a new friend through an online game. ☐ Yes ☐ No

6. I unfriended, unfollowed or blocked someone I used to be friends with. ☐ Yes ☐ No

7. I sent or received a picture of someone without their permission. ☐ Yes ☐ No

8. I took a screen shot of a private text conversation and sent it to someone. ☐ Yes ☐ No

9. I received or sent, or know someone who received or sent, a hurtful, mean or hate motivated text or text message. ☐ Yes ☐ No

10. I felt threatened or know someone else who has felt threatened, by something online. ☐ Yes ☐ No

11. I was supportive to someone who experienced cyberbullying. ☐ Yes ☐ No

SCENARIO WORKSHEET

Scenario 1: Every time Hayley posts a picture on Instagram, a girl named Jessica—who has many more friends and followers than Hayley—writes a sarcastic or nasty comment. Yesterday Hayley posted a picture of herself at the beach and Jessica wrote, "OMG, you're so pale. Is that why you went to the beach?"

Is this cyberbullying or mean behavior? Why?

Why do you think Jessica is doing that?

How do you think Hayley feels?

What should Hayley do?

Scenario 2: A group of five friends participate regularly on a group chat. Three of them went shopping together the day before and the other two are mad about it because they weren't invited. They start arguing with each other, calling each other names on the group chat. Jasmine, one of the three friends who didn't get invited, takes a screen shot of the text argument and sends it to her other friends.

Is this cyberbullying or mean behavior? Why?

Why do you think Jasmine sent the screen shot to her other friends?

How do you think all of the friends in this scenario feel?

What should they all do?

Scenario 3: Brandon and Jose are friends online—they "met" through a video game they play together. They live near each other but have some mutual friends. Jose has suggested they get together which made Brandon uncomfortable and he has started accusing Jose of being gay. Brandon has a picture that Jose sent to him being goofy that he sent around to a bunch of their mutual friends and he keeps implying on Snapchat that Jose is gay.

Is this cyberbullying or is it mean behavior? Why?

Why do you think Brandon is doing that?

How do you think Jose feels?

What should Jose do?

NAVIGATING A DIGITAL WORLD
Tips for Youth

Before going online...

☑ Set Guidelines

Make some rules together with your family before you go online, like the time of day and length of time you can use technology, and sites and apps you are allowed to use. Don't bend the rules or use unapproved apps without their permission.

☑ Limit Electronic Use

Be self-aware of how often you are on your phone, computer and other electronic devices. Make sure you are keeping a healthy balance between digital and in-person activities.

☑ Consider What It Means to Be Responsible Online

Keep in mind that no digital message is completely private, including texts, private/direct messages, etc. Others may be watching your online activity, and law enforcement can recover all messages—even if you deleted them. Using your phone or the Internet to embarrass, threaten, harass or hurt others is irresponsible and can have serious consequences.

☑ Understand Digital Behavior

Be aware that many apps, social media sites and cell service providers have rules about behavior. If you break them, your account—and every account in your home—could be disabled or canceled. Law enforcement may become involved in serious situations.

While online...

☑ Be Respectful of Others

Consider whether your actions contribute to creating a positive digital community. Don't write mean things to or about others, spread rumors/gossip or post things that might make others feel unsafe or uncomfortable, even if you mean it as a "joke." Never share others' *private* information, messages, photos or videos without their permission.

☑ Be a Positive Role Model

Model positive digital behavior by writing supportive posts and messages and applauding positive content that affirms people and communicates respect. Don't follow along when others are behaving negatively and remember to press pause and think before hitting "send."

☑ Engage in Respectful Dialogue

If you choose to engage in online discussions about controversial topics or issues, remember to always pause and think: *Is this how I want my ideas to be expressed online?* Focus your discussion on the ideas and not the individual(s) with whom you're communicating. It's okay to agree to disagree.

☑ Don't Confide in People You Don't Know

It is very easy for people to lie about who they are online. Use caution when sharing personal information or discussing your life with someone you meet online.

☑ **Never Meet a Stranger without Parental Approval**

Don't arrange to meet up in-person with people you have met online without your family's permission.

☑ **Maintain Privacy and Safeguard Security Information**

Don't share personal or private information online—like your full name, school name, home address, phone number and personal photos—with people you don't know or trust. Use the privacy and security features for social media apps you use. Keep passwords and PINs to yourself, but share this information with your parents/guardians. They'll trust you more if you're open with them and they can help you if a serious problem occurs.

☑ **Be Cautious of Messages from Strangers**

Don't open messages or attachments from people you don't know. In many instances it may be best to just delete them and even report them.

☑ **Keep Electronics in View at All Times**

Don't leave electronic devices out of sight because they can be hacked or stolen.

What can I do if I *experience* cyberbullying?

☑ **Don't Respond**

Don't respond to bullying or inappropriate messages, but save them as proof.

☑ **Act as an Ally**

Support people who are targets of mean behavior and bullying by reaching out to the target and/or telling the aggressor to stop. Report what is happening through the site's anonymous reporting procedures or tell a trusted adult in your life what is happening.

☑ **Communicate Issues with a Trusted Adult**

Talk about problems you experience or witness online with an adult that you trust, like a family member, teacher or school counselor.

☑ **Report Behavior/Incidents**

Always report cyberbullying, hate messages, inappropriate sexual content and threats (including possible suicide attempts) to an adult family member, school staff or the police right away. Use ADL's online Cyber-Safety Action Guide to find out how to report inappropriate content to popular online companies, including reporting abuse to apps if available. For serious or continuing problems, file complaints with Internet Service Providers, social media companies, e-mail services, Web sites, cell phone companies, etc. They can find the offenders and take further action.

☑ **Ask for Assistance in Reporting**

If you don't feel comfortable reporting problems yourself, ask an adult to do it for you. Keeping the people close to you aware of what's going on and seeking their support helps when you are targeted.

☑ **Stop and Reject Communication**

Block the cell phone numbers and electronic communication (e.g., posts, texts, etc.) of people who are sending unwanted messages. Change your phone numbers, e-mail addresses, screen names and other online information, if necessary.

☑ **Log Off!**

When in doubt about what to do, log off or shut down and ask for help from a trusted adult.

22. HOW MEDIA PERPETUATE BIAS

TIME
45 minutes

COMMON CORE STANDARDS
Writing, Speaking and Listening,
Language

STRATEGIES AND SKILLS
define terms, large and small group
discussion, small group work, create
media

KEY WORDS AND PHRASES
advertisement, commercial, dispels,
exclusion, media, narrowcasting

Rationale

The purpose of this lesson is for students to understand how bias manifests itself through different forms of media. Media has a powerful impact on our lives and because there is often bias, stereotyping and a lack of diversity embedded in it, it is important to understand media's impact and how to combat its effectiveness in conveying those messages. This lesson provides an opportunity for students to learn more about media and its different forms, reflect on how bias is embedded in media and create a piece of media that challenges bias and stereotypes.

Objectives

- Students will understand what media is and consider the different forms of media in their lives.

- Students will reflect on various forms of media and the extent to which it both perpetuates bias and dispels stereotypes.

- Students will create their own pieces of media that are bias-free and/or ones that dispel stereotypes.

What's Needed

Handouts and Resources: Flip the Media Script Worksheet (one for each student)

Other Material: Board/smart board, chart paper, markers

Advance Preparation:

- Place signs around the room with different forms of media. Choose 5–6 from the list in Procedure #3. Suggestions include: TV shows, video games, music videos, movies, advertisements, social media but could include: TV shows, video games, YouTube videos, movies, advertisements, social media.

- Prepare the list of questions in Procedure #8 to be posted on the board/ smart board or on chart paper.

Procedures

1. Begin the lesson by asking students: *What is media?* Define **media** as the system and organization of communication through which information is spread to a large number of people.

2. Explain that media includes every broadcasting and narrowcasting medium such as newspapers, magazines, TV, radio, billboards, phone and Internet.

3.  With students, brainstorm a list of media forms, which will include the following. Record on the board/smart board and have students take notes.

   — TV shows

   — TV news

   — Radio

   — TV commercials

   — Internet

   — Apps and games

   — Social media (Instagram, Snapchat, Facebook, Twitter, Pinterest, etc.)

   — Online news

   — Billboards

   — Video games

   — Podcasts

   — Magazines (paper or online)

   — Music videos

   — Newspapers (paper or online)

   — Ads on apps, websites or computer games

   — Movies

   — Internet shows

   — YouTube and other online videos

4. Review with students the definitions of stereotypes and bias and forms of bias/discrimination.

   Stereotype: An oversimplified generalization about a person or group of people without regard for individual differences. Even seemingly positive stereotypes that link a person or group to a specific positive trait can have negative consequences and are often rooted in painful histories.

   Bias: An inclination or preference either for or against an individual or group that interferes with impartial judgment.

FLIPPED CLASSROOM IDEA

Make a short video of you going over a list (#3) of different forms of media. You can also share which ones you use regularly and which ones you use less often.

Forms of Bias: ableism, ageism, anti-immigrant bias, anti-Muslim bias, antisemitism, anti-trans bias, classism, heterosexism, racism, religious bias, sexism, weightism

5. Point out to students the posted signs of media forms. Create new ones if students have noted ones that particularly resonate and post them.

6. Instruct students to move to the form of media that they are most interested in discussing with classmates.

7. After finding their spots in the room, explain to students that they will be responding to a list of questions in order to reflect on the extent to which they see stereotypes, bias or exclusion (lacking inclusion or diversity) in forms of media. They will have the opportunity to switch once or twice to a new spot with a new media form, time permitting. Ask students to identify one person who will take notes on their discussion. Allow 5–10 minutes for the discussion.

8. Post this list of questions on the board/smart board or chart paper and read aloud, allowing for a few minutes in between each question for students to respond.
   – What do you like about this form of media?
   – What don't you like?
   – What are examples of bias or stereotypes in this form of media?
   – What are examples of exclusion (certain groups of people not included, being left out) in this form of media?
   – What are examples that dispel bias and stereotypes, portray people in non-stereotypical ways and/or are inclusive?

   As time permits, have students move once or twice to a new form of media to discuss with the same five questions.

9. Have students go back to their seats and engage them in a discussion by asking the following questions:
   – Was it easy or difficult to come up with examples of bias in the media?
   – Can anyone share an example that came up in their group discussion?
   – Was it easy or difficult to come up with examples of exclusion in the media?
   – Can anyone share an example that came up in their group discussion?
   – Was it easy or difficult to come up with examples that dispel bias or stereotypes?
   – Can anyone share an example that came up in their group discussion?
   – What did you learn from this experience?

10. Divide students into small groups of 4–5 students each. Explain that students are going to "flip the script" and come up with a media presentation that is explicitly inclusive (includes a diversity of people/characters), or that dispels stereotypes.

11. Distribute *Using the Flip the Media Script Worksheet* to each student. Explain that as a group they should first decide on what form of media they would like to use (video, advertisement, video game, etc.). Next, they should decide what message they want to convey. It can either be inclusive in a way that it typically is not or it can serve to challenge or dispel a common stereotype. If students do not have time to bring the project to fruition, it can be assigned as a homework project over the next few days.

12. Have each group present their media presentation.

Extension Activities

- Have students conduct a content analysis looking at one form of media in a comprehensive way. A content analysis is a technique for interpreting and coding materials and then drawing conclusions based on their findings. Have students choose a particular TV show, video game, movie or series of advertisements and go through it methodically and count the incidents of stereotypes, bias or exclusion they see. They can then compile their results in a chart/graph, infographic or PowerPoint presentation.

- Have students interview a parent, grandparent or other older family member or family friend about media over their lives. Students can ask questions about the forms of media the person was exposed to when they were younger, the bias they saw in media then, and their reflections on changes they have seen in media bias from their childhood to the present. The interview can be audio or video recorded and shared with the class or students can write a summary of their interview in essay form.

FLIP THE MEDIA SCRIPT WORKSHEET

GROUP MEMBERS:	
FORM OF MEDIA:	

PREPARATION DETAILS

What will be the message?

How does the media example….

a. Dispel a stereotype?

b. Send an anti-bias message?

c. Convey an inclusive message?

What materials are needed?

TIMELINE FOR COMPLETING THE PROJECT

Task	Who is Responsible	Date Completed

23. THE ESCALATION OF HATE

Rationale

The purpose of this lesson is for students to understand how hate escalates and that the seeds of hate can quickly grow from biased ideas to violence. This concept is an important one in motivating people to act on the seeds of hate and bias so that they do not escalate to that point. This lesson provides an opportunity for students to understand how hate escalates, reflect on examples in history where hate led to violence and analyze a story through the lens of hate escalation.

Objectives

- Students will reflect on examples of hate and bias in history when people were hurt or killed because of an aspect of their identity.

- Students will understand the *Pyramid of Hate* and the various components of the escalation of hate.

- Students will analyze a story based on real events through the lens of the *Pyramid of Hate*.

What's Needed

Handouts and Resources: *Pyramid of Hate Categories*; *Pyramid of Hate* and *Jared's Story* (one of each for each student); *Imagine a World Without Hate®* video (2013, 80 secs., Anti-Defamation League, www.adl.org/imagine-a-world-without-hate)

Other Material: Chart paper (at least 10 sheets), markers; plain white paper and markers/colored pencils; Internet access, screen or LCD projector, speakers

Advance Preparation: Make copies of the *Pyramid of Hate Categories* and cut into individual strips so there is enough for each student to receive one and the five different categories are evenly distributed; set aside.

TIME
45 minutes

COMMON CORE STANDARDS
Reading, Writing, Speaking and Listening, Language

STRATEGIES AND SKILLS
draw, large and small group discussion

KEY WORDS AND PHRASES
escalation, harassment, heterosexism, lynching, threatened, unfamiliar words in *Pyramid of Hate*

Procedures

1. Begin the lesson by giving each student a piece of plain white paper. Using markers and colored pencils, have students draw a picture of something that is very important to them. The picture could be of their home, family, friends, pet, their place of worship, dance studio or anything else that is very special in their lives.

2. When the pictures are completed, have students hold them up so everyone in the class can see; ask a few students to share their pictures and describe what the picture is and why the people, places or things in the picture are important to them.

3. Collect the pictures and ask students, "How would you feel if I threw the pictures into the garbage can or tore them up? How would you feel knowing that something that symbolized something important to you is now going to be destroyed?" Explain to students that you are not really going to ruin their pictures but will display them around the room as a reminder that everyone has people, places and things that are special and important and no one has the right to destroy them.

4. Engage students in a discussion by asking the following questions:

    - Have you ever heard or read about a school, community building or place of worship that was spray painted with hateful words or symbols? Please explain.

    - Have you ever heard or read about a person being hurt or killed because of her or his race, religion, sexual orientation or some other aspect of their identity (e.g., gender, gender identity, national original, disability)? Explain what you remember about the situation.

    - What does the word "hate" mean to you?

    - Do you know of other situations where a person has been the victim of a hateful act?

    - Why do you think some people do hateful things to other people or their property?

    - Do you think that name-calling, believing or spreading rumors and misinformation, or stereotyping and other bias can eventually lead people to more hateful attitudes and behaviors? If so, how?

5. Using the *Pyramid of Hate* handout as a guide, draw a large pyramid on the board/smart board or a piece of chart paper and label it "Pyramid of Hate." Divide the pyramid into five sections by drawing horizontal lines. Label the five sections of the pyramid from **bottom to top**: (1) Biased Attitudes, (2) Acts of Bias, (3) Systemic Discrimination, (4) Bias-Motivated Violence and (5) Genocide. Explain to students that this pyramid represents the way that hate can escalate if it is not challenged. Define any of the words with which students may be unfamiliar.

6. Distribute a *Pyramid of Hate Category* strip to each student and divide students into five groups according to the category they received. Explain that each group should take 5–7 minutes to work together to come up with ideas and examples for their assigned category. Distribute paper and pens/pencils to each group for students to jot down notes of their examples.

7. Have each group share back what they came up with, starting with Biased Attitudes and ending with Genocide. As students share their examples from each category, write in those examples on the pyramid you drew in Procedure #5.

8. Distribute the *Pyramid of Hate* handout to each student. (This one has examples provided for each section.) Have them take note of what is included in the handout compared to what they came up with in their small groups. Go over the pyramid briefly, explaining how it works and providing definitions for certain words that may be unfamiliar to students.

9. Engage students in a discussion by asking the following questions:

    —   Why do you think this is called the "Pyramid of Hate?"

    —   How does the shape of a pyramid show (or not) how hate escalates?

    —   What are other ways this escalation of hate might be illustrated?

    —   Do you think that most people, at some time or other, have bias?

    —   Do you think that most people have done individual acts of prejudice?

    —   What are some things that might make it easier for people to continue to move up the pyramid or continue the escalation of hate?

    —   Once someone's actions start moving up on the pyramid, do you think it's difficult to stop? Why or why not? What might cause the escalation to stop?

    —   At what point in the pyramid do you think it's easiest for people to interrupt the escalation of hate, if they decide to do so? Why?

    —   Who is hurt by hate and violence?

10.  Distribute *Jared's Story* to each student and either read it aloud as a class or have students read it silently. Explain that it is based on real life events. Make sure that students have their copies of the *Pyramid of Hate* out and you have it projected on the board/smart board while reading the story.

11. When students are finished reading, have them identify specific examples of the pyramid components (e.g., examples of rumors, name-calling, stereotyping, etc.) and write the examples in the appropriate area on the *Pyramid of Hate* you have on the board or chart paper.

12. Engage students in a discussion by asking the following questions:

    —   Does this story sound familiar at all to you?

    —   How does this story illustrate the *Pyramid of Hate* model?

    —   What role did heterosexism play in the violence directed at the boy?

    —   Who was hurt by the events that took place in this situation?

    —   What do you think of the action taken by the student who overheard the boys threatening Jared?

    —   What do you think you would have done in the same situation?

    —   Do you think something like what happened to Jared could happen at this school? Why or why not?

    —   What must individuals do to stop the escalation of hate?

    —   What must communities do to stop the escalation of hate?

    —   How will everyone benefit if the escalation of hate is interrupted and stopped?

FLIPPED CLASSROOM IDEA

Make a video of you reading aloud *Jared's Story* and ask 2–3 of the discussion questions at the end of your reading for them to reflect upon.

13. End the lesson by showing the ADL video, *Imagine a World Without Hate*®. Afterwards, engage students in a discussion by asking the questions below:

— What happens in the video?

— What feelings did you experience while watching the video?

— What is the message of the video?

Extension Activities

- Using the same components in the *Pyramid of Hate,* have students design another model that illustrates the escalation of hate. It can be an original illustration, computer design or a model. In addition to the model, students should provide written instructions as to how this model illustrates the escalation of hate.

- Have students research contemporary examples of hate directed at people because of their sexual orientation, race, gender identity, religion or ethnicity, immigration status (e.g., Leo Frank, Emmett Till, Matthew Shepherd, James Byrd, Jr., latest murders of transgender women of color, etc.). Have students create *Pyramid of Hate* models that illustrate how things like misinformation, rumors, stereotypes, bias, discrimination and scapegoating contributed (or might have contributed) to the escalation of hate that resulted in violent acts. Students should consider the role that online hate sites or media may have played in these cases. Students can create a PowerPoint and/or research paper with their findings.

PYRAMID OF HATE CATEGORIES

Genocide

Bias-Motivated Violence

Systemic Discrimination

Acts of Bias

Biased Attitudes

PYRAMID OF HATE

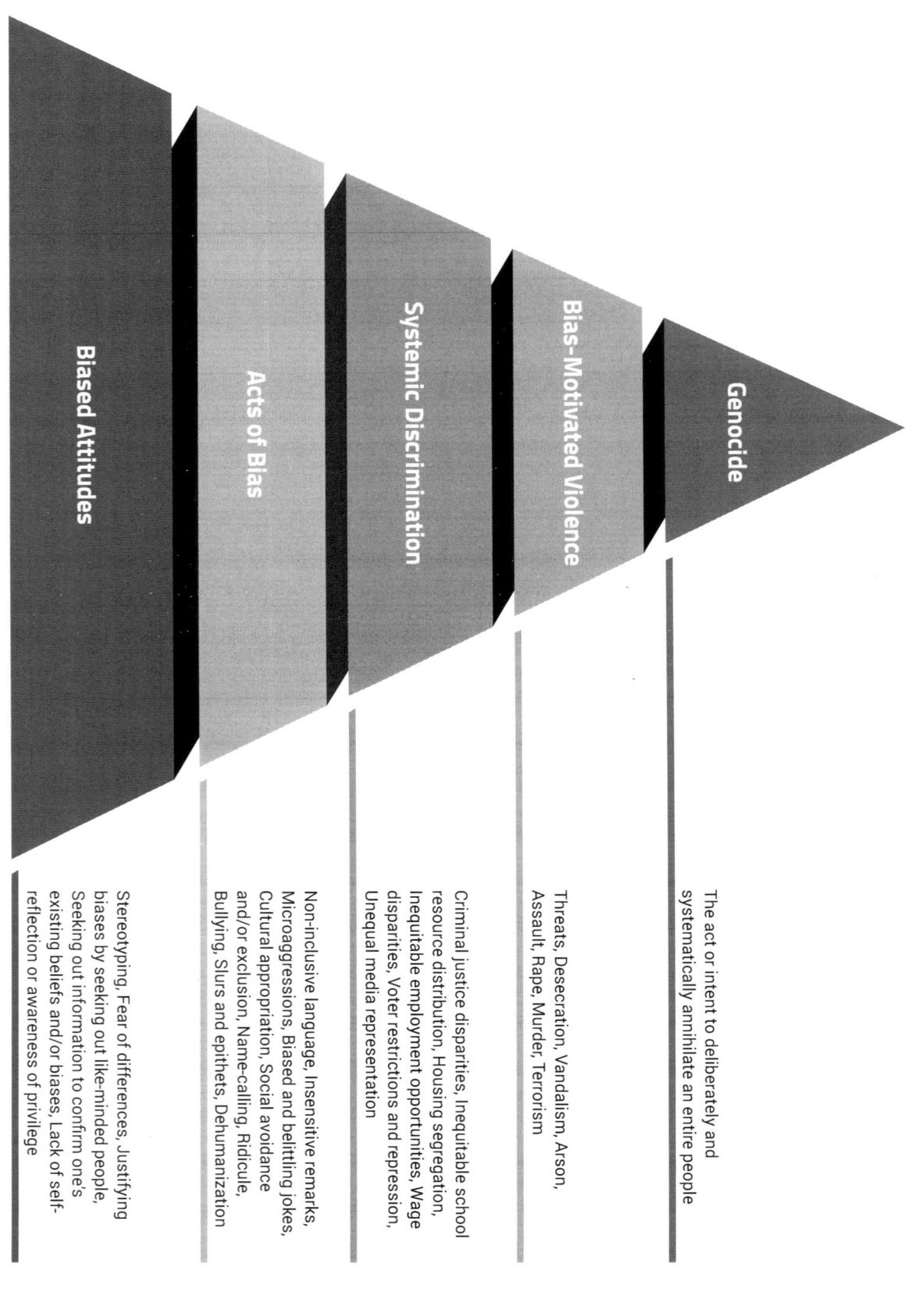

Biased Attitudes

Stereotyping, Fear of differences, Justifying biases by seeking out like-minded people, Seeking out information to confirm one's existing beliefs and/or biases, Lack of self-reflection or awareness of privilege

Acts of Bias

Non-inclusive language, Insensitive remarks, Microaggressions, Biased and belittling jokes, Cultural appropriation, Social avoidance and/or exclusion, Name-calling, Ridicule, Bullying, Slurs and epithets, Dehumanization

Systemic Discrimination

Criminal justice disparities, Inequitable school resource distribution, Housing segregation, Inequitable employment opportunities, Wage disparities, Voter restrictions and repression, Unequal media representation

Bias-Motivated Violence

Threats, Desecration, Vandalism, Arson, Assault, Rape, Murder, Terrorism

Genocide

The act or intent to deliberately and systematically annihilate an entire people

JARED'S STORY

In one school, a group of boys began whispering and laughing about Jared, another boy in their class that they thought was gay. They began making comments when they walked by him in the hall. Soon, they started calling Jared insulting anti-gay slurs. By the end of the month, they had taken their harassment to another level, tripping him when he walked by and pushing him into a locker while they yelled slurs. The seriousness of their conduct continued to escalate and one day after school, they followed Jared home, surrounded him and two of them held him down while the others punched and kicked him. They told him that if he told anyway, they would "get him back" and one of the boys threatened to bring his father's gun into school the next day to kill Jared. At this point, another student overheard the threat and the police were notified.

UNIT V. CHALLENGING BIAS AND INJUSTICE

Now that students have learned what bias and discrimination are, a critical next step is for them to develop the tools, skills and motivation to do something about it. It is so important that people, especially young people, do not feel powerless in the face of hate and injustice. Because tweens and teens are very sensitive to unfairness and injustice in the world and possess the desire, energy and idealism to do something about it, they are powerful agents for change. This can take the form of individual actions like challenging biased language or learning to be an ally, or it can take place on a larger level by them getting involved in social justice activism. We need to harness middle school students' desire for justice and fairness and provide the information, skills and inspiration to challenge prejudice, biased language, inequity, oppression, discrimination and injustice.

In Unit V, the final section of the curriculum, students will examine the different roles we play in incidents of bias and bullying including target, aggressor, bystander and ally. To help them explore the different ways to be an ally, middle schoolers will learn about six ways to be an ally and consider how to move from being a bystander to being an ally. Young people will reflect on their experiences with hearing and responding to biased comments and will practice responses for handling those remarks by considering the impact they want to have. Cyberhate, or online hate, is something young people may experience online and they will learn more about it and how to use counterspeech and other strategies for addressing it. Students will understand the difference between equality and equity and reflect on how they are similar and different. Gaining knowledge in how other communities have stood up to hate will help middle schoolers identify examples of hate in their own school, community, country and the world. Finally, students will reflect on what issues of injustice are most important to them and will then develop social action projects that address those issues.

24. ROLES WE PLAY IN BIAS AND BULLYING

Rationale

The purpose of this lesson is for students to understand the different roles we play when witnessing bias and bullying. Reflecting on how to move from bystander to ally is a critical step in making a difference when it comes to bias and bullying. This lesson provides an opportunity for students to understand the four roles (aggressor, ally, bystander and target), gain insight into how we play all these roles at different times and explore ways to move from being a bystander to an ally.

Objectives

- Students will understand and define aggressor, ally, bystander and target.
- Students will reflect on experiences they have had playing each of these roles.
- Students will consider ways to move from being a bystander to an ally.

What's Needed

Handouts and Resources: The Roles We Play and Determining How to Be an Ally (one of each for each student)

Other Material: Board/Smart board, chart paper, markers

Advance Preparation: Write the following words on separate sheets of chart paper and set aside: AGGRESSOR, ALLY, BYSTANDER, TARGET.

Procedures

1. Begin the lesson by reminding students about the specific lessons on bias and the different forms of bias, bullying and identity-based bullying they have learned about. Explain that today they are going to discuss

TIME
45 minutes

COMMON CORE STANDARDS
Writing, Speaking and Listening, Language

STRATEGIES AND SKILLS
turn and talk, large group discussion, act out roles, define terms

KEY WORDS AND PHRASES
aggressor, ally, bystander, target

the different ways we deal with bias and bullying. Ask students, "What are some things you can do (or have done) when you have witnessed or experienced bias or bullying?" Have a few students share their responses but this should be a brief discussion.

2. Explain to students that you are going to say out loud four different words that illustrate the roles we can play in bias and bullying situations. For each word, you will ask students to say or do something that represents the word. Tell students if they don't know the word, they can either guess or not do anything. Ask students to stand up at their desks (or if you have open space, they can stand here) and say the first word: "aggressor." Then tell students, one bullet point at a time, to do the following:

   — Make a facial expression to illustrate the word aggressor.

   — Make a body movement that illustrates the word aggressor.

   — Make a sound that illustrates the word aggressor.

   — Use your hands to illustrate the word aggressor.

   After each representation, have students take a few seconds to look around the room at each other. After "aggressor," use the same process for the other three words in this order:

   — target

   — bystander

   — ally

3. When you have gone through all four words and representations, have students sit down at their seats and engage them in a discussion by asking the following questions:

   — Was it difficult or easy to come up with a facial expression, body movement, hand movement or sound for each word? Please explain.

   — What did you notice when you looked around the room?

   — How did you feel while you were doing each of the representations for each word?

   — What did you learn by doing this activity?

FLIPPED CLASSROOM IDEA

Make a short video of you defining the four words (aggressor, ally, bystander and target) and share an example for each.

4. Explain that they are going to define the four words, which are all roles that we play in bias and bullying situations. Write the four words on the board/smart board and elicit a definition for each and come to the following definitions. Post the definitions on the board/smart board.

Aggressor: Someone who says or does something harmful or malicious to another person intentionally and unprovoked.

Ally: Someone who speaks out on behalf of or takes actions that are supportive of someone who is targeted by bias or bullying, either themselves or someone else.

Bystander: Someone who sees bias or bullying happening and does not say or do anything.

Target: Someone against whom mistreatment is directed.

5. Hang up your pre-made chart paper signs around the room with the words: AGGRESSOR, ALLY, BYSTANDER, TARGET with a few markers at each station. Give students 5–7 minutes to circulate around the room, stop at each station and write words, phrases, or a short (2–3 sentence) situation/story they associate with the word.

   If time permits, read aloud everything on all four of the sheets or have students quickly walk around the room and read what's on the chart paper. Engage students in a brief discussion by asking:

   — What do you notice about the words, phrases, etc.?

   — Did we all agree or did we see the roles differently? Please explain.

6. Ask students to raise their hands if they have ever been an aggressor, then target, then bystander, then ally.

7. Explain that we all have probably played all of these roles at different times or may do so in the future. Distribute *The Roles We Play* handout to each student and explain that they will be filling in the chart based on experiences they have had. Give students 10 minutes to fill out the sheets.

   Then, have students turn and talk with a person sitting next to them and share what they wrote with their partner, going through each of the four roles and highlighting one of the roles and a time it was most significant and why.

8. Engage students in a class discussion by asking the following questions:

   — Was it difficult or easy to identify times you were in each of the roles? How so?

   — Did you notice that you gravitate more to one role than the others?

   — Do you play different roles in different situations? Please explain.

   — What did you learn by reflecting on your experiences?

9. Explain to students that they are now going to focus on the times they have been bystanders because in many situations of bias or bullying, there are many more bystanders than there are aggressors, targets and allies. Ask, "Would anyone like to share a time when they were a bystander when witnessing bias or bullying?" If students are reluctant to share, you can have students turn in their *The Roles We Play* handouts and you can share some of their responses aloud, making sure to leave off any details or names that would identify specific people or situations.

10. Read aloud 3–5 bystander situations from the students' handouts, being careful not to identity anyone's name or particular situation. As you read each one, give students a few minutes to reflect on the situation and then write down (on a piece of paper or using the *Determining How to Be an Ally* handout) how the bystander in that situation can move from being a bystander to being an ally. Emphasize to students that they should come

NOTE 6

You can have students close their eyes and raise their hands and you can count if you think they are more likely to be honest and open with their responses.

up with ideas that are realistic and ones they could see themselves actually doing. Then ask students to share some of their ideas.

11. Engage students in a discussion by asking the following questions:
    - Was it easy or difficult to come up with ways to move from being a bystander to an ally?
    - Why do you think so many people are bystanders to bias or bullying?
    - What do you think would help more people be able to be an ally rather than a bystander?
    - What did you learn during the course of this lesson?

Extension Activities

▪ Have students analyze a television program, movie or video game and highlight the different characters in the story and the roles that they played (aggressor, target, ally, bystander). Students can then focus on one character and write a short essay on the role(s) that person played, using examples from the program.

▪ Have students write a fiction story about someone who was a bystander and moved from that role into the role of ally.

THE ROLES WE PLAY

BOX A: TARGET	BOX B: AGGRESSOR
Describe a time when someone's words or actions hurt you.	Describe a time when your words or actions hurt someone.

BOX C: BYSTANDER	BOX D: ALLY
Describe a time when you saw an act of prejudice taking place and you didn't do anything. Why do you think you didn't do anything?	Describe a time when you saw an act of prejudice and you took action as an ally or a confronter. Why did you choose the actions you did?

DETERMINING HOW TO BE AN ALLY

1 Short Description of Bystander Situation

What could the person do to move from being a bystander to being an ally?

2 Short Description of Bystander Situation

What could the person do to move from being a bystander to being an ally?

3 Short Description of Bystander Situation

What could the person do to move from being a bystander to being an ally?

4 Short Description of Bystander Situation

What could the person do to move from being a bystander to being an ally?

25. WHAT DOES IT MEAN TO BE AN ALLY?

Rationale

The purpose of this lesson is for students to understand the various ways to be an ally. Ally building behavior is a critical tool for young people to address bias and bullying in their lives. This lesson provides an opportunity for students to learn the different ways to be an ally, reflect on their own experience and work in small groups to come up with ally behaviors based on situations of bias and bullying.

Objectives

- Students will understand the different ways to be an ally.
- Students will reflect on different ways that they acted as an ally.
- Students will explore scenarios around bias and bullying and consider ways they can move from bystander to ally.

What's Needed

Handouts and Resources: *6 Ways to Be An Ally* and *From Bystander to Ally Worksheet* (one of each for each student); *Bullying Scenarios*

Other Material: Board/Smart board, chart paper, markers

Advance Preparation:

- Using the *6 Ways to Be an Ally* handout, write each way on a separate sheet of chart paper and set aside.
- (Optional) Download and reproduce the color version of *6 Ways to Be an Ally* at www.adl.org/education/resources/tools-and-strategies/6-ways-to-be-an-ally-en-espanol. Available in English and Spanish.
- Select 4–5 *Bullying Scenarios* and cut into strips of individual scenarios.

Procedures

1. Begin the lesson by asking students if they remember the definition of

TIME
45 minutes

COMMON CORE STANDARDS
Reading, Writing, Speaking and Listening, Language

STRATEGIES AND SKILLS
concentric circles, large and small group discussion

KEY WORDS AND PHRASES
supportive

ally from the previous lesson. Remind them of the definition by reading it aloud and recording it on the board/smart board:

Ally: Someone who speaks out on behalf of or takes actions that are supportive of someone who is targeted by bias or bullying, either themselves or someone else.

2. Ask students, "What are some of the different ways you can be an ally to someone who is the target of bullying or bias?" Remind them of the activity in the previous lesson where they thought of ways to move from bystander to ally.

FLIPPED CLASSROOM IDEA

Make a short video of you reading aloud *6 Ways to Be an Ally* and sharing a quick example for each.

3.  Distribute the *Six Ways to Be an Ally* handout to each student. Have students take turns reading each of the six ways described in the handout and ask if there are any questions. Place the six ways to be an ally signs around the room and point them out to students. Have students look around the room, consider each of the six ways and decide which of the six they want to talk about more. When you signal it's time to move, all of the students will select their spot in the room based on which of the six ways they have selected. Once they are situated, explain that they will spend 5–10 minutes in their groups and will discuss the following questions with each other:

   — Why did you choose this spot?

   — Have you ever observed someone being an ally in this way?

   — Have you ever been an ally in this way?

   — What do they think is helpful about being an ally in this way? What is not helpful?

4. When the time is up, have students come back to the large group and engage them in a discussion by asking:

   — Why did you choose the spot you chose?

   — Were you surprised by what others in your group shared?

   — What are some of the ways you have either been an ally or witnessed others being allies?

   — What ways are you most comfortable being an ally?

   — In what ways would you have to stretch yourself to be an ally?

NOTE 5

If you don't have the space to make a circle in the room, you can create two lines and have students move down the line or they can keep switching partners based on where they are seated.

5. Instruct students to count off by twos so that half the members of the class are designated as #1s and the other half are designated as #2s. Have students who are #1s form a large circle in the center of the room, facing outward. Ask students who are #2s to form a second circle outside the first circle and to face a partner in the inside circle. Explain to students that they will be using this structure (concentric circles) to discuss the topic of being an ally with several different people.

You will be asking a number of questions and each pair will have **two minutes** to respond to the question (one minute each). Explain that during the first minute, one person in the pair will respond to the question, while the other person listens. Explain that you will signal when one minute is up by calling "change." At this signal, the first speaker will become the listener and the second person will share his or her response to the same question or statement. Explain to the class that at the end of each question, after both members of the pair have responded, you will instruct the outside circle (those students who are #2s) to move one space to their left, joining a new partner for the next question.

— Share about a time you (or someone you know) supported a target.

— Share about a time you (or someone you know) didn't participate in bullying or bias that was taking place.

— Share about a time you (or someone you know) told aggressors to stop.

— Share about a time you (or someone you know) informed a trusted adult about bias or bullying.

— Share about a time you (or someone you know) got to know someone instead of judging them.

— Share about a time you (or someone you know) acted as an ally online.

6. Have students come back to the large group and engage them in a discussion by asking:

— In what ways is it easy to be an ally?

— In what ways is it difficult to be an ally?

— What do you think young people need in order to act as an ally more often than they do?

7. Divide students into groups of 4–5 students each and distribute one of the selected *Bullying Scenarios* and the *From Bystander to Ally Worksheet* to each group. Instruct students to choose someone to read the scenario aloud and then have students talk together about what happened in the scenario, what type of bias and/or bullying is happening and how they or the bystanders in the scenario could be an ally. Remind them to think about the six different ways to be an ally and tell them they are not limited to just one idea. Give students ten minutes for this small group work. As they are discussing the scenarios and ways to be an ally, they should complete their *From Bystander to Ally Worksheet* as a group.

8. After students complete their small group work, have each group present their scenario to the class and share what they came up with in terms of their ways to be an ally.

9. Engage students in a discussion by asking the following questions:

— How did you work together in your group?

— Did you agree or disagree about the ways to be an ally?

— Did you tend to gravitate towards one way to be an ally or different ways?

— What factors should be considered when deciding how to be an ally?

— What did you learn by doing this activity?

Extension Activities

▰ Have students write a story about when they witnessed bias or bullying and were a bystander but wished they were able to be an ally and how.

▰ Have students find a news story about a teenager who acted as an ally to someone else, either another teenager or someone else. Possible sources to find stories are: *The New York Times* Learning Network: Teenagers in the Times (www.nytimes.com/column/learning-teens-in-the-times) and *The Huffington Post:* Teen (www.huffingtonpost.com/teen/). Have students read the news story, write a summary of it and identify how the teenager was an ally. Other possible ways to present could be a letter to the editor in support of the teen ally.

6 WAYS TO BE AN ALLY

Here are some simple things you can do to be an ally to targets of name-calling and bullying. And remember—always think about your safety first when deciding the best way to respond.

1. Support targets, whether you know them or not.

Show compassion and encouragement to those who are the targets of bullying behavior by asking if they're okay, going with them to get help and letting them know you are there for them. Ask what else you can do and make sure they know they're not alone.

2. Don't participate.

This is a really easy way to be an ally because it doesn't require you to actually do anything, just to not do certain things—like laugh, stare or cheer for the bad behavior. By refusing to join in when name-calling and bullying occur, you are sending a message that the behavior is not funny and you are not okay with treating people that way. The next step is to speak up and try to put a stop to the hurtful behavior.

3. Tell aggressors to stop.

If it feels safe, tell the person behaving disrespectfully to cut it out. You can let them know you don't approve on the spot or later during a private moment. Whenever you do it, letting aggressors know how hurtful it is to be bullied may cause them to think twice before picking on someone again.

4. Inform a trusted adult.

Sometimes you may need extra help to stop the bullying. It's important to tell an adult who you trust so that this person can be an ally to you as well as the target. Telling an adult when you see someone engaged in bullying is never "tattling" or "snitching." So don't think twice—reach out to a parent, teacher, guidance counselor, coach or someone else who will get involved.

5. Get to know people instead of judging them.

Appreciate people for who they are and don't judge them based on their appearance. You may even find that they're not so different from you after all.

6. Be an ally online.

Bullying happens online, too, and through the use of cell phones. Looking at mean web pages and forwarding hurtful messages is just like laughing at someone or spreading rumors in person. It is just as hurtful, even if you can't see the other person's face. All the rules above are just as important to follow when texting and on social media. So online and offline—do your part to be an ally to others.

BULLYING SCENARIOS

Angie has been good friends with the same group of girls for the past two years. They always hang out on the weekends and have their own table in the cafeteria next to your friends' table. A few months ago, Angie's father lost his job and her family moved to a small apartment building in a different part of town. One day at lunch, you overhear several of Angie's friends asking her, "Aren't you afraid to live in that part of town?" as they give each other a look and roll their eyes. Today, you and your friends notice when Angie tries to sit down in an empty seat at her friends' table, they say they are saving it for someone else.

After social studies class, you are talking with a group of students about the Middle East because it was just discussed in class; you are specifically discussing war in that area. Several students say that they think it is okay to limit Muslim immigration because they could be terrorists or associated with terrorists. One student says she thinks we should be fighting wars in that area because Muslims treat women like second-class citizens. She mentions that women are required to cover their heads and faces to show their shame about their bodies. Although your friend Samira, who wears a hijab (head covering), is silent during the conversations, she looks very uncomfortable and a little angry.

Marcus is your Biology lab partner. When you notice he hasn't been in class the whole week, you ask another student, Mollie, who sits next to him in homeroom, if she knows where he is. Mollie says that some of the boys in your class have been teasing him and spreading rumors that Marcus is gay since the beginning of school; they often whisper about him and also sent a text message around about it. Mollie says that Marcus saw the text messages a few days ago and rushed out of the school building and hasn't been seen since. She says he's thinking about transferring schools because he's tired of being harassed.

DeQuan is good friends with Omar and Luke (all eighth graders), who have been best friends for years but are currently not speaking with each other. The reason is that Omar is furious with Luke after hearing that Luke went on a date with Elana, a girl Omar has liked all of middle school. Omar digs out an old photo of Luke from before he transferred to their school and before he lost fifty pounds. One day when DeQuan is over at his house, Omar gets a hold of a picture of a very overweight fifth-grader and texts it to Elana with a message saying "Just thought you should know what your boyfriend really looks like."

A student named Kaya always sits alone at recess and never gets asked to play. She doesn't dress like most of the other girls; she normally wears a Star Wars t-shirt and a baseball cap. Today, another student named Ella walks by her, calls her a "loser" and flips her cap off. Other students are watching this and start laughing out loud.

Josh is one of the only Jewish kids at his school. Whenever his social studies teacher talks about Israel, everyone looks at him but they don't say anything. He has a lot of friends but none of them are Jewish. When he brings matzoh to school for lunch during Passover, his friends and some other kids ask him what it is and why he's eating it and start to tease him about it. They try to shove a piece of bread in his mouth to see if he will eat it.

Every day after math class, Sam tells Carlos—who has a para because of some special needs—that he is stupid and shouldn't even try. Sam convinces others in the class to join in by making mean jokes and one day says to Carlos, "I don't know why you're in the high math class. You're in special ed and not smart enough to be in our class. You should be in the low math class." Carlos is embarrassed and doesn't know what to say.

Helena finds out from her twin brother that several of the boys at school have been posting "Top 10" lists on an Instagram page. The list includes "top ten faces," "top ten butts," etc. Helena tells some of her friends and it spreads around school so that most of the girls find out and are upset about these degrading lists. A few of them talk to their guy friends who they think will be sympathetic. They are upset when they find out that some of these guys contributed to the lists and suggest that the girls are being "too sensitive" because it's just a joke.

There's a new student at school named Ana who recently moved to your town from El Salvador. Ana doesn't speak much English but she is trying to learn. Gaby, another Latina girl befriends her and offers to help her with her homework and practice English with her. When they talk together, they speak mainly in Spanish and they notice that several kids are whispering about them. Gaby asks them, "Just say out loud what you want to say" and they reply with "If you two can't speak English, you need to go back from where you came."

FROM BYSTANDER TO ALLY WORKSHEET

What is happening here?

_____

_____

_____

_____

What kind of bias/bullying is going on and how do you know?

_____

_____

_____

_____

_____

You are the bystander in this situation. What can you realistically do to be an ally to the target? Include as many different ideas as you can think of.

_____

_____

_____

_____

_____

_____

_____

26. CHALLENGING BIASED COMMENTS

TIME
45 minutes

COMMON CORE STANDARDS
Speaking and Listening, Language

STRATEGIES AND SKILLS
large and small group discussion

KEY WORDS AND PHRASES
belittle, challenge, impact, intent, obstacle, tone

Rationale

The purpose of this lesson is for students to match their intent and impact when challenging biased comments. In the moment when a biased comment is made, sometimes the impact of our response doesn't match how we intend it. This lesson provides an opportunity for students to reflect on their experiences with hearing and challenging biased comments, gives them practice in responding in the moment and helps them explore what they need to be able to challenge biased comments in the future.

Objectives

- Students will explore their experiences with hearing biased comments.
- Students will reflect on intent and impact and what happens when they don't match.
- Students will practice challenging biased comments while trying to match their intent with the impact.

What's Needed

Handouts and Resources: What Is Your Intent? (one for each student)

Procedures

1. Begin the lesson by reminding students about the definition of bias and the different forms of bias (see lessons 17, "What is Bias?" and 19, "Forms of Bias and Discrimination"). Explain to students that they have already discussed being an ally in the previous lesson and are now going to talk about other ways to address biased comments. Ask students, "Can you think of any time recently when you heard a biased comment?" Remind students not to use individual names. Have students share a few examples and if relevant, ask them whether they or someone else said anything when the comment was made.

2. Divide students into groups of three to engage in small group discussions about their experiences with challenging bias. Explain to students that they will respond to three questions, taking turns responding to each question. The triad will have a total of three minutes for each question so each person will get one minute to respond. Read the questions one-at-a-time, allowing triads the three minutes to respond. Then move onto the next question:

   — Share about a recent time when you heard a biased comment. What happened? Did you say anything and if so, what did you say? Did you want to say something but didn't and how so?

   — What concerns did you have about challenging the comment? What prevented you from saying or doing something?

   — What would help or enable you to challenge biased comments when you hear them? What do you need to do this?

3. Have students come back to the large group and engage them in a discussion by asking the following questions:

   — What kinds of biased comments have you heard?

   — Do you find yourself usually, often, rarely or never able to challenge biased comments?

   — Do you find it difficult or easy to challenge biased comments? How so?

   — What are some of the obstacles in being able to challenge biased comments?

   — What do you need in order to be able to challenge biased comments?

4. Tell students that they are going to do an activity that helps them better understand intent and impact by taking them through a series of movement activities. Ask, "What is intent?" Explain that **intent** is what someone hopes to accomplish in a given situation, their goals. Then ask, "What is impact?" Explain that the **impact** on someone is the outcome or effect your actions have on them. Explain that sometimes our intent and impact do not match. Ask, "Can anyone think of a time when your intent and impact didn't match?"

5. Have students count off by 1s and 2s (1, 2, 1, 2, 1, 2 and so on) so that half the class are #1s and half are #2s. Have students who are #1s form a line on one side of the room and when they are situated, have the #2s form another line in front of the first line, positioning themselves so each person has a partner from the opposite line.

6.  Explain to students that you are going to call out a statement of intent such as "to refuse" and students, in their pairs, will perform an action that communicates that intent. Students can use facial expressions, hand or body gestures or physical movements to convey

NOTE 4

If you don't have space to do this activity, ask in advance whether it can be done in the hallway or find another room. If that's not possible, have students do the exercise with partners near their seats.

FLIPPED CLASSROOM IDEA

Make a short video of you acting out facial expressions, hand or body gestures or physical movements that convey different intents such as "to refuse," "to support" and "to exclude."

their intent. (Remind students that no obscene gestures, violent actions or direct body contact is permitted and there should be no speaking or verbal communication.)

Before having students do this in pairs, model the activity by asking for a volunteer who will stand facing you. State that the intent is "to refuse." You will then perform an action that represents this intention such as crossing your arms and shaking your head.

7. Explain to students that they will take turns in their pairs performing the different intentions. First, #1s will perform their intent and then #2s will perform the next one until you get through all of them as follows (there are ten total but each will only take a few seconds):

    — to protect   — to belittle
    — to attack   — to reject
    — to exclude   — to accept
    — to include   — to engage
    — to support   — to stop

8. Have students return to their seats and engage them in a discussion by asking the following questions:

    — What was it like when you were the one performing the actions?
    — What kind of reaction did you get from your partner?
    — Which actions or gestures had the most impact on you and why?
    — Which actions had the least impact on you and why?
    — What is the connection between intent and impact?
    — What does "tone" have to do with impact?
    — What did you learn from doing this activity?

9. Explain that the next part of the activity allows students to practice various responses to bias-related statements using intent as the guiding factor in their choice of words and tone. Distribute the handout, *What Is Your Intent?*, and review it with the class, having students take turns reading aloud each of the examples. Explain that being clear about your intention is important for helping you decide what to say and how to say it. Also point out that the handout contains guidelines and suggestions but each situation requires a different response based on many factors.

10. Have students pair up with the person from the previous activity. Explain that you will read a biased comment from the list below. For each comment, students will challenge the biased statement in some way. Explain that even though they are responding "on the spot" to the comment, they should think about their intent and try to say something where the impact will match their intent, taking guidance from the handout *What Is Your Intent?* or another idea that comes to mind. Read the statements one at a time, giving students time to respond. Start with #2 students and then alternate back and forth between #2s and the #1s. Do as many statements as time permits and insert other comments as you see fit.

    — Last weekend's dance was so gay.
    — You're Jewish? Your nose isn't big enough to be Jewish. Just kidding.
    — Don't be a retard and answer the question!
    — You're pretty good at basketball, for a girl.
    — I'm not racist, but I'm tired of hearing about how bad black people have it.

- I can't understand why he's dating her. He could easily get a girl who isn't so fat.

- I wish all the Muslims would just go back to Pakistan or wherever they're from.

11. Have students come back together and engage them in a discussion by asking the following questions:

   - What feelings came up as you were doing this activity?

   - What did you learn about yourself from doing this activity?

   - Was it easy or difficult to come up with an "on the spot" response? How so?

   - What responses had the most impact on you and why?

   - How will this activity help you to respond to harmful and biased comments in the future?

Extension Activities

■ Have students create posters or pictures (with illustrations or photos) that include one of the biased comments from the activity above (or other ones they have heard) and a response or challenge to that comment with an illustration that goes along with it.

■ Have students create a class video that uses one or more biased comments and illustrates a range of challenging responses to that comment, having several different students provide responses to each of the comments. Consider sharing the video with other classes in the school.

WHAT IS YOUR INTENT?

Responding immediately is not always the best way to challenge bias. Assess the safety of the situation. Once you have determined the situation is safe, *consider the suggestions below.*

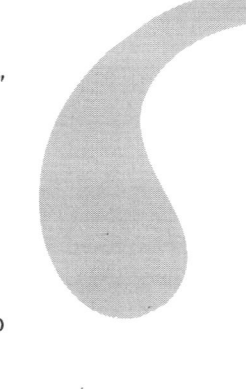

● **To inform**
Counter the person's comment with facts.

- — "Stereotypes like that are hurtful and simply not true."

- — "I recently participated in a peer leadership program and learned that..."

● **To express your feelings**
Use "I" statements.

- — "I cannot believe you said that. I find that comment to be very offensive."

- — "I would appreciate it if you didn't use language like that around me because it makes me uncomfortable."

- — "I used to feel that way too, but then I found that comments like that exclude people so now I try not to say things like that."

● **To build empathy**
Encourage them to try to understand how the person feels.

- — "How would you like it if someone said something like that about you?"

- — "Someone once said something like that to me and it really hurt."

● **To challenge the person's intentions**
Help them to consider the impact of their words.

- — "What did you mean by that?"

- — "I'm sorry, I don't understand why you would say that."

- — "What was your intent?"

- — "You may be joking, but the impact of what you said is not funny."

● **To stop the behavior**
Help them to consider the impact of their words.

- — "Please stop saying hurtful things like that."

- — "I would appreciate it if you didn't make hurtful comments like that around me."

- — "Seriously? That is not ok to say."

27. ADDRESSING BIAS ONLINE: COUNTERSPEECH

Rationale

The purpose of this lesson is for students to understand how bias manifests itself online and how counterspeech can be used to address it. Finding appropriate ways to challenge hate online (from reporting it to counterspeech) is an important tool in students' ability to address bias and hate. In this lesson, students will have an opportunity to reflect on hate speech they have seen online, discuss ways to respond to and challenge cyberhate and create their own counterspeech.

Objectives

- Students will reflect on their experiences with online hate speech.
- Students will understand what cyberhate is and explore examples.
- Students will brainstorm ways to respond to cyberhate and consider counterspeech as a viable option.
- Students will create some responses to cyberhate using counterspeech.

What's Needed

Handouts and Resources: *Definition of Cyberhate* (one for each student or project on board/smart board); *Old Navy Ad Twitter Post; This is Wholesome* video (2014, 30 secs., Honey Maid, www.youtube.com/watch?v=2xeanX6xnRU); *Love* video (2014, 2 mins., Honey Maid, www.youtube.com/watch?v=cBC-pRFt9OM)

Other Material: Board/Smart board; 8½" x 11" paper or chart paper, markers; Internet access, screen or LCD projector

Advance Preparation: Create 8½ x 11 inch (at least) signs that say: STRONGLY AGREE, AGREE, IN BETWEEN/NOT SURE, DISAGREE AND STRONGLY DISAGREE, with each word/phrase on its own sign. Post them on the wall around the classroom along a continuum from left to right, beginning with STRONGLY AGREE.

TIME
45 minutes

COMMON CORE STANDARDS
Reading, Writing, Speaking and Listening, Language

STRATEGIES AND SKILLS
large and small group discussion, develop and express opinions, create counterspeech

KEY WORDS AND PHRASES
blunt, counterspeech, cyberhate, freedom of speech, miscegenation

Procedures

1. Begin the lesson by explaining to students that they are going to do an activity where they listen to some statements and decide to what extent they agree or disagree with the statement. (Make sure the signs are hung up around the room on the wall.) Remind students about the difference between a fact and an opinion and explain that they will be indicating their opinion about each statement by positioning themselves along an imaginary line, depending upon whether they agree or disagree with a statement.

2. Select a large open space and indicate the position of an imaginary line with the farthest right point representing a "STRONGLY AGREE" response and the farthest left point a "STRONGLY DISAGREE" response. In between these two positions, indicate "AGREE," "IN BETWEEN/NOT SURE," and "DISAGREE" along the continuum.

3. Read each statement below, requesting students to take a few minutes to decide where they stand on the statement and then have them walk silently to that place and observe where others choose to stand:

    — Technology is an extremely important part of our lives.

    — I like sharing information online because I can be more honest and blunt.

    — Teenagers are more likely to post negative and mean content using technology than in real life.

    — Most of what I see online is positive and upbeat.

    — There isn't much you can do about the hate and mean behavior you see online.

    — I don't like when I see bias and hate online but freedom of speech allows people to do it.

    — The best way to deal with hateful content online is to shut it down.

4. After everyone has chosen their spot, have students spend 3–5 minutes talking amongst themselves about why they are standing where they are.

5. After students are finished going through all the statements, engage them in a class discussion by asking the following questions:

    — Was it easy or difficult to decide where to stand? Were some statements easier to decide and some more difficult?

    — How did it feel when most people had the same response as you?

    — If there was a time when you were alone in where you chose to stand, how did it feel?

    — Did you ever feel you needed to explain where you chose to stand? If so, why did you feel this way?

    — Did you ever decide to change your position when you saw you did not agree with a majority of the group, or after hearing others' points of view?

6. Ask students, "What is online hate speech, also known as cyberhate?" With students, define cyberhate as follows and either distribute the *Definition of Cyberhate* handout to each student or project the definition on the board/smart board.

    Cyberhate: Any use of electronic communications technology that attacks people based on their actual or perceived race, ethnicity, national origin, religion, sex, gender, sexual orientation, disability or disease to spread bigoted or hateful messages or information. These electronic communications technologies include the Internet (i.e., websites, social networking sites, user-generated content, dating sites, blogs, online games, instant messages and email) as well as other information technologies.

7. Ask if students have any questions. Students may ask about the differences between cyberhate and cyberbullying. Remind students what **cyberbullying** is: the intentional and repeated mistreatment of others

through the use of technology, such as computers, cell phones and other electronic devices. You can explain that cyberbullying can be a form of cyberhate and both terms have similarities which include the following:

— They both use electronic communications and technology to direct negative messages to someone and they both can target a person because of their identity group, using slurs, comments and pictures/photos.

— Cyberhate is not always directed at a specific person but instead can be directed at a group of people generally (e.g., Black people, Jewish people, LGBTQ people).

— Cyberhate can include using slurs or sexist, racist, or homophobic, etc. language without attacking an individual person.

— Conversely, as a form of bullying, cyberbullying intentionally targets an individual or group of individuals, and while mean-spirited, does not always include hate speech or references to identity. For example, cyberbullying can include posting mean comments and mocking someone using texts and posting embarrassing pictures of an individual but may not include the use of slurs or other prejudicial references.

8. Ask students for examples of cyberhate they have seen, heard about or witnessed. Share an example such as the following backlash to an Old Navy ad.

Explain that in 2016, Old Navy posted an advertisement on Twitter that featured an interracial family. Within hours of posting the ad, there were extreme negative reactions to it, with people using hashtags such as #BoycottOldNavy and #WhiteGenocide in addition to messages such as "Stop promoting miscegenation or else I'm taking my $$$ elsewhere!!!" and "I don't shop at stores that are anti-White and promote race mixing." However, another set of responses surfaced soon thereafter, with people expressing their rejection of the biased messages and many posting photos of their own interracial families using the hashtag #LoveWins.

(For more information visit www.nytimes.com/2016/05/05/us/upbeat-interracial-ad-for-old-navy-leads-to-backlash-twice.html)

9. Ask students:

— What's happening here?

— What form of bias and/or discrimination was playing out?

— What did people do in response?

10. Ask students, "In thinking about being an ally, what are some ways to be an ally to someone or a group that is targeted for cyberhate? What can we do about cyberhate?" Have students call out their ideas and record on the board/smart board. If not mentioned, make sure the list includes the following ideas:

— Talk with family, friends and classmates about what you have seen.

— Respond directly to the person (if you deem it appropriate and safe).

— Learn more about how you can combat specific forms of bigotry and hate speech.

— Report it. (You can show students ADL's *Cyber-Safety Action Guide,* which lists social media and other Internet companies (e.g., YouTube, Yahoo) where you can access the companies' cyberhate policies and links to register your complaint.)

— Applaud positive content that affirms people and communicates respect for diversity.

— Be an ally in one of the 6 ways to be an ally.

— Speak out about it amongst your friends and online community.

FLIPPED CLASSROOM IDEA

Have students watch the Honey Maid *Love* video and consider what aspects of bias were operating.

11. Explain that some of the strategies above would be considered to be "counterspeech," similar to the response to the Old Navy ad backlash.

12. Ask students, "Have you ever heard the term counterspeech? What do you think it means?" Explain that **counterspeech** is a process of exposing hate speech for its dishonest, false and hurtful content, setting the record straight, and promoting the values of respect and diversity.

13. 📷 Explain to students that they are going to learn more about counterspeech by watching two short videos. Show this video of a Honey Maid commercial, *This is Wholesome* (30 seconds). Immediately afterwards, show *Love* (2 minutes). Engage students in a discussion by asking the following questions:

    — What's happening here?

    — How did you feel while watching it?

    — What kind of bias was operating in the original response to the Honey Maid commercial?

    — What was the response and why do you think it inspired that response?

    — How did people respond and how is it an example of counterspeech?

    — What message is conveyed through the video?

14. Divide students into small groups of 4–5 to develop at least one response to cyberhate using counterspeech. Explain to students that their ideas can come from something they know about it, read about or the Honey Maid example discussed above. First have a brief brainstorming session with the whole class of different possibilities for how to express the counterspeech, including the following examples:

    — Make a video.

    — Write a blog.

    — Write a comment to a Instagram, Snapchat, Facebook or Twitter posting.

    — Write a comment in response to a hateful article.

    — Create a Tumblr, Facebook page, Twitter or Instagram account in support of someone who is a target of cyberhate.

    — Create a word cloud with your message.

15. Give students 10 minutes to work on their projects. They should decide what the hate speech is they will focus on, what strategies they will use to address it and then execute their plan. At this point, it can be something simple but if interest is high, this could be a longer term project that takes several class periods to complete.

16. Have students share their examples of counterspeech with the rest of the class when completed.

Extension Activities

▰ Have students find examples of cyberhate either online directly or stories about cyberhate in the news. They should then work (independently or with a partner) to create a plan for addressing the hate which can include a variety of strategies including others mentioned in Procedure #10 above.

▰ Have students write a letter to an Internet company or product that is in response to cyberhate. In the letter, they should include where they saw the cyberhate, the extent of it, an example or two and what they feel the company should do about it.

DEFINITION OF CYBERHATE

Any use of electronic communications technology that attacks people based on their actual or perceived race, ethnicity, national origin, religion, sex, gender, sexual orientation, disability or disease to spread bigoted or hateful messages or information. These electronic communications technologies include the Internet (i.e., websites, social networking sites, user-generated content, dating sites, blogs, online games, instant messages and email) as well as other information technologies.

OLD NAVY AD TWITTER POST

 Old Navy Official ✓
@OldNavy

 Follow

Love from our family to yours

Old Navy ad with interracial family prompts social media outrage — and supp...
An Old Navy sales ad showing an interracial family drew ugly responses on Twitter, as well as a flood of support from others defending diversity.
today.com

28. EQUALITY AND EQUITY

TIME
45 minutes

COMMON CORE STANDARDS
Writing, Speaking and Listening, Language

STRATEGIES AND SKILLS
define terms, small group work

KEY WORDS AND PHRASES
affirmative action, civil rights, equality, equity, parity, prohibits, special education, suffrage

Rationale

The purpose of this lesson is to help students understand equality and equity and how they are similar and different. While most people understand the concept of equality, equity is a term that is not as well known and important especially when understanding social justice. This lesson provides an opportunity for students to understand equality and equity, reflect on examples and the differences between them and create an original drawing that illustrates the difference.

Objectives

- Students will reflect on an illustration about equity and equality.
- Students will understand how equality and equity are similar and different.
- Students will explore examples of equity and equality.
- Students will create an original drawing that illustrates the differences between equality and equity.

What's Needed

Handouts and Resources: Equality vs. Equity Illustration; Equality and Equity Definitions and *Small Group Discussion Worksheet* (one of each for each student); *Examples of Equality and Equity* (one for each group)

Other Material: Board/Smart board, paper, pencils/pens

Advance Preparation: Copy and cut the *Examples of Equality and Equity* into individual strips.

Procedures

1. Begin the lesson by projecting the *Equality vs. Equity Illustration* on the board/smart board and asking someone to read the words out loud. Then

have students take out a piece of paper and write for one full minute what the picture and the words mean to them.

2.  Get students back together and engage them in a discussion by asking the following questions:

   — What was your first reaction to the picture?

   — Describe what you see in the picture.

   — What does the picture mean to you?

   — How did you come to that conclusion?

   — Based on this picture, what is the difference between equality and equity?

FLIPPED CLASSROOM IDEA

Have students look at the *Equality vs. Equity* picture the night before and write down their thoughts and reactions to what it means to them.

3. Ask students, "Based on the picture, how would you define equality? Then ask: Based on the picture, how would you define equity?" Write the following definitions of equality and equity on the board/smart board or distribute the *Equality and Equity Definitions* handout to each student and have a student read them each aloud.

   Equality: Everyone having the same rights, opportunities and resources. Equality stresses fairness and parity (or uniformity) in having access to social goods and services.

   Equity: Everyone getting what they need in order to have access, opportunities and a fair chance to succeed. It recognizes that the same for everyone (equality) doesn't truly address needs and therefore, specific solutions and remedies (which may be different) are necessary.

4. Clarify any questions students may have about the two definitions. If you want to explain the difference using a simple example, say this:

   Pretend that one child in the class has a broken arm, another student has a cut on her finger and another child banged his knee and it is swollen.

   Then ask, "If I give a band-aid to each of these students, will it fix each of their problems? Why or why not?"

   Elicit from students that people do not always need the exact same thing. Each of these students needs something but what each of them needs is different and only one of them needs a band-aid. Explain that in our society, people should be treated with fairness and have the same opportunities, which does not necessarily mean that everyone gets or needs the exact same thing.

5. Engage students in a discussion by asking if they can come up with an example of equality. If students don't offer any examples, you can provide the following example of equality:

   Prior to 1920, nearly 100 years ago, women were not allowed to vote. There were several generations of women suffrage supporters who were involved in a movement to achieve voting rights for women, which they finally achieved in August 1920.

6. Ask students if they can come up with an example of equity; this may be more challenging. If they can't come up with any examples, provide the following example of equity:

   The Individuals with Disabilities Education Act (IDEA) is a law that ensures services to children with disabilities and those services are tailored to children's individual needs. The law requires that states provide early intervention, special education and related services to more than 6.5 million eligible infants, toddlers, children and youth with disabilities.

7. Place the *Examples of Equality and Equity* strips on a table or desk in different parts of the room. Then either divide students into six groups and randomly assign each group to one of the examples or tell students the category for each and allow them to decide which group in which to participate.

8. When everyone is situated, distribute the *Small Group Discussion Worksheet* to each student. Have one student read the example out loud to the rest of their small group and discuss what they think it means. Then, as a group, complete the worksheet, having someone record the responses (in note form) on the *Small Group Discussion Worksheet*. Give students 10–15 minutes for this task.

   Answer Key for Teachers Only (question #1): 1. Equality, 2. Equity, 3. Equality, 4. Equity, 5. Equity, 6. Equality and Equity

9. When small group work is completed, have each group present their examples of equality or equity and share how they responded to some or all of the questions. Allow a few minutes for asking and answering questions after each group presents.

10. Reflecting again on the picture discussed at the beginning of the lesson (project again for them to look at), have students create an original drawing that illustrates the difference between equality and equity. Their ideas can generate from the examples discussed in the lesson, another form of discrimination or something else. This may require more time and additional research. If that is the case, assign the additional work for homework. You may also choose to allow students to work on this in pairs.

11. Have students share their drawings by placing them around the room and having students do a gallery walk to view all of them. Engage students in a brief discussion by asking the following questions:

    — How was it to come up with the difference between equality and equity?

    — How would you describe the difference now?

    — What did you learn?

Extension Activities

▪ Based on the *Examples of Equality and Equity,* have students choose one of those for further research and investigation. Have them learn more about the issue, relevant statistics and if possible, interview adult family members about what their experience may be with the issue. Have students write a research paper or create a PowerPoint based on what they learned.

▪ Have students consider an issue or topic in which equity has not yet been achieved. In small groups, have them brainstorm what the issue is, what equity would look like and identify steps that would need to be taken in order for equity to be achieved.

EQUALITY VS. EQUITY ILLUSTRATION

Interaction Institute for Social Change | Artist: Angus Maguire

EQUALITY AND EQUITY DEFINITIONS

Equality

Everyone having the same rights, opportunities and resources. Equality stresses fairness and parity (or uniformity) in having access to social goods and services.

Equity

Everyone getting what they need in order to have access, opportunities and a fair chance to succeed. It recognizes that the same for everyone (equality) doesn't truly address needs and therefore, specific solutions and remedies (which may be different) are necessary.

EXAMPLES OF EQUALITY AND EQUITY

1. The **Fair Housing Act** protects people from discrimination when they are renting, buying or securing financing for any housing. Specifically, protections cover discrimination because of race, color, national origin, religion, sex, disability and whether there will be children living there. This act makes it illegal to refuse to rent or sell housing, have different terms or conditions for sale or rental of housing, refuse to make a mortgage loan and more to members of these groups.

2. The **Voting Rights Act** was designed to address racial discrimination in voting. It prohibits discrimination based on race, and requires certain jurisdictions to provide bilingual assistance to voters. Section 5 of the Act requires federal "preclearance" before certain jurisdictions (i.e., specified jurisdictions with a history of practices that restricted minority voting rights) may make changes in existing voting practices or procedures. The Act also provides the Department of Justice with the authority to appoint observers and examiners to monitor elections to ensure that they are conducted fairly. In 2013, the Supreme Court, in a case called *Shelby County* v. *Holder*, struck down key provisions of the Voting Rights Act of 1965.

3. **Marriage equality** provides the ability for same-sex couples to get married in the same way that opposite sex couples can get married. It grants the same rights to both gay/lesbian and heterosexual couples. Prior to marriage equality being the law in all 50 states, some states allowed same-sex couples to marry and some states did not.

4. **Affirmative action** policies are those in which an institution or organization actively engages in trying to improve opportunities and access for historically excluded groups in U.S. society. Affirmative action policies often focus on employment and education. In colleges and universities, affirmative action refers to special admission policies that increase access to education for groups that have been historically excluded or underrepresented, such as women and people of color.

5. **Title I** funds provide financial assistance to local educational agencies and schools with high numbers or high percentages of children from low-income families to help ensure that all children meet challenging state academic standards. Federal funds are currently given through pre-set formulas that are based primarily on census poverty estimates and the cost of education in each state.

6. The **Americans with Disabilities Act (ADA)** makes it unlawful to discriminate in employment against a qualified individual with a disability. The ADA also provides for "reasonable accommodation," which means making changes or adjustments to a job or work environment so that a qualified applicant or employee with a disability can participate in the job application process, perform the essential functions of a job, or enjoy benefits and privileges of employment equal to those enjoyed by employees without disabilities. For example, reasonable accommodation may include: providing or modifying equipment or devices, part-time or modified work schedules, providing readers and interpreters, and making the workplace readily accessible to and usable by people with disabilities.

SMALL GROUP DISCUSSION WORKSHEET

Directions: Discuss amongst your group what you think your assigned example of equality and equity means and answer the questions below.

1. Is this an example of equity or equality? Please explain your thinking.

2. What else do you know about this? What else do you want to know?

3. What form of discrimination or injustice is happening here?

4. Why is equality or equity needed in this case?

5. What more needs to be done?

29. **COMMUNITY ACTIONS**

Rationale

The purpose of this lesson is for students to reflect on experiences of hate in their school, community, country and the world. Learning about how other communities have stood up to hate can provide inspiration and a sense of empowerment to young people that they can do something about the bias and hate they see. This lesson provides an opportunity for students to learn about how one community stood up to hate, identify examples in their own lives of hate and bias and begin thinking about what can be done about it.

Objectives

- Students will consider ways that members of a community can work together against bias and hate.
- Students will learn about ways that the people of a specific town fought bias and hate in their community.
- Students will identify examples of hate in their own school, community, country or the world and begin to reflect on what can be done about it.

What's Needed

Handouts and Resources: Community Alliance Square and *How a Town Fought Hate* (project or provide one of each for each student)

Other Material: Board/Smart board, *Post-it Notes*® (4–8 per student), chart paper, markers

Advance Preparation: Write the following words on four separate sheets of chart paper and set aside: (1) OUR SCHOOL, (2) OUR TOWN/NEIGHBORHOOD/CITY, (3) OUR COUNTRY and (4) THE WORLD.

TIME
45 minutes

COMMON CORE STANDARDS
Reading, Writing, Speaking and Listening

STRATEGIES AND SKILLS
brainstorm, turn and talk, large group discussion

KEY WORDS AND PHRASES
community, graffiti, harassment, institution, intimidated, Ku Klux Klan, swastika

Procedures

1. Begin the lesson by explaining that students will examine some of the things that members of towns, communities or neighborhoods do to fight bias, prejudice and hate. Review with students the ways they have learned about being an ally both online and in person.

2. Ask students to try to imagine the following events and pay attention to how they feel while listening to each scenario.

   — You are sitting in your home when a large object (like a brick) comes flying through the window, narrowly missing you and sending pieces of glass everywhere.

   — Swastikas are painted on the wall of a synagogue you see on your way to school.

   — Racist graffiti is painted outside the community center where you and your friends play basketball.

   — The Ku Klux Klan and other organized hate groups hold a rally in your community, spreading negative and hateful messages about your cultural group or cultural groups to which many of your friends belong.

3. Have students call out the different feelings they had while listening to the events and record the words on the board/smart board. Then ask, "What do you notice about the words and feelings on the board?"

4. Engage students in a class discussion by asking the following questions:

   — How do you think people feel when they are the targets of hateful words and actions like the ones you just heard about?

   — How do you think other community members, who are not the targets but who live there, feel when others are targeted?

   — What can people do to show they are allies?

   — What can institutions (such as schools, police, newspapers, government, community-based organizations, houses of worship, businesses, etc.) do to show they are allies?

   — What are the possible risks in getting involved in such actions?

   — Do you think it is more or less effective for individuals or institutions to speak out against bias and hate?

   — What might happen if everyone remained a bystander in these situations?

5. Using the scenarios described at the beginning of the lesson, have students turn and talk with a partner and share a few ideas they have about some actions people and institutions in the community might take together to show that they are allies to those who have become the targets of bias and hate. Have students spend five minutes sharing with each other; one person should jot down their ideas. Then have students come back to the whole group and share their ideas and record on the board/smart board under the heading "Community Responses to Bias and Hate." They may include ideas such as the following:

   — Organize a rally or demonstration in the town.

   — Write letters to a local newspaper stating that hate actions are unacceptable.

   — Sign and/or circulate a petition.

   — Tear down hate posters and seek permission to paint over graffiti.

   — Write letters to local officials to join with them to fight hate.

6. Explain to students that responses can include one-time actions (like signing a petition) or ongoing or long-term actions (like holding regular community meetings). On the board/smart board or chart paper share the

Community Alliance Square handout, filling it in together with students' ideas and using the ones already noted as examples.

7.  / ↗ Distribute the *How a Town Fought Hate* handout to each student. Give students 10 minutes to read the article or read aloud together, with students taking turns.

8. Engage students in a discussion by asking the following questions:

   — In what ways did the people of Billings show that they were allies to those who were targets of hate?

   — Were the ally behaviors one-time actions, long-term actions or a combination of both? How so?

   — What kinds of risks did the people of Billings take when they decided to take action against what was happening in their community?

   — What are some of the possible risks people take (in general) when they decide to become allies?

   — What do you think the community of Billings should do to continue sending the message that hate has no place there?

9. Ask students for some examples of bias and hate in (1) our school, (2) our town/neighborhood/city, (3) our country and (4) the world. Distribute 4–8 *Post-it Notes®* to each student and have them write down their examples on post-its. As students are recording their examples, put the four pieces of chart paper prepared in advance around the room. When students are done, have them post their notes on the appropriate piece of chart paper. When students finish pasting their post-its around the room, either have students walk around the room to see all the notes or have a student read aloud what is on each sheet. Save the charts or the examples on there for the next lesson, "Social Justice in My World."

10. Engage students in a brief discussion by asking the following questions:

   — Was it easy or difficult to come up with examples of hate and bias? How so?

   — What did you notice as you walked around the room (or listened to what was on each paper)?

   — What do you think we can do about the bias and hate in our school, community and world?

Extension Activities

▰ Have students develop a Community Alliance Square for one of the examples of bias and hate that they shared in the lesson. Have them think through the steps it would take to implement their ideas and what they would need to execute at least one of their ideas.

FLIPPED CLASSROOM IDEA

Make a short video of you reading aloud *How a Town Fought Hate* and then ask some of the questions in #8 for students to consider.

↗ **ALTERNATIVE**

Instead of the *How a Town Fought Hate* story, you can share this incident that occurred in New York City: "Subway Riders Rise Up To Clean Swastikas From New York Train" by Nina Golgowski, *The Huffington Post*, www.huffingtonpost.com/entry/subway-riders-clean-swastikas_us_589728a8e4b0c1284f265adb. Read the article aloud (or have students read silently) and then adjust the questions in #8 as needed.

■ Invite someone from a local government agency to speak with the class about what programs and policies are in place to ensure that community members are safe from bias and hate. Have students prepare a list of questions in advance for the guest and have students write up the interview in essay format afterwards.

COMMUNITY ALLIANCE SQUARE

	INDIVIDUAL ACTION	COMMUNITY ACTION
One-time	▰ Interrupt a biased joke ▰ Sign a petition	▰ Paint over hateful graffiti ▰ Attend a rally
Ongoing	▰ Make a commitment to always interrupt biased language and jokes	▰ Hold monthly community meetings to discuss areas of concern and develop an action plan

HOW A TOWN FOUGHT HATE

In the mid-1980s, some hate groups declared the northwestern part of the United States to be their "homeland." These hate groups were becoming more and more violent in the region. In 1986, the Aryan Nations organization declared its intention to make the region a place where only Whites and Christians could own property, vote, conduct business, bear arms and hold public office. Incidents of harassment and violence against "minority" groups became more and more common. It was not long before Billings, Montana, a city in southern Montana found itself the target of a series of hateful incidents. Billings, with a population of approximately 82,000 people, is the largest city in Montana and the commercial, shipping and processing center of a region that produces cattle, wheat and sugar beets. Billings is the gateway to Yellowstone National Park, the Crow Indian Reservation and the Little Bighorn Battlefield National Monument.

In 1993, Ku Klux Klan fliers were distributed around Billings, tombstones in the Jewish cemetery were overturned, the home of a Native American family was spray painted with swastikas, members of an African-American church were intimidated and bricks were thrown through windows of homes that displayed menorahs for the Jewish holiday of Chanukah.

Rather than accept what was happening in their community, people decided to take a stand against hate. Those who were not targets, became allies to those who were. City officials and law enforcement officers made strong statements against the activities. The Painters Union formed a work force to paint over the graffiti. Religious and community leaders sponsored human rights activities. The local newspaper printed full-page menorahs for display in homes and businesses throughout the town. Most of the 10,000 people who decided to display the menorahs were not Jewish; they displayed the symbols to show that they were unwilling to accept hate in their community. In a show of support, people attended religious services at an African-American church where the congregation was being harassed and intimidated by members of hate groups.

Actions by the people of Billings, Montana became a model for other communities around the country who also spoke out against hate. The motto for such community actions became known as "Not in Our Town."

30. SOCIAL JUSTICE IN MY WORLD

Rationale

The purpose of this lesson is for students to create a social action project that addresses an issue of injustice that is important to them. Conveying the idea that young people can do something about the injustice they see in the world is an important message and motivation for engaging in social activism. This lesson provides an opportunity to identify what issues are important to them, consider a variety of social action projects and implement a project that changes the world in some way.

[**NOTE:** The poetry reading and writing part of this lesson assumes that students have had some instruction in and exposure to the form, elements and figurative language in poetry. Included in the lesson is a sample poem to read aloud, a poetry worksheet and elements of poetry that students will use to write their own poems.]

Objectives

▰ Students will identify what issues of bias, hate and injustice are important to them and write a social justice poem about it.

▰ Students will consider social action projects that would address the inequities stemming from the issues of bias, hate and injustice.

▰ Students will develop and implement a social action project around an issue of injustice in their school, community or world.

What's Needed

Handouts and Resources: I, Too; Poetry Worksheet; Elements of Poetry; 10 Ways to Engage in Activism and *Social Action Project Planning* (one of each for each student)

TIME
60 minutes

COMMON CORE STANDARDS
Reading, Writing, Speaking and Listening, Language

STRATEGIES AND SKILLS
turn and talk, write poems, large and small group discussion, brainstorm

KEY WORDS AND PHRASES
activism, poetry elements (words from handout)

FLIPPED CLASSROOM IDEA

Have students watch a video reading of "I, Too" from *The Great Debaters* film at www.youtube.com/watch?v=TuRQDrySOVQ.

Procedures

1.  Begin the lesson by reading aloud the poem, "I, Too" by Langston Hughes. To get students to think a little bit about form and poetry elements, engage students in a brief discussion by asking the following questions:

   — How do you feel while listening to the poem?

   — What is the message of the poem?

   — What form does it use?

   — What are some of the images and symbols in the poem that are meaningful?

   — What figurative language is used?

2. Bring out the list of examples of bias, hate and injustice in their school, community, country or world completed during Lesson 29, "Community Actions". Ask students if they want to add any issues to the list. Conduct a brief brainstorming session so that the list of ideas includes a wide range of examples. The list might look something like this:

   — Bullying in my school

   — Police violence against black and Latino men

   — Girls not being able to get educated like Malala

   — Lack of wheelchair accessibility in buses and on streets

   — Animals being abused by their owners

   — Girls getting dress-coded at school

3. Have students reflect on the list and decide on one topic that is important to them. Explain that they are going to write a poem about that issue of bias, hate or injustice. Have students either close their eyes or free their minds in some way and ask the following questions about their issue/topic:

   — When you think about your example of bias and hate, how do you feel?

   — What pictures or images do you see in your mind?

   — What sounds do you hear? Smells?

   — What words, phrases or sayings come to mind?

   — What is a vivid example of this bias? What can be done about this injustice?

4. Next, have students write their issue at the top of a piece of paper and write down their thoughts and feelings from the reflection that include words, phrases, ideas, images and feelings they want to convey with the poem. Have students turn and talk with a partner, sharing their words

and phrases and each taking turns asking each other questions. After sharing with their partner, they can add additional words or phrases to the list that came up during their discussion.

5. If you haven't already done poetry with your students or if you want to review, distribute and go over the *Elements of Poetry* handout, talking about each element and how it can be used in poetry. Then give students 15–20 minutes to write their poems, either beginning with free writing or a combination of free writing and using the *Poetry Worksheet* questions and responses.

6. Depending on how long you give students to complete their poems (you could use the writing process with conferencing and revising), have students practice and then perform their poetry aloud. Consider video or audio taping their oral presentations of their poems or inviting other classes and family members in for a performance of their poetry read aloud.

7. After constructing their poems about the issues, begin to brainstorm solutions to those issues by asking students to think about the examples of bias, hate and injustice that they wrote poems about or that their classmates wrote. Ask students, "In these situations of bias or injustice, what would social justice or the lack of hate look like? What do we need and how do we get there? What steps do we need to take?" After initial brainstorming, distribute the *10 Ways to Engage in Activism* handout to each student, reading the ideas aloud. Based on these ideas, do another round of brainstorming of ideas about what can be done about bias, hate and injustice.

8. Based on the topics of bias and injustice identified in the previous activity, identify 4–5 social action projects of highest interest to students. You can do this by trying to come up to consensus or if that doesn't work, you may want to have individual students speak on behalf of choosing a particular issue and then have the class vote. The list could look something like this:
   − Design and circulate a petition about police violence
   − Hold anti-bullying workshops in my school
   − Make a video about biased language
   − Write letters to my congressperson about anti-LGBT legislation in my state

9. Based on the 4–5 ideas, have students select one of the ideas for a social action project they want to pursue and begin talking together as a group about what they are going to do to address the problem. They can begin by brainstorming ideas and beginning to complete the *Social Action Project Planning* form. Over the next few weeks or longer, have students engage in a process for bringing their projects to fruition.

Extension Activities

■ After completing their social action projects, have students write another poem about the way they used activism to make a difference in their school, community or world. They can then merge the two poems together (the one about the issue and the one about their activism) to come up with a new poem.

■ Have students interview their parents, adult family members or friends of the family about their experience with activism, reflecting on their experiences as youth themselves or about others they knew who engaged in activism. They can create the questions in advance and while they are conducting the interview, either take notes and write the interview up in essay format or videotape the interview and make it available for others to watch.

I, TOO

By Langston Hughes

Langston Hughes (1902-1967)
Photographer Jack Delano

Courtesy of the Library of Congress Prints
and Photographs Division, LC-USZ62-43605.

I, too, sing America.

I am the darker brother.
They send me to eat in the kitchen
When company comes,
But I laugh,
And eat well,
And grow strong.

Tomorrow,
I'll sit at the table
When company comes.
Nobody'll dare
Say to me,
"Eat in the kitchen,"
Then.

Besides,
They'll see how beautiful I am
And be ashamed—

I, too, am America.

ELEMENTS OF POETRY

▶ **Alliteration**

The repetition of initial sounds on the same line or stanza.

▶ **Metaphor**

Figure of speech which makes an implicit, implied or hidden comparison between two things or objects that are very different but have some characteristics common between them.

▶ **Personification**

The projection of characteristics that normally belong only to humans onto inanimate objects, animals, deities, or forces of nature.

▶ **Repetition**

The repetition of the same word throughout the poem to emphasize significance.

▶ **Rhyme**

The repetition of sounds within different words, either end sound, middle or beginning.

▶ **Rhythm**

The flow of words within each meter and stanza.

▶ **Simile**

Figure of speech that makes a comparison, showing similarities between two different things. Unlike a metaphor, a simile draws resemblance using words "like" or "as."

▶ **Symbol**

Something that represents something else through association, resemblance or convention.

POETRY WORKSHEET

MY TOPIC:
Central theme of message or poem
Some words, phrases, ideas, images and feelings I want to convey with the poem
What form do I want to use (e.g., free verse, ballad, haiku, acrostic, ode, etc.)?
What mood or tone do I want to convey to the reader?

POETRY ELEMENTS
(Refer to the *Elements of Poetry* handout to determine and list below the elements you will use in your poem.)

Poetry Element	How I Might Use It

10 WAYS TO ENGAGE IN ACTIVISM

Young people are powerful agents for change.

Our country has a long history of youth-led movements that brought about significant social change. Young people have advocated for child labor laws, voting rights, civil rights, school desegregation, immigration reform and LGBT rights. Through their actions, the world has changed. Because young people often have the desire, energy and idealism to do something about the injustice they see in the world, they are powerful agents for change.

Our work in education helps students examine implicit and overt forms of bias and discrimination and as a result, educators often feel a responsibility to provide students with the structure, opportunity and tools to do something about the injustice they see in the world. Transforming students' feelings of anger, sadness and hopelessness into concrete actions that can make the world better is a vital teaching opportunity. Voting is one way to get your voice heard but there are a myriad of ways young people can make a difference.

Below are ideas for bringing social activism into the classroom and outside of the school walls. These are lifelong skills and attitudes that teach students about citizenship and that there is something you can do when faced with injustice. The strategies can be acted upon individually, organized together as a group and young people can join with a larger effort that is taking place locally or nationally. The tactics also bring opportunities for students to read, write, research, think critically and talk with each other.

1. Educate others.

As students learn about an issue they care about, their natural instinct is to share their new knowledge and insight with others. Encourage this by providing live and online opportunities for them to teach others, including their classmates, younger students and adults in their lives. This can include school assemblies, community forums, teach-ins, peer education programs and social media forums. Include opportunities to share the information in interesting ways (written, art, theatre, etc.) and they should also give other students the chance to explore their own thoughts and feelings about the topics. Youth who want to know more may be more likely to learn from another young person.

2. Advocate for legislation.

Change comes about in a variety of ways and one of these is through legislative change. For example, the primary advocates for the DREAM Act have been young people known as the DREAMers, who have a personal investment in the issue. With your students, provide opportunities for them to learn about the history and impact of legislative change like the Civil Rights Act of 1964. Help them analyze proposed legislation in relation to their goals and assess the extent to which it will have an impact. They can study research that examines the extent to which legislation impacted injustice. Have students push for legislation by working with other groups with similar goals, building coalitions and writing letters to their legislators to advocate for specific local, state and federal laws.

3. Run for office.

Student government provides a chance for students to have a positive impact in their school and learn about how government works on a small scale. It gives youth the experience to reflect on and consolidate their own positions on important school issues, learn how to communicate those positions, build relationships with others and become a good listener in understanding constituent (i.e., other students) needs. It is also good practice for the future in getting involved in politics. Elected positions are not the only way to get involved; students can also become involved in groups like the Gay-Straight Alliance (GSA), peer training or other task forces that are working to improve their school.

4. Demonstrate.

Marching in the streets enables students to express themselves while meeting and connecting with other people who feel passionate about the same issues. Demonstrations and protests can be uplifting and empowering and can help students feel like they are part of a larger movement. In preparing to attend a demonstration or protest, have students consider what their goals are in attending the event and think through what message they want to convey. They can create posters, prepare songs or chants and practice symbolism that conveys their thoughts and feelings. They should consider whether they want to go individually or organize a group of students from their school to go together, make transportation arrangements and ensure that safety concerns are addressed.

5. Create a public awareness campaign that includes social media.

There are many ways to develop or participate in a public awareness campaign Educating people about an issue in order to inspire change can take place in school, in the community and online. Creating signs and posters using art and photography can be very effective as can videos and live speeches; these are all useful skills that young people can learn. In recent years, the use of social media to raise public awareness has been largely driven by young people and is a useful vehicle for raising issues and effecting change. The use of blogs, social networking sites such as Facebook, Instagram and Tumblr, videos, memes and online petitions are just a few examples of how words travel fast online and can incite quick and effective action.

6. Do a survey about the issue and share the results.

Understanding what people think and why is helpful in bringing about social change. Students can learn more about public opinions on issues by participating in surveys themselves and also reading about them. They can also create their own surveys. Using paper surveys or online surveys, students can gain insight into how other students in their school or the larger community feel about an issue. This is useful in organizing others and addressing their concerns and needs; at the same time it builds math, critical thinking and interpersonal skills.

7. Raise money.

Raising money is a concrete way for students to contribute to community or national efforts to address injustice. From organizing a bake sale around a local issue to fundraising on a larger scale for a national concern like racial disparities in the criminal justice system, raising money helps students feel like they are part of something bigger and backs the cause. Fundraisers can include selling items, auctions, entertainment, sponsoring events and more.

8. Write a letter to a company.

Students can reach out to companies or organizations that they feel have done something unfair or biased. This is a small act but can be an important experience for them in making a difference. For example, if students want to change the ways toy companies use gender role stereotypes to package and sell their toys or games, have them write letters to toy or video game companies and explain why they think their practices are biased. In crafting a well-written letter with evidence and a clear statement of what needs to change, students learn useful skills in persuasion and at the same time, it has a made a difference.

9. Engage in community service.

In addition to organizing and advocating on a large scale, students should be encouraged to engage in community service on issues they care about. For example, if they are concerned about the stereotypes and violence directed at homeless people, in addition to advocating for legislation or attending a demonstration, students can also donate their time to help out in a homeless shelter or soup kitchen. Serving the people who are directly impacted gives young people firsthand knowledge of the situation, deepens their understanding and builds empathy.

10. Get the press involved.

Help students understand that bringing publicity to their issue amplifies the message, gets more people concerned and potentially has a greater impact. They can write a press release, do an interview, write an op-ed in their local paper or invite a reporter to see what they are doing and write something about it. This sharpens their own message and serves to bring that message to a larger group of people.

SOCIAL ACTION PROJECT PLANNING

Group Members: _____

What is the issue of hate, bias or injustice our group is addressing: _____

Social action project: _____

Goal	Activities/Actions	Timeline	People	Resources
What do we want to happen? What is the end result we hope to achieve?	What actions and activities are needed to reach our goal?	When will specific tasks be started and completed?	Who will do what?	What is needed to complete each specific task: supplies, people, permissions, space, funding, etc.

APPENDIX. CORRELATION OF LESSONS TO THE COMMON CORE LEARNING STANDARDS

Unit I. Setting a Respectful Classroom Tone

Content Area/Standard	L1	L2	L3	L4	L5
Reading					
R.7: Integrate and evaluate content presented in diverse media and formats, including visually and quantitatively, as well as in words.		X	X	X	
Writing					
W.1: Write arguments to support claims in an analysis of substantive topics or texts, using valid reasoning and relevant and sufficient evidence.	X				
W.2: Write informative/explanatory texts to examine and convey complex ideas and information clearly and accurately through the effective selection, organization, and analysis of content.					X
W.3: Write narratives to develop real or imagined experiences or events using effective technique, well-chosen details and well-structured event sequences.		X		X	
W.4: Produce clear and coherent writing in which the development, organization, and style are appropriate to task, purpose and audience.				X	X
W.7: Conduct short as well as more sustained research projects based on focused questions, demonstrating understanding of the subject under investigation.					X
Speaking and Listening					
SL.1: Prepare for and participate effectively in a range of conversations and collaborations with diverse partners, building on others' ideas and expressing their own clearly and persuasively.	X	X	X	X	X
SL.2: Integrate and evaluate information presented in diverse media and formats, including visually, quantitatively and orally.			X		
SL.3: Evaluate a speaker's point of view, reasoning and use of evidence and rhetoric.	X	X	X		
SL.4: Present information, findings and supporting evidence such that listeners can follow the line of reasoning and the organization, development and style are appropriate to task, purpose and audience.		X	X		
SL.5: Make strategic use of digital media and visual displays of data to express information and enhance understanding of presentations.	X		X		

Content Area/Standard	L1	L2	L3	L4	L5
Language					
L.3: Apply knowledge of language to understand how language functions in different contexts, to make effective choices for meaning or style, and to comprehend more fully when reading or listening.		X		X	
L.5: Demonstrate understanding of figurative language, word relationships and nuances in word meanings.		X	X	X	

Unit II. Identity and Differences

Content Area/Standard	L6	L7	L8	L9	L10
Reading					
R.1: Read closely to determine what the text says explicitly and to make logical inferences from it; cite specific textual evidence when writing or speaking to support conclusions drawn from the text.		X			
R.3: Analyze how and why individuals, events or ideas develop and interact over the course of a text.		X			
R.6: Assess how point of view or purpose shapes the content and style of a text.		X			
R.7: Integrate and evaluate content presented in diverse media and formats, including visually and quantitatively, as well as in words.				X	
R.9: Analyze how two or more texts address similar themes or topics in order to build knowledge or to compare the approaches the authors take.		X			
Writing					
W.2: Write informative/explanatory texts to examine and convey complex ideas and information clearly and accurately through the effective selection, organization and analysis of content.	X	X			X
W.3: Write narratives to develop real or imagined experiences or events using effective technique, well-chosen details and well-structured event sequences.	X	X		X	X
W.4: Produce clear and coherent writing in which the development, organization and style are appropriate to task, purpose and audience.	X				
W.6: Use technology, including the Internet, to produce and publish writing and to interact and collaborate with others.	X	X			X
W.7: Conduct short as well as more sustained research projects based on focused questions, demonstrating understanding of the subject under investigation.		X	X		X
W.8: Gather relevant information from multiple print and digital sources, assess the credibility and accuracy of each source, and integrate the information while avoiding plagiarism.	X		X		
W.9: Draw evidence from literary or informational texts to support analysis, reflection and research.		X			
Speaking and Listening					
SL.1: Prepare for and participate effectively in a range of conversations and collaborations with diverse partners, building on others' ideas and expressing their own clearly and persuasively.	X	X	X	X	X
SL.2: Integrate and evaluate information presented in diverse media and formats, including visually, quantitatively and orally.	X				

Content Area/Standard	L6	L7	L8	L9	L10
SL.3: Evaluate a speaker's point of view, reasoning and use of evidence and rhetoric.				X	X
SL.4: Present information, findings, and supporting evidence such that listeners can follow the line of reasoning and the organization, development and style are appropriate to task, purpose and audience.	X	X	X	X	
SL.5: Make strategic use of digital media and visual displays of data to express information and enhance understanding of presentations.	X	X	X		X
Language					
L.3: Apply knowledge of language to understand how language functions in different contexts, to make effective choices for meaning or style, and to comprehend more fully when reading or listening.				X	X
L.4: Determine or clarify the meaning of unknown and multiple-meaning words and phrases by using context clues, analyzing meaningful word parts, and consulting general and specialized reference materials, as appropriate.	X	X			
L.5: Demonstrate understanding of figurative language, word relationships and nuances in word meanings.		X		X	
L.6: Acquire and use accurately a range of general academic and domain-specific words and phrases sufficient for reading, writing, speaking and listening at the college and career readiness level; demonstrate independence in gathering vocabulary knowledge when considering a word or phrase important to comprehension or expression.	X	X	X	X	

Unit III. Analyzing Where We Get Information

Content Area/Standard	L11	L12	L13	L14	L15	L16
Reading						
R.1: Read closely to determine what the text says explicitly and to make logical inferences from it; cite specific textual evidence when writing or speaking to support conclusions drawn from the text.	X	X		X	X	
R.2: Determine central ideas or themes of a text and analyze their development; summarize the key supporting details and ideas.		X		X		
R.3: Analyze how and why individuals, events or ideas develop and interact over the course of a text.					X	
R.6: Assess how point of view or purpose shapes the content and style of a text.	X	X		X		
R.7: Integrate and evaluate content presented in diverse media and formats, including visually and quantitatively, as well as in words.		X		X		X
R.9: Analyze how two or more texts address similar themes or topics in order to build knowledge or to compare the approaches the authors take.	X	X		X		
Writing						
W.1: Write arguments to support claims in an analysis of substantive topics or texts, using valid reasoning and relevant and sufficient evidence.	X	X	X			X
W.2: Write informative/explanatory texts to examine and convey complex ideas and information clearly and accurately through the effective selection, organization and analysis of content.		X		X	X	
W.3: Write narratives to develop real or imagined experiences or events using effective technique, well-chosen details and well-structured event sequences.		X	X		X	
W.4: Produce clear and coherent writing in which the development, organization and style are appropriate to task, purpose and audience.	X			X		
W.5: Develop and strengthen writing as needed by planning, revising, editing, rewriting or trying a new approach.	X					
W.6: Use technology, including the Internet, to produce and publish writing and to interact and collaborate with others.				X		
W.7: Conduct short as well as more sustained research projects based on focused questions, demonstrating understanding of the subject under investigation.	X		X			X

Content Area/Standard	L11	L12	L13	L14	L15	L16
W.8: Gather relevant information from multiple print and digital sources, assess the credibility and accuracy of each source, and integrate the information while avoiding plagiarism.	X		X	X		
W.9: Draw evidence from literary or informational texts to support analysis, reflection and research.	X					
W.10: Write routinely over extended time frames (time for research, reflection and revision) and shorter time frames (a single sitting or a day or two) for a range of tasks, purposes, and audiences.			X			
Speaking and Listening						
SL.1: Prepare for and participate effectively in a range of conversations and collaborations with diverse partners, building on others' ideas and expressing their own clearly and persuasively.	X	X	X	X	X	X
SL.2: Integrate and evaluate information presented in diverse media and formats, including visually, quantitatively and orally.		X	X	X		X
SL.3: Evaluate a speaker's point of view, reasoning and use of evidence and rhetoric.	X	X	X	X		X
SL.4: Present information, findings and supporting evidence such that listeners can follow the line of reasoning and the organization, development and style are appropriate to task, purpose and audience.			X	X	X	
SL.5: Make strategic use of digital media and visual displays of data to express information and enhance understanding of presentations.					X	X
Language						
L.3: Apply knowledge of language to understand how language functions in different contexts, to make effective choices for meaning or style, and to comprehend more fully when reading or listening.					X	
L.5: Demonstrate understanding of figurative language, word relationships and nuances in word meanings.	X					X
L.6: Acquire and use accurately a range of general academic and domain-specific words and phrases sufficient for reading, writing, speaking and listening at the college and career readiness level; demonstrate independence in gathering vocabulary knowledge when considering a word or phrase important to comprehension or expression.				X		X

Unit IV. Understanding Bullying, Bias and Injustice

Content Area/Standard	L17	L18	L19	L20	L21	L22	L23
Reading							
R.1: Read closely to determine what the text says explicitly and to make logical inferences from it; cite specific textual evidence when writing or speaking to support conclusions drawn from the text.			X	X	X		X
R.2: Determine central ideas or themes of a text and analyze their development; summarize the key supporting details and ideas.					X		
R.7: Integrate and evaluate content presented in diverse media and formats, including visually and quantitatively, as well as in words.	X	X	X	X			X
Writing							
W.1: Write arguments to support claims in an analysis of substantive topics or texts, using valid reasoning and relevant and sufficient evidence.		X					
W.2: Write informative/explanatory texts to examine and convey complex ideas and information clearly and accurately through the effective selection, organization and analysis of content.	X						X
W.3: Write narratives to develop real or imagined experiences or events using effective technique, well-chosen details and well-structured event sequences.	X	X		X		X	
W.4: Produce clear and coherent writing in which the development, organization and style are appropriate to task, purpose and audience.		X					X
W.6: Use technology, including the Internet, to produce and publish writing and to interact and collaborate with others.	X			X		X	
W.7: Conduct short as well as more sustained research projects based on focused questions, demonstrating understanding of the subject under investigation.				X			X
W.8: Gather relevant information from multiple print and digital sources, assess the credibility and accuracy of each source, and integrate the information while avoiding plagiarism.				X			X
Speaking and Listening							
SL.1: Prepare for and participate effectively in a range of conversations and collaborations with diverse partners, building on others' ideas and expressing their own clearly and persuasively.	X	X	X	X	X	X	X
SL.2: Integrate and evaluate information presented in diverse media and formats, including visually, quantitatively and orally.		X			X	X	

Content Area/Standard	L17	L18	L19	L20	L21	L22	L23
SL.3: Evaluate a speaker's point of view, reasoning and use of evidence and rhetoric.	X		X	X	X	X	X
SL.4: Present information, findings and supporting evidence such that listeners can follow the line of reasoning and the organization, development and style are appropriate to task, purpose and audience.	X	X	X	X			X
SL.5: Make strategic use of digital media and visual displays of data to express information and enhance understanding of presentations.				X		X	X
Language							
L.3: Apply knowledge of language to understand how language functions in different contexts, to make effective choices for meaning or style, and to comprehend more fully when reading or listening.			X				X
L.4: Determine or clarify the meaning of unknown and multiple-meaning words and phrases by using context clues, analyzing meaningful word parts, and consulting general and specialized reference materials, as appropriate.			X	X	X		
L.5: Demonstrate understanding of figurative language, word relationships and nuances in word meanings.				X			
L.6: Acquire and use accurately a range of general academic and domain-specific words and phrases sufficient for reading, writing, speaking and listening at the college and career readiness level; demonstrate independence in gathering vocabulary knowledge when considering a word or phrase important to comprehension or expression.	X		X		X	X	X

Unit V. Challenging Bias and Injustice

Content Area/Standard	L24	L25	L26	L27	L28	L29	L30
Reading							
R.1: Read closely to determine what the text says explicitly and to make logical inferences from it; cite specific textual evidence when writing or speaking to support conclusions drawn from the text.		X				X	X
R.3: Analyze how and why individuals, events or ideas develop and interact over the course of a text.						X	
R.4: Interpret words and phrases as they are used in a text, including determining technical, connotative and figurative meanings, and analyze how specific word choices shape meaning or tone.							X
R.5: Analyze the structure of texts, including how specific sentences, paragraphs and larger portions of the text (e.g., a section, chapter, scene, or stanza) relate to each other and the whole.							X
R.6: Assess how point of view or purpose shapes the content and style of a text.		X					X
R.7: Integrate and evaluate content presented in diverse media and formats, including visually and quantitatively, as well as in words.				X			X
Writing							
W.1: Write arguments to support claims in an analysis of substantive topics or texts, using valid reasoning and relevant and sufficient evidence.				X	X		
W.2: Write informative/explanatory texts to examine and convey complex ideas and information clearly and accurately through the effective selection, organization and analysis of content.	X	X				X	
W.3: Write narratives to develop real or imagined experiences or events using effective technique, well-chosen details and well-structured event sequences.	X	X				X	X
W.4: Produce clear and coherent writing in which the development, organization and style are appropriate to task, purpose and audience.		X		X		X	X
W.5: Develop and strengthen writing as needed by planning, revising, editing, rewriting or trying a new approach.							X
W.6: Use technology, including the Internet, to produce and publish writing and to interact and collaborate with others.							X

Content Area/Standard	L24	L25	L26	L27	L28	L29	L30
W.7: Conduct short as well as more sustained research projects based on focused questions, demonstrating understanding of the subject under investigation.					X		
W.8: Gather relevant information from multiple print and digital sources, assess the credibility and accuracy of each source, and integrate the information while avoiding plagiarism.					X		X
W.9: Draw evidence from literary or informational texts to support analysis, reflection and research.							X
Speaking and Listening							
SL.1: Prepare for and participate effectively in a range of conversations and collaborations with diverse partners, building on others' ideas and expressing their own clearly and persuasively.	X	X	X	X	X	X	X
SL.2: Integrate and evaluate information presented in diverse media and formats, including visually, quantitatively and orally.	X		X	X			X
SL.3: Evaluate a speaker's point of view, reasoning, and use of evidence and rhetoric.		X			X		X
SL.4: Present information, findings and supporting evidence such that listeners can follow the line of reasoning and the organization, development and style are appropriate to task, purpose and audience.				X	X		X
SL.5: Make strategic use of digital media and visual displays of data to express information and enhance understanding of presentations.			X	X	X		X
Language							
L.4: Determine or clarify the meaning of unknown and multiple-meaning words and phrases by using context clues, analyzing meaningful word parts, and consulting general and specialized reference materials, as appropriate.							X
L.5: Demonstrate understanding of figurative language, word relationships and nuances in word meanings.	X		X	X	X		X
L.6: Acquire and use accurately a range of general academic and domain-specific words and phrases sufficient for reading, writing, speaking and listening at the college and career readiness level; demonstrate independence in gathering vocabulary knowledge when considering a word or phrase important to comprehension or expression.	X			X	X		X

BIBLIOGRAPHY

Books

Alexander, Michelle. *The New Jim Crow: Mass Incarceration in the Age of Colorblindness.* New York: The New Press, 2012.

Au, Wayne, Bill Bigelow, and Stan Karp. *Rethinking Our Classrooms: Teaching for Equity and Justice,* Vol. 1. Milwaukee: Rethinking Schools, 2007.

Ayers, William, Jean A. Hunt, and Therese Quinn, eds. *Teaching for Social Justice: A Democracy and Education Reader.* New York: The New Press, 1998.

Banks, James A. *Educating Citizens in a Multicultural Society,* 2nd ed. New York: Teachers College Press, 2007.

Bigelow, Bill, Brenda Harvey, Stan Karp, and Larry Miller. *Rethinking Our Classrooms: Teaching for Equity and Justice,* Vol. 2. Milwaukee: Rethinking Schools, 2004.

Bodine, Richard J., Donna K. Crawford, and Fred Schrumpf. *Creating the Peaceable School: A Comprehensive Program for Teaching Conflict Resolution,* Program Guide, 2nd ed. Champaign: Research Press, 2003.

Bolgatz, Jane. *Talking Race in the Classroom.* New York: Teachers College Press, 2005.

Coloroso, Barbara. *The Bully, the Bullied and the Bystander: From Preschool to High School—How Parents and Teacher Can Help Break the Cycle of Violence.* New York: William Morrow Paperbacks, 2009.

Darling-Hammond, Linda, Jennifer French, and Silvia P. Garcia-Lopez, eds. *Learning to Teach for Social Justice.* New York: Teachers College Press, 2002.

Delpit, Lisa. *"Multiplication is for White People": Raising Expectations for Other People's Children.* New York: The New Press, 2012.

Delpit, Lisa. *Other People's Children: Cultural Conflict in the Classroom.* New York: The New Press, 2006.

Elias, Maurice, Joseph Zins, and Roger P. Weissberg. *Promoting Social and Emotional Learning: Guidelines for Educators.* Alexandria: Association for Supervision and Curriculum Development, 1997.

Fergus, Edward, Pedro Noguera, and Margary Martin. *Schooling for Resilience: Improving the Life Trajectory of Black and Latino Boys.* Cambridge: Harvard Education Press, 2014.

Garbarino, James, and Ellen deLara. *And Words Can Hurt Forever: How to Protect Adolescents from Bullying, Harassment, and Emotional Violence.* New York: Free Press, 2003.

Gay, Geneva, ed. *Becoming Multicultural Educators: Personal Journey Toward Professionalism.* San Francisco: Jossey-Bass, 2003.

Harry, Beth, and Janette Klingner. *Why Are So Many Minority Students in Special Education?: Understanding Race and Disability in Schools,* 2nd ed. New York: Teachers College Press, 2014.

Howard, Gary R. *We Can't Teach What We Don't Know: White Teachers, Multiracial Schools,* 2nd ed. New York: Teachers College Press, 2006.

Kozol, Jonathan. *Savage Inequalities: Children in America's Schools.* New York: Broadway Books, 2012.

Lee, Enid, Deborah Menkart, and Margo Okazawa-Rey, eds. *Beyond Heroes and Holidays: A Practical Guide to K-12 Anti-Racist, Mulitcultural Education and Staff Development.* Washington, DC: Teaching for Change, 2007.

Lewis, Amanda E., and Myra Bluebond-Langner, eds. *Race in the Schoolyard: Negotiating the Color Line in Classroom and Communities.* Piscataway: Rutgers University Press, 2003.

Nieto, Sonia, and Patty Bode. *Affirming Diversity: The Sociopolitical Context of Multicultural Education,* 6th ed. Old Tappan: Pearson, 2011.

Schniedewind Nancy, and Ellen Davidson. *Open Minds to Equality: A Sourcebook of Learning Activities to Affirm Diversity and Promote Equity,* 4th ed. Milwaukee: Rethinking Schools, 2014

Stern-LaRosa Caryl, and E.H. Bettmann. *Hate Hurts: How Children Learn and Unlearn Prejudice.* New York: Scholastic, 2000.

Tatum, Beverly. *Can We Talk About Race?: And Other Conversations in an Era of School Resegregation.* Boston: Beacon Press, 2008.

Turner-Vorbeck, Tammy, and Monica M. Marsh, eds. *Other Kinds of Families: Embracing Diversity in Schools.* New York: Teachers College Press, 2007.

Wiseman, Rosalind. *Masterminds and Wingmen: Helping Our Boys Cope with Schoolyard Power, Locker-Room Tests, Girlfriends, and the New Rules of Boy World.* New York: Harmony Books, 2014.

Wiseman, Rosalind. *Queen Bees and Wannabees: Helping Your Daughter Survive Cliques, Gossip, Boyfriends, and the New Realities of Girl World.* New York: Harmony Books, 2009.

Zinn, Howard, and Rebecca Stefoff. *A Young People's History of the United States.* For Young People Series. New York: Seven Stories Press, 2009.

Children's and Young Adult Books

Books Matter: The Best Kid Lit on Bias, Diversity and Social Justice, www.adl.org/books-matter
  ADL's online bibliography of recommended children's and young adult books about bias, bullying, diversity and social justice. This collection of books is representative of the excellent anti-bias and multicultural literature available for educators and parents of children and teenagers. All the titles in Books Matter have been reviewed by ADL staff and are frequently updated with new and noteworthy books. Integrated into Books Matter is ADL's Book of the Month feature, which highlights a book every month and includes a *Book Discussion Guide* with vocabulary, discussion questions, extension activities and additional resources (see also www.adl.org/book-of-the-month).

Organizations

Association for Middle Level Education (AMLE), www.amle.org
  AMLE is the leading international organization advancing the education of all students ages 10 to 15, helping them succeed as learners and make positive contributions to their communities and to the world. AMLE is committed to helping middle grades educators.

Collaborative for Academic, Social and Emotional Learning (CASEL), www.casel.org
  CASEL is the nation's leading organization advancing the development of academic, social and emotional competence for all students. Their mission is to help make evidence-based social and emotional learning (SEL) an integral part of education from preschool through high school.

Facing History and Ourselves, www.facinghistory.org
  Facing History and Ourselves is an international educational and professional development organization whose mission is to engage students of diverse backgrounds in an examination of racism, prejudice, and antisemitism in order to promote the development of a more humane and informed citizenry.

The Gay, Lesbian and Straight Education Network (GLSEN), www.glsen.org
  GLSEN is the leading national education organization focused on ensuring safe schools for all students.

Gender Spectrum, www.genderspectrum.org
  This site provides an array of resources and services that helps to create gender sensitive and inclusive environments for all children and teens.

International Bullying Prevention Association (IPBA), www.ibpaworld.org
  IPBA advances bullying prevention best practices by convening research-based forums, advocating best practices, promoting positive school climate and collaborating across disciplines, sectors and fields.

Morningside Center for Teaching Social Responsibility, www.morningsidecenter.org
  Morningside Center works hand in hand with educators to help young people develop the values, personal qualities and skills they need to thrive and contribute to their communities—from the classroom to the world.

PACER's National Bullying Prevention Center, www.pacer.org/bullying
  The Center unites, engages, and educates kids, teens, parents and communities nationwide to address bullying.

Rethinking Schools, www.rethinkingschools.org
   Rethinking Schools is a nonprofit publisher and advocacy organization dedicated to sustaining and strengthening public education through social justice teaching and education activism. Their magazine, books and other resources promote equity and racial justice in the classroom.

Share My Lesson, www.sharemylesson.com
   Share My Lesson is a place where educators can come together to create and share their very best teaching resources. This free platform gives access to high-quality teaching resources and provides an online community where teachers can collaborate with, encourage and inspire each other.

StopBullying.Gov, www.stopbullying.gov
   StopBullying.gov provides information from various government agencies on what bullying is, what cyberbullying is, who is at risk, and how you can prevent and respond to bullying.

Teaching Tolerance, www.tolerance.org
   Teaching Tolerance is dedicated to reducing prejudice, improving intergroup relations and supporting equitable school experiences for our nation's children by providing free educational materials to teachers and other school practitioners.

Welcoming Schools, www.welcomingschools.org
   A project of the Human Rights Campaign Foundation, Welcoming Schools offers tools, lessons and resources on embracing family diversity, supporting transgender and gender-expansive youth and preventing bias-based bullying.

GLOSSARY

This glossary includes terms used throughout the curriculum.

ableism
Prejudice and/or discrimination against people who have disabilities, including temporary, developmental, physical, psychiatric and/or intellectual disabilities.

activism
Engaging in activities that are meant to achieve political or social change; this also includes being a member of an organization which is working on change.

advertising
Speech, writing, pictures or films/video meant to persuade people to buy something.

ageism
Prejudice and/or discrimination against older people based on the belief that older people are inferior, incapable or irrelevant. Ageism also describes the Prejudice and/or discrimination of people who are too young to have social independence.

aggressive
Pursue what one wants or needs without regard to the other person, using harsh language, strong resistance or physical force.

aggressor
Someone who says or does something harmful or malicious to another person intentionally and unprovoked.

ally
Someone who speaks out on behalf of or takes actions that are supportive of someone who is targeted by bias or bullying, either themselves or someone else.

anti-immigrant bias
Prejudice and/or discrimination against people who are of immigrant origin, transnational or outside the dominant national identity or culture.

anti-Muslim bias
Prejudice and/or discrimination against people who are Muslim based on the belief in stereotypes and myths about Muslim people, Islam and countries with predominantly Muslim populations.

antisemitism
Prejudice and/or discrimination against people who are Jewish based on the belief in stereotypes and myths about Jewish people, Judaism and Israel.

anti-trans bias
Prejudice and/or discrimination against people who are transgender and/or non-binary (identifying as neither a man nor a woman) based on the belief that cisgender (gender identity that corresponds with the sex one was assigned at birth) is the norm.

assertive
Express thoughts and feelings and asking for what you want and need without violating the rights of others.

avoidance
Ignore or delay the problem or conflict, hoping it resolves itself or goes away without confrontation.

bias
An inclination or preference either for or against an individual or group that interferes with impartial judgment.

bullying
The repeated actions or threats of action directed toward a person by one or more people who have or are perceived to have more power or status than their target in order to cause fear, distress or harm.

bystander
Someone who sees bias or bullying happening and does not say or do anything.

classism
Prejudice and/or discrimination against people who are from low-income or working-class households based on a social hierarchy in which people are ranked according to socioeconomic status.

clique
A small group of people who spend time together and who are not friendly to other people.

communication
The act of using words, sounds, signs or behaviors to exchange information or express your ideas, thoughts, feelings, etc. to someone else or a group of people.

community
A group of people who live in the same area such as a city, town or neighborhood or who share common characteristics or interests.

conflict
An argument, fight, disagreement or struggle over something.

consensus
General agreement.

counterspeech
A process of exposing hate speech for its dishonest, false and hurtful content, setting the record straight, and promoting the values of respect and diversity.

culture
The patterns of daily life learned consciously and unconsciously by a group of people. These patterns can be seen in language, governing practices, arts, customs, holiday celebrations, food, religion, relationships, family roles, clothing, etc.

cyberbullying
The intentional and repeated mistreatment of others through the use of technology, such as computers, cell phones and other electronic devices.

cyberhate
Any use of electronic communications technology that attacks people based on their actual or perceived race, ethnicity, national origin, religion, sex, gender, sexual orientation, disability or disease to spread bigoted or hateful messages or information. These electronic communications technologies include the Internet (i.e., websites, social networking sites, user-generated content, dating sites, blogs, online games, instant messages and email) as well as other information technologies.

disability
A mental or physical condition that restricts an individual's ability to engage in one or more major life activities (e.g. seeing, hearing, speaking, walking, breathing, performing manual tasks, learning, working or caring for oneself).

discrimination
The denial of justice, resources and fair treatment of individuals and groups (often based on social identity), through employment, education, housing, banking, political rights, etc. Discrimination is an action that can follow prejudicial thinking.

diversity
Means different or varied. The population of the United States is made up of people belonging to diverse groups characterized by culture, race, ethnicity, nationality, gender, sexual orientation, ability, etc.

empathy
The ability to identify with or experience the feelings and thoughts of others.

equality
Everyone having the same rights, opportunities and resources. Equality stresses fairness and parity (or uniformity) in having access to social goods and services.

equity
Everyone getting what they need in order to have access, opportunities and a fair chance to succeed. It recognizes that the same for everyone (equality) doesn't truly address needs and therefore, specific solutions and remedies (which may be different) are necessary.

ethnicity
Refers to a person's identification with a group based on characteristics such as shared history, ancestry, geographic and language origin, and culture.

facts
Absolutely true statments (something that truly exists or happened).

gender
The socially-defined "rules" and roles for men and women in a society. Dominant western society generally defines gender as a binary system—men and women—but many cultures define gender as more fluid and existing along a continuum.

gender identity
Relates to a person's internal sense of their own gender. Since gender identity is internal, one's gender identity is not necessarily visible to others.

gossip
Information that is shared about the behavior and personal lives of other people

heterosexism
Prejudice and/or discriination against people who are lesbian, gay, bisexual, queer and/or asexual, based on the belief that heterosexuality is the norm.

identity
The qualities, beliefs, etc. that make a particular person or group different from others.

identity-based bullying
Refers to any form of bullying related to the characteristics considered unique to a person's identity, such as their race, religion, sexual orientation or physical appearance.

impact
The outcome or effect your actions have on someone.

implicit bias
The unconscious attitudes and stereotypes and unintentional actions (positive or negative) toward members of a group merely because of their membership in that group. These associations develop over the course of a lifetime beginning at a very early age through exposure to direct and indirect messages. When people are acting out of their implicit bias, they are not even aware that their actions are biased. In fact, those biases may be in direct conflict with a person's explicit beliefs and values.

injustice
A situation in which the rights of a person or a group of people are ignored, disrespected or discriminated against.

intent
What someone hopes to accomplish in a given situation; their goals.

interest
Something that concerns or arouses the curiosity of a person.

language
The system of words or signs that people use to express thoughts and feelings to each other. (There are approximately 7000 languages spoken in the world today).

media
The system and organizations of communication through which information is spread to a large number of people.

miscommunication
Failure to communicate clearly.

misinformation
False or misleading information.

name-calling
The use of language to defame, demean or degrade individuals or groups.

nationality
Solely refers to a person s citizenship by origin, birth, or naturalization.

opinions
What people feel, think and believe; there can be a wide range of opinions or points of view about something.

individual bias
Includes individual acts of bias, meanness or exclusion.

perspective
A way of looking at or thinking about facts and/or situations or point of view.

prejudice
A premature judgment or belief formed about a person, group or concept before gaining sufficient knowledge or by selectively disregarding facts.

propaganda
Information that is shared and spread in order to influence public opinion and to manipulate other people's beliefs, often to promote or publicize a particular political cause or point of view.

race
Refers to the categories into which society places individuals on the basis of physical characteristics (such as skin color, hair type, facial form and eye shape).

racism
Prejudice and/or discrimination against people of color based on a socially constructed racial hierarchy that privileges white people. Differences in physical characteristics (e.g., skin color, hair texture, eye shape) are used to support a system of inequities.

religion
An organized system of beliefs, observances, rituals and rules used to worship a god or group of gods.

religious bias
Prejudice and/or discrimination against people who belong to one or more religious groups or no religious group based on the belief in a correct or sanctioned faith system.

rumor
Information or a story about someone that is spread that has not been proven to be true.

sexism
Prejudice and/or discrimination against women, based on the belief in a natural order based on sex that privileges men.

sexual orientation
Determined by one's emotional, physical and/ or romantic attractions. Categories of sexual orientation include, but are not limited to, **gay, lesbian** (attracted to some members of the same gender), **bisexual** (attracted to some members of more than one gender) and **heterosexual** (attracted to some members of another gender).

skill
An ability to do something well which comes from one's knowledge, practice or aptitude.

social change
When elements of a society are altered or changed in some way, including the changes in society's institutions, behaviors, rules or social relationships.

socioeconomic status
An individual's or family's economic and social position in relation to others, as measured by factors such as income, wealth and occupation.

stereotype
An oversimplified generalization about a person or group of people without regard for individual

differences. Even seemingly positive stereotypes that link a person or group to a specific positive trait can have negative consequences and are often rooted in painful histories.

systemic bias
Includes policies and practices that are supported by power and authority (in institutions) and that benefits some and disadvantages others.

talent
A special natural ability or aptitude.

target
Someone against whom mistreatment is directed.

teamwork
A cooperative effort in which a group of people work together for a common goal or cause.

weightism
Prejudice and/or discrimination against people who are larger than the socially constructed norm for body size.